PRAISE FOR
THE ROBOT-PROOF
RECUITER

'*The Robot-Proof Recruiter* is a well-researched argument against the technology-first craze of the 21st century. Katrina Collier makes a compelling case for human-powered leadership at the front and centre of the hiring process, ensuring applicants and candidates are neither forgotten nor marginalized.'
Laurie Ruettimann, HR writer, speaker and entrepreneur, and podcast host of Let's Fix Work

'Wow – this is gold! There are some books you read once and never look at again and then there is *The Robot-Proof Recruiter*. Katrina Collier has managed to produce a resource that should be mandatory reading for every recruiting organization in the world. Why? In this modern tech age where robots, automation and artificial intelligence encroach upon every border of our lives, there is a propensity to forget that the reason for such advances is so that people will have more time to do other things; like connecting with other people. Alas, we do not, and nowhere is that more evident than in the recruiting industry – a people business.

It seems that in these days and times, empathy and interpersonal skills are dwindling commodities and the golden rule is forgotten in the candidate journey. Why else do we have the "ghosting" phenomenon of candidates ditching companies? Or, the negative reputation of recruiters in general? And let us not overlook the negative company reviews that proliferate online. What these issues have in common is that somewhere along the way manners were swapped for selfish concerns. So, how do we turn these trends around? What is a better way to promote opportunities online? How best should a recruiter handle an intake meeting? How can a company prove it is worth a candidate's time? How can one write job descriptions that don't unintentionally exclude certain demographics? Katrina Collier has the answers to these questions and others that, honestly, I had not considered before.

For two decades, I've been involved with the recruitment industry. When I began reading this book, my expectation was that it would refresh what I already knew – instinctively. It did so much more – it made me think, and that is not something I take for granted. If you, like me, think you are so experienced that there is nothing new to be learned about optimizing the recruitment experience then I dare you to pick up this book. I double dare you to put it back down after reading a few of its easy-to-read chapters and thoughtful summaries. And if you are new to the field of recruiting, consider this the forgotten manual you were supposed to read on day one. It will set you on the right recruitment course now and in perpetuity.'
Jim Stroud, talent acquisition innovator and author, and vlogger and podcaster at JimStroud.com

'Recruitment was, is and always has been about human interactions. Yet more than ever the recruitment field is affected by various tools and by artificial intelligence. *The Robot-Proof Recruiter* contains a ton of practical tips for recruiters and hiring managers on how to improve the candidate experience, communicate better with candidates and better use the technology advancements we have at our disposal. This book teaches recruiters about marketing, referrals and the power of social networks – all of which are must-have skills for 21st-century recruiters and HR professionals. It is a great guide that will help recruiters implement these modern methods and tools in their work, and is well worth reading and rereading. Every time you do so you will discover something new.'
Jan Tegze, Senior Recruiting Manager, author of *Full Stack Recruiter* and Founder of Sourcing.Games

'Katrina Collier has written a must-read business book for the modern recruitment professional. Highly practical, thoroughly enjoyable and engaging, this is a real page turner. Read this book – and become a recruiter worth talking to.'
Louise Triance, Managing Director of UK Recruiter

'I'll preface this by saying that I don't enjoy most books on recruitment, as the industry tends to idolize outdated techniques and ideologies. But once I started reading *The Robot-Proof Recruiter* I couldn't put it down. I found myself nodding and smiling the whole way through the book. I hope every recruiter reads this and relearns the art of being human in the ever-changing technology-driven recruitment landscape. A must-read for all people in all facets of hiring, be it agency, internal or a hiring manager.'
Troy Hammond, Founder and CEO of Talent Army

'This book is a friendly reminder that no amount of technology and data can take the place of human interaction. In *The Robot-Proof Recruiter*, Katrina Collier details the skills needed by today's full-life-cycle talent acquisition teams in order to stay relevant and not become obsolete. Even though Katrina and I sometimes see technology's role in recruiting differently, we can both agree that the difference between an "OK" recruiter and a top-performing recruiter lies in their ability to build genuine relationships. This book contains great practical advice, tested examples, and recommendations even the most seasoned recruiter will find valuable.'
Jackye Clayton, TA speaker and trainer, and Director of Customer Success at HiringSolved

'Human-first recruiting strategies will put you at the front of the pack, no matter what technological changes occur. At all points of the recruiting process candidates want to be treated as humans and that is exactly what this book delivers. This isn't old-school stuff, but new-school twists that help you leverage technology to show you are worthy of a candidate's time and attention. When you have over 25 years of experience, it's easy to think you have all the answers. In this case, Katrina Collier does!'
Hannah Morgan, Job Search Strategist at Career Sherpa, and 'On Careers' writer at US News & World Report

'*The Robot-Proof Recruiter* is a fantastic call to action for any recruiters looking to keep the edge on our AI competition. Full of insight from Katrina Collier and leading industry peers, it is backed up with examples

and easy-to-do-why-don't-you-do-it-already ideas and data. As a practitioner I highly recommend this book to anyone looking for ways to up their game as a rounded recruiter, in-house or agency.'
Sophie Power, Senior Talent Professional and DBR Community Admin

'Coming from the HR vendor space, I am incredibly grateful to Katrina Collier for designing the ultimate framework for a healthy cooperation between recruiters and technology. *The Robot-Proof Recruiter* offers a practical guide on the recruitment process from A to Z, helping to successfully navigate the online world and build a humane recruitment process. Packed with real-life examples and Katrina's brilliant humour, the book is a pleasure to read; it also gives a platform to many incredible people from the industry. This is a must-read for all HR professionals of the modern age.'
Yulia Kuzmane, speaker, and Director of Sales and Customer Success at Amazing Hiring

'Some days it feels like most recruiters were raised by wolves. Without formal training, skills are passed down from the previous generation, and there is little standardization. When hiring recruiters, the focus is still on years of experience rather than on excellence or the value the recruiter brought to a company. Consequently, recruiting has one of the largest gaps between "competent" and "great" relative to any other job I can think of.

Competent recruiters follow instructions, taking the meagre training their first few bosses gave them and calling it gospel. Great recruiters take what they learn via experiments and fine-tune their approach. They put themselves in the candidates' shoes to find ever-more-effective ways of attracting and persuading.

The best recruiters, like Katrina, see the whole system, breaking each element into its components and finding new ways to make them better. She knows that every element within the hiring process can be made better with a little more thought, cleverness, brains and heart.

Think of this book as the handbook an entire industry needs to use to level up. From big ideas to "use this software to solve this very specific problem", this book is a field manual for better recruiting, helping junior recruiters see a better way forward and sparking "why didn't I think of that?" moments in senior recruiters.

If you make your living attracting and hiring talent, these are the instructions you need to become your best recruiter, regardless of experience and level.'

James Ellis, Employer Brand Consultant and host of The Talent Cast podcast

'Just when you thought we didn't need another "how to recruit" book, along comes Katrina Collier's *The Robot-Proof Recruiter* and does things differently. Collier's background in experienced and targeted recruiting empowers her stance that there are just some things that technology can't do better than a recruiter who is passionate and who, more importantly, gives a damn about talent.

In a period when recruiting automation and LinkedIn recruiting tools are touted as the go-to solution for placements, recruiters of every level will enjoy (and likely identify with) the storytelling aspect of this overview, which is complemented with various technical and tactical recruiting tips including, but not limited to, search, marketing, engagement, branding, and even managing hiring managers.

The Robot-Proof Recruiter has a place in every recruiter's library – especially in the libraries of those who believe that robots are coming for their job!'

Chris Hoyt, President and co-owner of CareerXroads

'*The Robot-Proof Recruiter* is an outstanding how-to guidebook for recruiters who want to stay ahead of the curve. Katrina Collier has pulled together a valuable and accessible resource – a great contribution to the industry.'

Hung Lee, Curator, Recruiting Brainfood

Be fabulous, Marjorie!

*For Dad, who never expected to hold
a book published on his 90th birthday
and signed by his daughter*

CONTENTS

FOREWORD

Can we automate being human? This was the question that was at the forefront of almost every recruiter's mind in 2017. During that time, it was hard to hide from the HR clatter and condemnation. Doomsday headlines littered recruitment blogs and popular business magazines. With the rise of artificial intelligence-powered companies, many critics were quick to point out that the recruitment process is broken and that AI will soon replace us all.

It was a supercilious prophecy fuelled by clickbait headlines and, at the time, the insecurity in our craft. How could a human-driven profession be replaced by robots?

In a period in which we all should have stood tall and cried 'Blasphemy!', oddly most recruiters were steadfastly ready to jump aboard the AI train. 'If you can't beat them, join them' became our AI anthem back then.

As easy as recruitment had become, recruiters were quick to admit defeat. For the first time in our profession, finding and messaging candidates had become effortless. Bulk messages, spammy in quality, rapidly filled potential candidates' inboxes, even though many of these 'candidates' were not qualified for the roles. The phone slowly became prehistoric. Some recruiters were actually doing everything they could to avoid human interaction!

I lived by the saying, 'If you act like a robot, then you will be replaced by one'.

With AI Armageddon approaching, we needed a superhero to rescue us. We were desperately seeking to be saved from our mind-numbing routine of copy, paste, send, repeat. We needed a champion, a combatant resistance against complacency, a resilient force to remind us to be human.

Long since I've known her, Katrina Collier has been our superhero against AI. She has been the head cheerleader for people and an essential enforcer behind the #BeHuman movement she coined. With her technology-proof shield, Katrina is an avid activist for recruiters to maintain a human-first approach. She believes that upholding this approach will make us impermeable to artificial intelligence and robots alike.

Katrina's was the voice recruiters needed in early 2017. While several people were quick to dismiss bad practices with robots, Katrina was one of the few leaders to show us how to progress. Fuelled with a heart-filled love for our industry and for the candidates that we work with, Katrina communicates a momentous motto to put humans first. She shows us how to use generations of best practices with modern technology in a manner that will make us sparkle in a crowd.

Katrina was the saviour I needed when, as Editor of SourceCon, I put together the programme for my second conference, 'We Control the Robots'. I'll never forget 15 March 2017, the final day of that SourceCon Spring conference. After lunch, 700 recruiters and sourcers piled into the main ballroom at the Anaheim Marriott Hotel. This was one of the first conferences of its time to address the growing presence of artificial intelligence and robotics. Up until the moment that Katrina took to the stage, most of the presentations had focused on the fact that AI is coming and how we can prepare for it. That day, Katrina had a different message for our SourceCon audience.

Upon Katrina taking the stage, the room was abuzz. Often on the third day of a conference, and after lunch, the audience can be drained and a little muted. This wasn't the scenario. Katrina took the stage to a roar of momentum and energy. Splashed across the screen was a simple question – the title of her presentation, 'Can we automate being human?'. Her presentation was filled with vivacity, hilarity and relatability. It was an interactive session that involved Katrina whisking mini orange human-like dolls into the audience every time someone engaged with her questions. She had the audience's attention and her message was simple – be human and be peculiar.

That day, Katrina challenged us to find something about ourselves that a robot could not find. It was a lesson that we could use when interacting with our most important clients, our candidates and our people. We all have something that makes us peculiar, something different from the person next to us. It might be easy for a robot to identify us, but problematic for a robot to know us. We all have silly habits, unique tastes and quirks. These peculiar traits are hard for robots to recognize.

In the end, Katrina had all of us on our feet. Positivity filled the air and the conference ended with an optimistic message – that the human-first approach is very much alive. That day, we learned how to beat the robots. It was also the day that we learned how important Katrina's message is to our profession.

You will soon understand Katrina's message and her philosophy. She is not naive about her work, her calling or the world. She has travelled widely, delivering her human-first approach to some of the most remote places across the globe. In person, she is full of charisma, tremendously enthusiastic and amiable, and has a sharp sense of humour. After spending five minutes with her you'll feel like you've known her your entire life.

This book is a forthright account for all talent acquisition professionals that will stand the test of time. It is relayed by an industry icon, a kind-hearted human looking to pass on as much advantageous information as she possibly can.

Shannon Pritchett,
Editor, SourceCon

PREFACE

Your purchase is helping end modern day slavery

From the moment I saw Ian Pettigrew, leadership coach and Retrak Trustee, post about the inaugural #ConnectingHRAfrica trip I knew I'd go and that it would irreversibly change me. It did – but, unplanned, it also changed the lives of others.

In my usual style, I decided to go in the blink of an eye. Completing the forms left me curious as to how I would contribute to this team of HR and L&D professionals, and even as I landed at Entebbe Airport in Uganda in 2016, I had little idea of how I would help the street children or Retrak charity's staff.

In the UK, access to training is a given. Many of us attend courses, implement 10 per cent and, even with the best intentions, discard the rest. This was not the case for the people working for Retrak in Kampala, Uganda. Keen to learn, they took 100 per cent of the skills our team of HR professionals shared and ran with it. Returning with another group of HR professionals in 2018, I was awed to see the cohesion of the team, working and supporting each other with such love, kindness and gratitude. Then there was the ripple impact of the work being passed on to the women in the outreach centres: Ian Pettigrew's brainchild is becoming a tidal wave.

When Retrak joined Hope for Justice the positive impact came full circle. Retrak works tirelessly to return children to a safe and loving home, and the programmes they run in the outreach centres empower women with business and parenting skills. By stemming the flow of children into the slums, they are reducing the number of children who end up in the sex trade or trafficked. Together with Hope for Justice, their aim is to end modern day slavery, by preventing exploitation, rescuing victims, restoring lives and reforming society.

Modern day slavery is where one person controls another by exploiting a vulnerability. It is often linked with human trafficking, of which London, UK appallingly is the global hub, and where a person is forced into a service against their will through physical, financial or psychological control.

As an ambassador, I have used my DisruptHR events to raise awareness of the work of Hope for Justice, and unexpectedly inspired others to volunteer for the 2018 and 2019 #ConnectingHRAfrica teams. Each volunteer has raised thousands of pounds, and selflessly contributed their time and expertise. I am excited to see the positive impact they will make in Ethiopia after witnessing their impact in Uganda.

The sponsors that have been attracted to my DisruptHR events donate directly to Hope for Justice, and even though these sums are life-changing, I always feel I can raise more money because even the smallest amount makes the most extraordinary difference in these communities.

Rather than receive royalties, my share of the proceeds from *The Robot-Proof Recruiter* is going directly to Hope for Justice. Not only will this book create a positive impact on the recruitment industry, it will be changing the lives of the most vulnerable: street children.

ACKNOWLEDGEMENTS

I love being part of the recruiting community and I needed the book to include thoughts from its members. I cannot thank enough the following people for sharing their time and expertise, either directly or indirectly, so that you would not only read my ideas but so that you would also hear from your industry peers.

Huge thanks to Ahmad Iman, Alison Mackay, Amy Miller, Andrew Gadomski, Angie Verros, Ashley Bush, Audra Knight, Aylin Halil, Ben Gledhill, Bennett Sung, Billy McDiarmid, Chris Hoyt, Chris Long, Chris Raw, Dale Clareburt, David Sankar, David Wolstenholme, Debi Eastaway, Denis Dinkevich, Derek Zeller, Derek-Murphy Johnson, Ellie Brown, Emma Crowe, Eva Balúchová, Evan F Herman, Gemma Matthews, Gerry Crispin, Glenn Martin, Hannah Morgan, Heidi Wassini, Hung Lee, Jacqui Barratt, James Ellis, James Whitelock, Jan Tegze, Jane Hatton, Jatinder Bansal, Jennifer Candee, Jeff Lovejoy, Joanne Ward, Katrina Kibben, Kay Kelison, Kelly Hartmann, Kelly Swingler, Kristen Graham, Lars Schmidt, Maisha Cannon, Mark Hopkins, Mark Lundgren, Mark Mansour, Matt Buckland, Maury Hanigan, Melanie Silverman, Michael Crouse, Michael Wright, Mike Massaro, Nathan Perrott, Noa Ferber, Ondřej Procházka, Patrick Caldwell, Pete Radloff, Rebecca Clarke, Russ Morgan, Sara Duxbury, Sarah Williams, Shane Gray, Shannon Smedstad, Simon Halkyard, Simon Jones, Sjamilla Van der Tooren, Sofia Broberger, Sophie Theen, Stacy Zapar, Stephen O'Donnell, Steve Levy, Steven Kosakow, Sue Ingram, Tangie Pettis, Ted Hewett, Teddy Dimitrova, Toby Culshaw, Tracey Parsons, Tris Revill, Trish McFarlane, Vanessa Raath and Wendy McDougall.

Then there are all the people behind the scenes who have supported and cajoled me through the highs and lows of writing my first book.

Richard Collier, the best ex-husband I have, you have read this book by osmosis when really you would prefer to read about cycling. Michelle Zelli, I am eternally grateful to you for showing me how to believe. Perry Timms, without your introduction and faith in me there wouldn't even be a book. Jim Stroud, you believed in my writing before I did. Pauline Richardson, you unknowingly made it possible for me to dedicate my time to writing, and to Mum and Caryn Morgan who made that happen, thank you. Shannon Pritchett, for your faith that I belong on the SourceCon stage inspiring sourcers to take a #BeHuman approach. Sue Ingram, Audra Knight, Mark Lundgren, Vanessa Raath, Jo-Dee Walmsley and Louise Triance, thank you for cheering me on from the start. Andy Swann, Alex Moyle and Mervyn Dinnen, thank you for all the insider knowledge. Alan Walker and Clair Bush, thank you for your tech advice when I was stuck.

For all the people who have awed me with their kind comments and messages of support, and even offers to buy this book without even knowing what it was about, thank you to each and every one of you.

To you, my reader, I am thankful that you are joining me on my quest to improve recruitment for everyone.

Introduction

Recruiters earned this reputation

Fifty-three per cent of people have left jobs or considered leaving their job because they think that their employers don't recruit or retain high-performing individuals.[1] The recruiter's job is pivotal to the success of the company yet our poor reputation is causing our own undoing.

In an attempt to save time and fill roles fast, recruiters have inadvertently turned the market against themselves so that now, in 2019, the market belongs to the people. People who don't like recruiters, people who don't want to reply to recruiters and people who are beginning to pay recruiters back.

Putting technology first and the human last was never going to create a positive outcome for recruiters, even if it was unintentional. For too long recruiters have used technology to spam, disrespect, ghost and even reject; using technology to cut the wrong corners, they have left people cold.

Encouraged by HR and recruitment technology providers, recruiters have irritated people with their bulk messages about irrelevant roles to the point that people have created the hashtags #recruiterspam and #recruiterfail, and a subreddit on Reddit called recruiting hell, to express their annoyance.[2] Recruiters have used technology to spray jobs onto social media, confusing it with an online job board; used technology to unveil email addresses to send me, me, me emails; and used technology to auto-post irrelevant content that ignores the etiquette of social media.

It is time to turn it around.

We are people

It was easy to decide upon *The Robot-Proof Recruiter* as the title for this book because I strongly believe that a human-first approach will make you irreplaceable by artificial intelligence and robots. It is true though, there is some incredible technology around, and some of it can even do a part of your job but throughout this book, I will show you how to put the human first and keep the technology in its supporting role so that you can drastically improve your human engagement and response rates.

This book is not written for high-volume recruitment. In fact, I have little expertise in high volume or early career recruitment. My expertise and experience are squarely in recruiting difficult-to-find, engage and recruit people, people who possess skills that are in demand. I have written this book for people recruiting people who will only respond to a high-quality human-first approach.

HR and recruitment industry jargon removes the human from the equation. People are not an acquisition, passive talent, active talent, human capital, a resource, a candidate, in-demand talent, talents, unicorns, purple squirrels, targets, perfect fits and other worse dysphemisms that I would prefer not to repeat. Nor are recruiters or sourcers job whisperers, talent magnets, unicorn hunters, career matchmakers, career whisperers or headhunters; recruiters are also people, helping other people secure their next job, contract or project.

For the sake of understanding though, throughout the book, I have used the industry terms that are easy to relate to including recruiter, sourcer, hiring manager, applicant, candidate, interviewee, employee and so on. I hope though that when you read the industry jargon that you remember that I really mean 'a human being with thoughts and feelings'.

I have used the term recruiter loosely to cover in-house recruiters, talent acquisition, HR, recruitment agents, staffing companies, sourcers, resourcers, researchers and anyone who is involved in the recruitment life cycle.

To agency recruiters, this book may sound like it is written for in-house recruiters and that is because, for brevity, I have used 'company' instead of using 'company, agency or client' or 'company or agency' and so on. The chapters that may seem exclusive to companies are still worth your time, especially if you wish to be consultative to your clients about managing their reputation and employer branding.

Transparency can hinder recruitment

When I started in my first full-time job 28 years ago, I had a manager who reduced me to tears regularly and who stressed out his second-in-charge so greatly that she used to be sick each lunchtime. He was deeply unpleasant but we stayed because the internet was yet to create transparency. In 1990, I couldn't see the thousands of jobs and the fear of being jobless was greater than the atmosphere in that office.

Fast-forward nearly three decades and technology has empowered the job seeker. For example, Olivia Bland, who took to Twitter on 29 January 2019 to share feedback about her interview with Web Applications UK.[3] She wrote, 'After a brutal 2 hour interview, in which the CEO tore both me and my writing to shreds (and called me an underachiever), I was offered the job' and attached a copy of her email to the company politely declining the offer. She did not feel that being made uncomfortable to the point of tears in an interview was appropriate.

What happened next is more damaging to the company's future recruitment. The story was picked up by the media, including the national press, and Olivia was soon to be heard on BBC Radio and TV.[4] Her tweet has also now been retweeted over 42,000 times.

Being inquisitive, I looked the company up on employer review site Glassdoor and was soon reading a review from 2016 that supported Olivia's claims of bullying. It wasn't the review that stood out but the reply by the CEO which started condescendingly with 'Are you sure you worked here?' and went downhill from there.

Putting aside your thoughts on Glassdoor and whether you think the reviews hold relevance or not, if you visit Web Applications UK's Glassdoor page, you will see the aforementioned review is now marked helpful by 122 people.[5] You will also find new reviews that have been found helpful by hundreds of people, including one that states 'I came here to post this after seeing the Twitter thing about that woman who was abused in an interview. I wanted people to know that everything she said was true.'

In the future, this company will have difficulty recruiting because of the impact of these reviews and their mention in the national press. In Chapter 4, you will hear how to handle reviews and balance them out genuinely so this doesn't happen to your company or client.

Technology hindering recruitment

Finding people isn't hard. There are so many tools available to use, from paid LinkedIn Recruiter licences to free Chrome add-ons. For too long the emphasis has been placed on using tools to find people and little on how to engage, which has caused an excessive amount of recruiter spam and a decrease in response rates. In this book, I am focusing on showing you how to engage people so they respond, I am asking you to use technology better and to take a little extra time up front so you save yourself hours later trying to find and engage with yet more people.

Pondering the state of sourcing for 2019, technical recruiter Mark Mansour tweeted, 'People fighting for the same people, businesses not investing in hiring on potential, CEOs still lying and saying talent is the most important thing for the upcoming year. Oh, and recruiters still too reliant on LinkedIn!'[6]

LinkedIn isn't always the answer

If you have followed my journey, it will come as no surprise that I don't drink LinkedIn's Kool-Aid. If LinkedIn spent as much time as Facebook does keeping people active on the platform before selling recruiters its user data, and if LinkedIn hadn't convinced recruiters that all people on the platform are looking for a job, then I may think differently.

LinkedIn has the lowest active user base after Facebook, Instagram, QZone, Reddit, Twitter and Douban yet it is the place recruiters can be found in greatest abundance due to a combination of LinkedIn's marketing and ease of searching.[7] But due to the large volume of irrelevant recruiter InMails, people with skills that are in great demand prefer to avoid the site or visit infrequently.

Sadly, it is not hard to find people mocking misguided LinkedIn messages. Rupert Murdog is a blog that starts with 'I'm a dog. I'm on LinkedIn. Sometimes recruiters contact me.'[8] Rupert shares examples of the messages he receives and it is a fine example of where automation has been too heavily relied upon. Though difficult to read without laughing, it is this noise that you are now trying to be heard over.

But even the best hyperpersonalized LinkedIn InMail, one that shows there was human input, can fall on deaf ears. In 2016, Paul Fenwick shared a tweet with a screenshot of an InMail he had received from Weston Fillman at Google.[9] The InMail included skills that were buried deep in Paul's LinkedIn profile and he called it 'Gold'. What struck me though was that it had taken Paul 10 months to open LinkedIn and see the message. The InMail was dated 13 July 2015 and seen on 11 May 2016, and though Weston and Paul did end up speaking, by sending the message on the wrong platform they had both lost a great opportunity.

In Chapter 5 on intake strategy sessions, you will hear about recruiting personas, which can help you discover where your future employees are most active so your messages are successful.

People use tech against recruiters

So big is the problem of recruiter spam caused by the wrong kind of automation, that people are using technology to ignore recruiters, some have even created bots to deal with the volume of irrelevant messages. At Reply.id you can supercharge your inbox with a free AI Gmail filter. They state 'You won't see any more recruiting emails in your inbox with our AI Gmail filter & autoresponder.' Emails are filtered to a subfolder and the autoresponder replies to recruiters asking them to answer questions, mostly about the relevance of the skills and location to the recipient. It is incredibly clever and easy to use but how sad that someone felt the need to create it in the first place.

Technology obstacles

Ever had a call from a robot? I received one yesterday about my non-existent 'car accident' that was obviously fake. It was annoying and it reminded me of the technology providers who will tell you that a bot can cold engage with people and successfully receive a response.

Don't get me wrong, bots do have their place and you will hear how Zalando and Yodel use chatbots to keep people engaged but these are people who have successfully arrived on their careers websites, they are not people avoiding contact with recruiters because they have been treated poorly for so long. These people deserve the extra effort and a human touch.

Recruiters know that referred applicants are the best quality of hire but do people know that they need to be referred to a company to get around a broken applicant tracking system (ATS)? In 'I applied to 13 top tech companies in Silicon Valley', software developer Tony Mai shared that initially his application to Airbnb was rejected by automated email but that 'I later realized I knew someone who works at Airbnb and reached out to him for a referral. I got contacted the next day and my Airbnb process went all the way to the onsite interviews.'[10] If Tony had not been proactive, this wouldn't have happened. Is your ATS stopping you from hiring great people?

Attitude obstacles

Technology highlights people's behaviour online. I appreciate my view of recruiter behaviour comes down to the network of people I have built and what LinkedIn, for example, chooses to show me but I don't think that I will be alone in being shocked by the increase in recruiters shaming and even bullying other recruiters and candidates online. Besides being damaging to their own reputations, and clearly visible in the activity section of their profile, it is also damaging to the industry as a whole. It creates yet more noise for great recruiters to battle through when trying to engage with people who are in demand.

There is no reason to mock candidates like this, 'If you're really looking to annoy the recruiter who's looking at your CV definitely write curriculum vitae at the top. Using four different fonts is a real winner too.' Instead, this recruiter could have given some great advice to job seekers that reflected well on her and her agency. In the next few chapters, you will hear more about the social media etiquette that helps grow a great community of interested people.

Recruiter behaviour + transparency = candidate ghosting

Ghosting is defined as the practice of ending a personal relationship with someone by suddenly and without explanation withdrawing from all communication.[11] There is an increase in candidate ghosting, where people disappear out of the hiring process and this is due to the buoyant job market, poor recruiter behaviour that has created disloyalty, and the ease with which people can keep looking for jobs or be approached about another job during the recruitment process.

Whenever I hear recruiters complaining about candidate ghosting I am surprised that they do not realize that recruiters have been ghosting candidates for years. Recruiters are known to not acknowledge applications, not return phone calls or emails, not deliver feedback after interviews and even not turn up for the interview.

It is easy to find examples of recruiter ghosting causing resentment online. On Twitter, consultant Valeska Magalhaes shared 'I hate it when they schedule a phone interview and don't show up or when they invite me for an interview at the company with two people and both are on vacation.'[12] In his article 'Have you been "ghosted" by an employer?' software engineer Yechiel Kalmenson shared 'I've had one company where they had me take a full day off work unpaid, so I could come to their office for an interview, only to never hear back and get no replies to my emails. I've had a friend who was ghosted after getting an offer!'[13] There are many comments from other developers, people possessing skills that are in high demand, sharing similar experiences and it is disappointing.

I feel Jordan Stewart's tweet sums up the way recruiters and hiring managers have been treating people the best, 'I had a 4 hour interview for a job, and the manager flew in from Florida to meet me and I never heard back from them. It is a different world.'[14]

This won't be the last time I mention ghosting, in Chapter 8 you will hear how to reduce the likelihood of people ghosting you in this candidate-driven market, and in Chapter 3 I will share the impact of not delivering feedback on ghosting. It deserves your attention because it is one of the biggest factors negatively impacting hiring.

Human first, technology second

In the 2019 HMC Trend Report, Principal Analyst Ben Eubanks expects a greater focus on the actual, practical impacts of artificial intelligence and shared concerns about over-automation, 'employers must be cautious about over-automating and potentially compromising the experience for candidates, employees, and customers.'[15] In my experience, automation has already damaged the reputation of recruiters and reduced candidate engagement, and recruiters need drastic action to put the human first and become robot-proof.

If you skip to the messaging chapter of this book, you will miss the formula that increases response rates, engages people through the whole hiring process and eases the pain of recruitment. The internet has created incredible transparency and it has given people access to information about your company or client that was hidden in the past.

Today a recruiter's job is not as simple as it used to be; today if you want to be heard in the 2.5 quintillion bytes of data produced each day, it takes all the elements below.[16] There are no shortcuts to the results, skip any, and your response rates and engagement will remain the same or worsen in the years ahead.

Over the course of the book you will learn why today recruiters now need to:

- be candidate-centric (human first);
- look worthy of someone's time under internet scrutiny;
- ensure their hiring managers and company also look good under review;
- conduct exceptional intake strategy sessions;
- create human-first job posts and messages;
- have efficient application, interview and rejection processes;

- ensure that people are taken care of during pre- and onboarding; and

- even ensure people are off boarded well for potential boomerang or referral hires.

It may seem overwhelming when you have a pile of requirements to fill and a hiring manager breathing down your neck, but I will also share the technology that you can use to support you in all these areas. Today, candidate engagement is at an all-time low and you can no longer ignore the change technology has created, you must embrace it.

Let me show you how to put the human first and technology second.

Notes

1 Randstad [accessed 11 April 2019] Your best employees are leaving. But is it personal or practical? Ranstad [Online] https://www.randstadusa.com/about/news/your-best-employees-are-leaving-but-is-it-personal-or-practical/ (archived at https://perma.cc/KE7A-AQQ5)

2 Recruiting hell [accessed 11 April 2019] r/recruiting hell, Reddit [Online] https://www.reddit.com/r/recruitinghell (archived at https://perma.cc/8YM3-T7KS)

3 Tweet from Olivia Bland [accessed 11 April 2019] Twitter [Online] https://twitter.com/oliviaabland/status/1090281095805980672 (archived at https://perma.cc/P6KT-BPNY)

4 Rubinstein, P (2019) [accessed 11 April 2019] The 'stress interview': a technique that goes too far? BBC, 2 February [Online] http://www.bbc.com/capital/story/20190201-the-stress-interview-a-technique-that-goes-too-far (archived at https://perma.cc/Q4AX-5T8N)

5 Employee reviews for Web Applications UK [accessed 11 April 2019] Glassdoor [Online] https://www.glassdoor.co.uk/Reviews/Employee-Review-Web-Applications-UK-RVW12360906.htm (archived at https://perma.cc/L98N-GMVL)

6 Tweet from Katrina Collier [accessed 11 April 2019] Twitter [Online] https://twitter.com/KatrinaMCollier/status/1073514556348133376 (archived at https://perma.cc/G3GS-Z4AH)

7 Statista [accessed 11 April 2019] Most popular social network sites worldwide as of January 2019, active users (in millions) Statista [Online] https://www.statista.com/statistics/272014/global-social-networks-ranked-by-number-of-users/ (archived at https://perma.cc/NK43-LF72)

8 Rupert Murdog [accessed 11 April 2019] tumblr [Online] http://iamrupertmurdog.tumblr.com/ (archived at https://perma.cc/K9ZX-5C7S)

9 Tweet from Paul Fenwick [accessed 11 April 2019] Twitter [Online] https://twitter.com/pjf/status/730215052750381056 (archived at https://perma.cc/4CVQ-QG3C)

10 Mai, T (2019) [accessed 11 April 2019] I applied to 13 top tech companies in Silicon Valley – talked to 9 – got onsite interviews at 5 – and offers from 3 of them, Medium, 20 February [Online] https://medium.com/@thetonymai/i-applied-to-13-top-tech-companies-in-silicon-valley-talked-to-9-got-onsite-interviews-at-5-22c7d5824095 (archived at https://perma.cc/YQ7J-X7U3)

11 Definition of ghosting [accessed 11 April 2019] Oxford Living Dictionaries [Online] https://en.oxforddictionaries.com/definition/ghosting (archived at https://perma.cc/5RUL-FH4A)

12 Tweet from Valeska Magalhaes [accessed 11 April 2019] Twitter [Online] https://twitter.com/Val_Mag/status/1048118342006067200 (archived at https://perma.cc/FJ4B-8BW6)

13 Kalmenson, Y (2018) [accessed 11 April 2018] Have you been 'ghosted' by an employer? DEV Community, 16 December [Online] https://dev.to/yechielk/are-millenials-ghosting-their-employers-407k (archived at https://perma.cc/U4Y2-FM8K)

14 Tweet from Hearty B [accessed 11 April 2019] Twitter [Online] https://twitter.com/DearBurlyMan/status/1078763907483951104 (archived at https://perma.cc/JHE4-ZJTW)

15 2019 HCM Trends Report [accessed 11 April 2019] upstartHR [Online] https://upstarthr.com/what-are-the-2019-trends-in-hr/ (archived at https://perma.cc/5ZXL-YSP6)

16 Data never sleeps 5.0 [accessed 11 April 2019] DOMO [Online] https://www.domo.com/learn/data-never-sleeps-5 (archived at https://perma.cc/7YU2-JLZR)

Candidate-centric recruiters beat robots

At the beginning of my career, companies were in charge. Employment was all about fear. How employees were treated didn't matter. There was no talk of mental health in the workplace, or health and wellbeing programmes, and certainly not any concern for employee engagement or its impact on productivity. You were lucky to have a job, be grateful for it.

There was no transparency; people could only see the few jobs listed in the Sunday newspaper or trade magazines. Parents still talked about a job for life, and you never, I mean never, left a job without having secured another one! Gaps in your career were unforgivable. Employment was all about the stick, senior management had long eaten the carrot.

Recruitment agents were in charge of supplying people to companies. They had their Rolodex of contacts and companies could not get hold of these candidates without paying a lofty placement fee. Online job boards were present but made little impact until much later, when people became confident using the internet and present in large numbers online.

In 2003 I entered the world of recruitment after seeing an advertisement in a newspaper. Like many recruiters, I fell into the industry. After a few false starts, including being appalled to discover that one agency didn't pay all of its contractors each month and enduring one that was full of badly behaving cowboys, I was placed by Tina Maddock into a professionally behaving technical recruitment agency.

Tina was one of the first recruiters to treat me, the candidate, as a high priority. To me, she sets the standard of how a candidate-centric recruiter should behave. At no point did I feel like a commodity, she coached, coaxed and supported me through the emotional ups and downs of many interviews. Her treatment taught me how to be a candidate-centric recruiter and to this day she is the only recruiter-to-recruiter, or rec-to-rec, I recommend.

My new agency also taught me the importance of treating my clients and candidates well. Early on I was encouraged to develop strong professional relationships by attending my clients' sites, sitting in on interviews, taking my contractors out to lunch and so on. My contractors were important to me because I wanted to keep them and I took it very personally when they were mucked about, which did not make me a favourite with the accounts team, but did win me the respect of my contractors, who would then refer their friends for roles. My clients appreciated my candidate-centric approach because it made their job easier.

I was and still think like a candidate-centric recruiter. Of course, in my agency days, I was finding people for jobs and not jobs for people and this difference is often misunderstood by a job seeker, but I always put the human first in the process. If I couldn't help a job seeker I would do my best to find someone who could and for my candidates, I remembered I have two ears and one mouth and used them in that order. I used my empathy, creativity, judgement and ability to build a community to keep my approach human first.

Somehow over the last decade, recruiters have got so overloaded with technology and tools, that they have forgotten the human in the hiring process. A human with feelings, thoughts and emotions. A human who doesn't want to have their time wasted reading irrelevant InMails and emails sent by time-poor recruiters. A human who spends time crafting and submitting an application and investing time interviewing for our jobs.

It has become the norm for recruiters to hide behind technology and complex processes to the point that there are thousands of articles and posts bemoaning 'recruiter spam', 'recruiter ghosting' and 'employer ghosting'. But in 2019, people with skills that are in high demand are hiding behind the same technology recruiters have been using to be unavailable. Candidates are keyboard warriors who don't need to reply to you if they don't like what they see. The term 'candidate ghosting' is being used in frustration by the very same recruiters who have been mistreating people for a decade.

Recruiters hoped that improving their messaging alone would be enough to increase candidate engagement but it is not. Trust needs to be built. Years of recruiters' reputations diminishing needs to be undone. To ensure you are not replaced by a robot in the years ahead, it is essential to place the human first and use the skills that technology cannot replace.

Feeling in-demand

There has only been one time when recruiters have had an inkling of what it is like to be a human with skills that are in high demand; in late 2017/early 2018, when the panic over the unknown impact of the incoming General Data Protection Regulation (GDPR) made companies across the world send us countless emails about the security of our data or asking us to opt back in.

Do you remember the feeling of receiving hundreds of bland emails that were constantly interrupting your flow? 'High priority' emails asking you to rejoin the email marketing list you were pretty sure you had never signed up to, so you could continue receiving their 'hot jobs'. Telling you your data was secure on a site you had last visited in 2012. It was crazy, I even received a letter from Australia about the data related to a bank account I closed in 2003 when I moved to London, UK. How frustrating it was to be hounded by people who were vying for your attention, demanding your action, when most of it was no longer relevant or of interest.

This is what it is like to be a developer, a data scientist, a nurse, a plasterer or any other occupation where there is a shortage of people. Here in London UK, there are around five job vacancies for every developer; imagine how many unsolicited emails and InMails they receive every single day.[1] I bet they dread opening their inbox or feel irked at the amount of spam. Keep their crazy inbox in mind, use your robot-proof skills and all you learn in this book, and you will succeed in gaining and holding the attention of people with in-demand skills.

Robot-proof skills

To make it as a recruiter in this candidate-driven market, you will discover in the following chapters why you need to look like a recruiter worth talking to, why your company and hiring manager also need to look worthy of someone's time, how to share the right information in the right way to gain and hold a candidate's attention, and how to use technology to put the human first through the entire recruitment experience.

Without using the following skills though, those that will never be replaced by AI or robotics, and without following the etiquette that creates a better connection with people in this transparent online world, it will all be in vain.

Curiosity

I believe curiosity is one of the most crucial skills a candidate-centric sourcer or recruiter can possess, that burning desire to know or learn more. It makes the best look further, delve deeper, ask more questions, listen for the unspoken, question the status quo and strive to do better. It makes the candidate feel heard and valued and begins the building of trust in the relationship.

They are the recruiters who are not upset when a tool that reveals email addresses disappears because they know they will work out how to find information in other ways. They are the recruiters disappearing down social media warrens looking for interesting pieces of information to engage people with, who stand out in the noise online because they have taken a moment to do their research. In an interview, they are the recruiters who seem genuinely interested because they ask questions in a conversational tone of voice.

They are the recruiters who don't play exclusively in the LinkedIn sandpit; they use their curiosity and talk to their colleagues or candidates to discover what forums or social networks they prefer and will be found sourcing there. They find ways to expand their reach and join recruitment and sourcing groups on Facebook to seek inspiration from their industry colleagues.

Flex your curiosity by:

- Being brave enough to ask questions you fear are dumb. It's worse to pretend that you understand something when you don't! Just ask them to explain it until you do get it.
- Tapping into your inner toddler's need to learn and ask questions relentlessly.
- Study up on the industry you are recruiting in by reading news and blogs.

Further reading

If you would like to hire recruiters who are naturally curious:

- An interesting post from CIO on why you should hire for curiosity: bit.ly/CIOCuriosity
- Character interview questions from Adecco USA: bit.ly/AdCuriosity
- A case study from SurveyMonkey about creating a culture of curiosity: bit.ly/SMCuriosity

---

Listen

As clichéd as it sounds, humans have two ears and one mouth, and the best recruiters use them in that order. It is not enough to be curious, it is essential to listen, to really listen.

The benefit of speaking to candidates face-to-face or on a live video chat is that you can see their non-verbal communication or body language, which creates context around what they are saying. It also means they can see yours so sit up, let go of any tension in your shoulders and focus completely on the speaker. Even on a voice call, you will listen better if you turn away from your computer screen and focus completely. Be sure to mute your email and notifications for distraction-free calls and videos too.

Ensure your interviewers also practise active listening or you could find an interview review like this impairing your future hiring, 'The hiring manager wasn't focused, didn't make eye contact and answered her phone during the interview!' or this, 'The person who interviewed me was snorting and wasn't listening to me.' In Chapter 5, you will hear about the importance of partnering with your hiring managers and the intake strategy session; this could also be a great time to find out how confident they feel interviewing and if they would like some coaching.

Listen further

- Social listening tools give you access to what people are saying about your company, industry and competitors across social media and the web, which will help you engage better with candidates and hiring managers. Marketing Land recommends six of the best in this article: bit.ly/SLTools

- Take an honest look at your listening skills with this online quiz from *Psychology Today*: bit.ly/STListTest and test your body language reading skills here: bit.ly/BodLangTest

- Podcasts can improve your listening skills. You could start with Glenn Martin's and my weekly podcast 'The #SocialRecruiting Show', which you will find at anchor.fm/social-recruiting-show and you can find many more on Recruiting Brainfood's 'Big list of podcasts': bit.ly/RecPodcasts

---

Empathy

Empathy is the ability to understand and share the feelings of another; this shouldn't be confused with sympathy, which is to feel pity for someone else's situation.

Humans are sentient beings with the power to perceive, reason and think. People can perceive more than your words, they can feel the energy or be a highly sensitive individual who can sense other people's feelings and thinking by the vibration they give off. Have you ever walked into a room and just known that the people in the room had been arguing? The tension hanging in the air in the silence; that awkward vibe. This is something to be aware of when creating the mental and physical space for an interview; to provide fairness to the interviewee try to leave any stress or grievance outside of the room or away from the phone call. Give yourself time to arrive fully prepared and calm, which may mean ditching back-to-back interviews.

To ensure you remain robot-proof, you will want to be empathetic through the entire recruitment process. Put yourself in the candidate's shoes, walk through your entire application process, look for the hiccups that create a poor candidate experience, think about their concerns around changing jobs, the new environment, the new commute and their fears about it all going wrong. Think mostly about how you would feel if you were treated the way your applicants and candidates are being treated as this will give you true empathy.

Further reading

- Advice for building empathy into your recruitment process: bit.ly/IndEmpathy
- How to develop empathy at work: bit.ly/EmpathyWork
- Take an online quiz to test your empathy: bit.ly/EmpQuotient

---

Self-awareness

One evening out for dinner at my favourite restaurant, I watched with bemusement a couple on a date. They were both immersed in their phones; she would look up and see him looking at his phone, then he would look up and see her looking at her phone. This went on for a while until I audaciously walked over, turned their phones over, and told them to talk to each other.

Mobile technology with its almost addictive need to share our lives on social media has become such an interrupter that it can be difficult to realize its impact without using our powers of self-awareness. The interviewer who, for example, answered her phone during the interview demonstrated a lack of self-awareness.

Personal transformation author, Debbie Ford, provides this definition, 'Self-awareness is the ability to take an honest look at your life without any attachment to it being right or wrong, good or bad.'[2] In a work context, this means knowing what you're good at while acknowledging what you still have yet to learn, and includes admitting when you don't have the answer and owning up to mistakes.

Self-awareness isn't easy and it is difficult to do without judgement, we can be our own harshest critics, but by being present in the moment and aware of how we are being perceived by people, in this case, our candidates, we will become better recruiters and deliver a better experience for all.

Certainty and clarity

I distinctly remember the feeling of wonderment, en route from Dulles Airport to keynote at RecruitDC in 2016, realizing that I had used my iPhone to board my flight, order and pay for my taxi, look up directions, text home and, as I sat in the Uber, complete my banking using my thumbprint to pass security. The satellite navigation gave me certainty that I was safe, I was watching my trip in real time and had the clarity of knowing exactly when I would reach the hotel.

The advancement in technology had me awed but now the ability to easily gain certainty and clarity by using their mobile phone is second nature to 63.4 per cent of internet users.[3] Candidate-centric recruiters understand that people crave certainty, the confidence that they know what is going on, and clarity, the ease of transparent communication. Throughout the book, you will see examples of how you can use technology to improve the recruitment experience for candidates by providing certainty and clarity.

Committed influencers

There are parts of this book you may consider skipping, wondering what onboarding or alumni management has to do with you, for example. Committed recruiters understand that though you may not be able to control a certain part of the process, it does impact your ability to recruit, so they are committed to improving it or finding a workaround that will. Be committed to putting the human first and influencing all those involved in the recruitment process the benefit of doing the same.

Further reading

- Six steps to build recruiting influence from Matt Charney: bit.ly/MCInfluence
- Dos, don'ts and case studies on building influence at work: bit.ly/HBR-Influence

Brave

It is human nature to seek closure and avoid ambiguity, to want explanations for things we don't understand so we can move on. Think of a time when a relationship or friendship was suddenly over and they would not give you an explanation. Your mind races, you play out scenarios, you look for understanding where there is none to be found. The lack of closure makes it hurt for the longest time.

Candidate-centric recruiters face the difficult conversations head on and don't leave people hanging and wondering. Recruiters reject more people than they will ever place into jobs. Yet many recruiters hide behind technology instead of delivering bad news, and our news is that they didn't get the job, not that we don't love them anymore. Always remember the heartache, use your empathy, and give people the news and the closure.

In Chapter 8, we will look at technologies that can be used to reduce the number of applicants, ease the rejection process and humanize the interview process.

Further reading

- Scientifically proven ways to deliver bad news: bit.ly/SPBadNews
- *Fire Well* might be about terminating an employee but in it, author Sue Ingram shares many tips to help you conduct a difficult conversation: bit.ly/SIFireWell
- Article outlining different styles of managing conflict and when to use them: bit.ly/ConStyles

Collaborators and community builders

The walls of the silos came down with the creation of the internet and in place of silos, a collaborative world of knowledge sharing developed. Traditionally a collaborator would be considered someone near like a co-worker, colleague, teammate or assistant, but now collaborators include people online, anywhere in the world, people you may never have met, your fans, followers and supporters, people within your industry and those that are not.

To collaborate is to work jointly on an activity or a project; robot-proof recruiters are great collaborators, they want to help people and create communities where people can network, ask, learn, grow and exchange ideas. In the final chapter, you will hear more about social and alumni referrals that can come from a well-managed community of potential employees and your ex-employees.

For inspiration on becoming collaborative, look at the people keeping these recruitment communities engaged and valuable, and join in the conversation:

- Shannon Pritchett: SourceCon.com is more than a blog or conference, it is a community of sourcers and now thanks to the chapter events started by Mark Lundgren, Natalie Glick and Iker Jusué in Europe, and Vanessa Raath in South Africa, knowledge sharing is more accessible to those outside the United States.

- Matt Buckland, Matt Bradburn and Kristian Bright are the founding members of DBR, the largest Slack community of in-house recruiters and, with help from people like Sophie Power, run a series of events around Europe: bit.ly/DBRCommunity

- Alan Walker: #ChatTalent is now more than a blog; it is its own online community for knowledge sharing and discussing talent and technology challenges: bit.ly/ChatTalent

- Alex Moyle: set up the RecruitingGym for recruitment agency leaders to collaborate and seek answers to the questions that are holding them back: bit.ly/RecruitingGym

- James Ballard: established The Business Transformation Network to add more value to his agency's clients by providing an online portal of exclusive content and events across the UK, Germany and the Nordics: bit.ly/BTN-TV
- Louise Triance: UKRecruiter is the home of a community of recruitment professionals in the UK: bit.ly/UK-Rec. They run events for in-house and agency recruiters across the UK and it is the birthplace of RecruiterZone, where you can participate in video shows on a wide range of topics: bit.ly/RecZone

Social behaviour in real life

If you can, before you proceed, please spend three minutes watching Jena Kingsley's YouTube video, 'Social networking in real life', which you will find here: bit.ly/SocNetRL. Take note when she mentions connecting, endorsing and introductions because they relate directly to platforms like LinkedIn, Viadeo and Xing.

In the video, comic Jena Kingsley demonstrates impeccably the inanity of online social behaviour, from creepily following people around, to asking for introductions (referrals) from a stranger, to endorsing people for their coffee-making skills. Many interactions we think nothing of doing online, we would never act out in real life.

Unexplained invites to connect

When Jena sits down at the table of two strangers and says creepily 'Will you accept my friendship?', I felt uncomfortable. In fact, I cringed. In this instance, she is referring to Facebook but it differs little from professional networking sites like LinkedIn.

Recruiters have been led to believe that everyone on LinkedIn is happy to connect to a stranger but are they? By connecting with you, I give you access to my contact details and the ability to message me through the platform for free. That is my gift to you when I accept.

Unfortunately, over the years this has been abused by people transferring contact details from LinkedIn to their own databases and then sending the new connection irrelevant mass messages. When GDPR came into force in May 2018 modernizing the laws that protect the personal information of European individuals and impacting those dealing with the personal information of individuals in Europe, it was hoped that there would be a reduction in this kind of behaviour but unfortunately, it still happens, whether intentionally or not.[4]

Remembering as you are asking to connect, that you are receiving the trust of shared contact information if they accept, makes adding a personal note to demonstrate your professionalism the only logical choice. Later in the book, you will get some great tips for using the 300 characters to write a sincere invitation to connect, which candidate-centric recruiters always use to stand out from all of the other recruiters vying for the attention of the invitee.

Growth hacking

I am all for recruiters trying different ideas and marketing methods to reach more people and build communities that are valuable to members in the most efficient way possible, but there are lines and when you cross those lines you can end up irreversibly damaging your reputation and even angering people, and people don't forget the way you make them feel.

One of the darkest things about social media is the ease with which you can mute someone who you find annoying and leave them completely unaware. Think of the people on Facebook you have remained friends with but have unfollowed so you don't see their posts. It's the same on other sites; you can mute people on Twitter and unfollow people on LinkedIn. If you don't follow the etiquette of social media or if you constantly behave objectionably, by being snide and critical or disagreeing just because you think it gains you visibility, you could end up with thousands of followers but nobody actually listening or engaging.

It is worth being aware of the following etiquette no-nos so you gain a positive reputation from sharing valuable posts and content, and from engaging in useful conversation, so you build a community that will be your fans and want to comment, share your posts and help.

Tagging etiquette   On LinkedIn, I accepted an invite to connect from someone I have never met or interacted with, which said 'Hi Katerina, Love to connect. I am about to embark on a huge content strategy exercise in 2019, bringing interviews, mentoring, training and video to my connection base. Watched a lot of your work, very cool.' Ignoring the extra 'e' in my name, I was impressed that he had included a personal note, so I checked his profile to ensure it was genuine and then accepted.

In retrospect, the wording of his invitation is unclear but it definitely did not read as 'I will be forcing you to pay attention to my content by tagging your name in my posts'. The first time I was tagged, I glanced at the post and I didn't comment, like or share the post, I simply felt vexed and by doing nothing, I did not raise the post's online visibility. But the second time it happened, I was tagged in a motivational quote. I always feel like motivational quotes are telling me how to think, feel or act so I find them especially irksome. His intention may have been to brighten up my day but I was now angry because he was wasting my irreplaceable time by forcing me to check what I had been tagged in.

Nipping it in the bud, he received my curt message, 'By accepting your connection request, I wasn't giving you permission to tag me in posts on a regular basis. Would you walk up to a stranger on the street and ram a piece of paper in their face? That's the real-life equivalent.'

Imagine it, you have popped out to buy some lunch, you're focused on your rumbling belly, what to eat and ensuring you do so within your finite lunch break, when suddenly a person jumps in front of you, stops you in your tracks, and says 'Read this!' (piece of irrelevance). How would you react?

By connecting with someone, their updates appear in your feed and you can then decide whether you wish to see and engage with them. If the update is interesting to you, you will open it, engage with it, you may even comment or share it. But if it is not, you will keep on going down your news feed. As you will learn in the next few chapters, sharing valuable and relevant information helps you become known, liked and trusted, which is an essential part of being a recruiter worthy of someone's valuable time.

There was an easy way for my new connection to gain my attention, share my content. He had already mentioned that he had watched my work so he could have shared a recent show, with a caption like 'You have to listen to this from Katrina Collier and Audra Knight, they drop so much knowledge about…' Shifting the focus to me, from his own content, wins my appreciation. If you are wanting to gain the attention of a specific person, share their content. Compliment the post, ensuring it shows you have read it, and in this instance, it is OK to tag them. 'This is a great post by [name] because it goes into detail about [subject], be sure to give it a read.' The person will receive a notification that you have shared their content, perfect.

Once trust is earned and you have invested the time to become known to the person through comments and messages, tagging them on a self-promotional post will evoke a completely different reaction. But you must do the work first! Audra and I regularly tag our show's fans in tweets to let them know who our guest is, and because they like us and support us, they retweet them and comment.

Hacking trust   Trust is defined in the *Oxford English Dictionary* as the 'firm belief in the reliability, truth, or ability of someone or something'.[5] Trust is gained and trust is earned. In the fickle world of social media, it is easy to gain notoriety but difficult to gain trust. It takes time to build and once it is lost, it is rare to regain it.

Part of growth hacking involves trying new ways of attracting people to a new community. Most recruiters build communities of potential new employees, you could call it a talent pool, but it may simply be your own network. Some recruiters grow communities of peers to network among and learn from. The best of these have taken years to evolve and are tight networks of supportive recruiters sharing their knowledge and wisdom be it on Slack or in a Facebook group. There is trust and a feeling of safety in these communities because of the values of the founding members and how well the communities are managed. You could even call them clubs due to their, often unwritten, moral codes of behaviour.

In a real-life scenario, would you break into a tennis or golf club? Would you hack into the computer system or open the lockers to steal the members' private data from their wallets? Would you then use this data to invite them to your unknown club just down the road? Of course not. You know it is illegal, unethical and, potentially, breaching GDPR.

So just because it is possible to scrape Slack's open application programming interface (API) and transfer member emails to a marketing email tool, and to use that data to send video messages to thousands of people with an exclusive invitation to join your community, doesn't mean you should. It is immoral and likely to backfire by irreversibly damaging your reputation. If it involves European personal data, you will have breached GDPR, which could also have costly implications.

There is a distinct difference between using a tool that uncovers an email address that is publicly available on the internet, to start a conversation with someone about something that could be immediately valuable to them, and accessing an API to mass email another community's members to invite them to your own.

Contrary to what Google may reveal when you search for 'recruiters are', most successful and well-regarded recruiters have high morals and don't cross lines just because the technology is available to do so. Communities are built on trust and you cannot hack trust.

Human first, tech second

Candidate-centric recruiters use technology to support their processes and not to replace the human touch. They are curious enough to look beyond the shiny new toy or outlandish claim and properly assess if the latest buzzword-laden bit of kit will actually help or hinder their recruitment process.

Matt Buckland, former recruiter now VP of Customer Advocacy at Workable, makes a valid observation:

> The biggest problem in HR Tech is that people don't want something to help them do the work, they want something to do the work for them, and the majority of vendors are happy to sell the silver bullet dream. People buy into artificial intelligence which is supposed to free them up to do other things but I'm yet to find anyone who has seen the tangible benefit of more free time, instead they now spend it being a slave to the new piece of technology. There is an overwhelming amount of misapplied technology. Vendors produce a product without an audience in mind, so call it 'HR TECH!' and claim it will fix the broken world of recruitment, an industry the vendors had no experience of until 5 minutes ago.

Through the book, you will hear more about using the available technology to ease your workload, and much of that comes back to questioning your processes and assessing the available technology more deeply, and discover how to use technology to put the candidate first. You will also hear how your industry peers put the human first and use technology to create a better experience for the candidate.

To become a robot-proof recruiter, one that won't be replaced by technology in the future, you want to embrace technology but let it know who is in charge and, in this market, that is the candidate.

Summary

- The internet irreversibly changed the recruitment industry, shifting power from the company to the employee or candidate.

- The only time recruiters felt what a person with in-demand skills thinks when they open their inbox to more irrelevant messages, was during the onslaught of privacy and consent emails preceding GDPR.

- To be a candidate-centric recruiter that gains and holds the attention of in-demand talent, recruiters must make use of the soft skills that cannot be replaced by AI or automation.

- Play out online scenarios in real life to help you adhere to the nuances of social media etiquette.

- Ensure the vendor can explain exactly how the technology will help the candidate experience and ease the hiring process before investing.

- Don't try to use technology as a solve-all solution; make sure that it is you who is in charge of the technology, rather than the other way around.

Notes

1 Stack Overflow [accessed 11 April 2019] Developer survey results 2018, Stack Overflow [Online] https://insights.stackoverflow.com/survey/2018 (archived at https://perma.cc/QF37-PXJB)

2 Quote from Debbie Ford [accessed 11 April 2019] Goodreads [Online] https://www.goodreads.com/author/quotes/7851.Debbie_Ford (archived at https://perma.cc/4TNQ-XZGW)

3 Statista [accessed 11 April 2019] Mobile phone internet user penetration worldwide from 2014 to 2019, Statista [Online] https://www.statista.com/statistics/284202/mobile-phone-internet-user-penetration-worldwide/ (archived at https://perma.cc/8KQU-R9SC)

4 Burgess, M (2019) [accessed 11 April 2019] What is GDPR? The summary guide to GDPR compliance in the UK, *Wired*, 21 January [Online] https://www.wired.co.uk/article/what-is-gdpr-uk-eu-legislation-compliance-summary-fines-2018 (archived at https://perma.cc/KJ2U-H24S)

5 Definition of trust [accessed 11 April 2019] Oxford Living Dictionaries [Online] https://en.oxforddictionaries.com/definition/trust (archived at https://perma.cc/KJ2U-H24S)

Show you are a recruiter worth talking to 02

When recruiters spend their days looking at the social media profiles of candidates, it is surprising how few recruiters complete their own. If we look at people, people will look at us, and while we would be most likely to look on a professional site like LinkedIn, Xing or Viadeo, they may simply run our name through a search engine. Are you making it easy for people to form a good impression of you or hiding behind incomplete or cryptic profiles?

If like me, you have an unusual name, how you present yourself online is even more important or you could be repelling candidates without even realizing. Discussing this with Ondřej Procházka, Technical Sourcer at Facebook, he added a more important point, 'Most people fear [technical] recruiters not understanding the role and their needs and simply wasting their time.' With such a shortage of people with STEM skills, this shouldn't have surprised me but it was the use of the word fear. They fear having their time wasted, which makes sense, it is a finite resource.

So not only do you need to be able to cut through the noise of this modern world, past all of the other recruiters and sourcers vying for a person's attention, past all of their thinking about the risks involved in changing jobs, you also need to make sure that you won't waste their time, and look worthy of their time.

A quick search of 'recruiters are' on Google, Bing and DuckDuckGo will reveal the words that people type into search engines to describe recruiters. It shows how poorly recruiters are perceived. It is important to neutralize the stereotypes and this chapter will show you how to present yourself online to appear worthy of the time and attention of a person who possesses skills that are in high demand.

Curiosity and the internet

In 1989 when Sir Tim Berners-Lee created the world wide web, do you think he realized how much he would aid our natural human curiosity? Larry Page and Sergey Brin used their own curiosity in 1996 when, wanting to improve search engine results, they created a new product called PageRank. Later renamed Google, today the company processes over 92 per cent of all search traffic.[1]

To over 4.2 billion internet users, it is second nature to open a web browser and research new products and services, ask for recommendations or referrals, read reviews and much more.[2] The world has become transparent and when you send a candidate a message or if they see your advertisement, they will look at you and form an opinion. How you present yourself has always been important, and online this is no different. If you've given little thought to your online profiles and presence you're not alone but in a world of noise and interruption, your recruiting will improve significantly if you stand out for all the right reasons.

The easiest way to check your online presence is to open an incognito window in Google and search for yourself. If you have a fairly common name or share one with a celebrity, you may be harder to find but for most of us our LinkedIn, Facebook and Twitter profiles rank well.

Even if you think the network you are using is personal, it is likely easy for people to find you there and the curious will want to see what you are really like before they place the future of their career in your hands. Let's look at what you could do on the big four networks to improve your online presence.

Profile pictures

According to LinkedIn, InMail response rates improve if your profile has a picture.[3] Yet when I ran a Twitter poll asking 'How much thought did you put into your LinkedIn profile picture?' a startling 16 per cent of you said none and 44 per cent said some.[4]

During the same research, a sourcer shared that she very nearly didn't accept her current job because the head of talent acquisition uses a panda cartoon as a profile picture. Aside from the fact this breaches LinkedIn's User Agreement, she simply couldn't believe this talent acquisition leader doesn't take LinkedIn seriously.

Professional profile pictures are definitely subjective and impacted by the business we want to represent. As recruiters we want to look approachable, competent and trustworthy but can we do that without wearing corporate attire if our office is 'dress down'? To provide an example of factors to consider when choosing a profile picture, sourcer Mark Lundgren and I ran two different photos through Photofeeler. The site lets strangers vote on your picture based on your chosen category of business, social or dating and decides if we are competent, likeable or influential. See page 32 for the results for our images in the business category (Figure 2.1).

What this shows is that profile pictures are subjective but there are key takeaways here. Consider the difference between Mark's first and second photos; the scores show that users of Photofeeler are much more receptive to the second image that is better lit, more positive and has better body language. However, also keep in mind my pictures. The difference between wearing my glasses, regular or purple hair, and my level of competency is quite fascinating. Arguably these are not major changes, but this highlights how small factors can make a difference.

Ultimately, you can find the best profile picture by seeing what draws you to others'. After running Sjamilla Van der Tooren's two profile photos through we discovered what works best! A smiling approachable face, using a photo taken by another, and a blurred background to draw people to genuinely smiling eyes (Figure 2.2).

If you'd like people to find your other social media profiles more easily, it pays to use the same profile picture across those networks so they will come up on a browser image search. It's also worth checking in your LinkedIn settings, under Account and Site Preferences, to make sure that your photo is 'visible to all LinkedIn members'.

A word on unconscious bias

Unconscious or implicit bias refers to the attitudes or stereotypes that affect our understanding, actions and decisions in an unconscious manner.[5] It impacts everyone, including candidates. To substantially

Figure 2.1   Profile picture results from Photofeeler for Mark Lundgren and the author

BUSINESS	20 VOTES
Competent	12%
Likable	6%
Influential	12%

BUSINESS	20 VOTES
Competent	86%
Likable	46%
Influential	94%

BUSINESS	20 VOTES
Competent	78%
Likable	91%
Influential	58%

BUSINESS	20 VOTES
Competent	45%
Likable	59%
Influential	26%

Figure 2.2 Profile picture results from Photofeeler for Sjamilla Van der Tooren

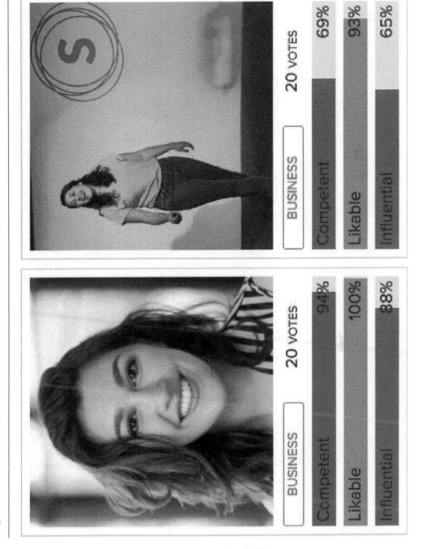

increase candidate response rates, I know of instances where foreign recruiters have created a second profile that better represents the local population. But be aware that the use of a fake LinkedIn profile not only breaches Clause 8.2a of the User Agreement, it also starts your hiring process off with a lie.[6] Instead use your social networks to build trust through your profiles, behaviour and value-adding posts.

Build out your profiles

Headlines and bio

You have mere seconds to get someone's attention so if you've hit their radar with your profile picture you need to quickly draw them in further with your headline or bio. It needs to have a purpose. You want to let people know what you're about while injecting confidence that you are trustworthy enough to place their career in your hands and worthy of their time.

Twitter bio

When I'm speaking at conferences my Twitter followers always increase. This rise comes from people I can tell are recruiters in attendance because they are using the conference hashtag. Yet if I look at their profiles I find them bare, which inhibits their ability to build a good following and succeed on Twitter.

On Twitter, the magic happens when you're following each other but you get mere moments to obtain that follow-back so make it easy by explaining who you are. And to stand out from other recruiters, your bio also needs to have some personality.

Some good Twitter bio examples

@AOChrisPiercy: Talent Acquisition Manager at @ao / @ao_jobs Love Hull FC, Hull City, Whisky and Crossfit but before that I need Developers in Manchester! #AOLetsGo #AOJobs

@Carole_Llamas: Sourcing Partner @Sky | #London | A #MusicLover | Passionate about #photography :)

@KatrinaMCollier: Candidate Engagement Author & Keynote | #HR #Recruitment Speaker | 🌐✈️♥️😺😺 | @DisruptHRLon Founder | @Retrak_Charity Ambassador | #BeHuman

---

We have all set the scene and made it easy to be followed, quickly. By using the @ symbol we are connecting our personal accounts to the company or careers Twitter account. Instead of just talking about work we have included our personal interests to give followers or candidates something else to engage with.

Side note: I am often asked, 'Do I tweet as myself or the company?' We are in a people business. We need to gain trust before people place their careers in our care. If you were looking for a job, would you want to deal with a faceless company or a real human?

Instagram bio

There are over 1 billion monthly Instagram users and, contrary to what you may hear, all generations use it.[7] People use the platforms that give them the best experience, so try not to rule it out before you have checked to see if your future recruits use it. You will hear more about how useful it can be for attracting talent in the next chapters.

If you use Instagram to share photos of your children, I recommend that you open a second account. Unlike Facebook and LinkedIn, where having two accounts breaches their user agreements, this isn't the case with Instagram. Keep your family account private and then have a public account that you use for recruitment and a mix of photos from outside of work. I'll expand on this a little later.

Like Twitter, the magic happens when someone follows you back so make it easy for them to get a sense of who you are from your bio.

Some good Instagram bio examples

@KatrinaMCollier: Candidate Engagement Author & Keynote | HR & Recruitment Speaker. 🐝✈️ traveller AU GB in London 🐶🐶 Retrak Ambassador ♥ #BeHuman #RobotProofRecruiter

@MNHeadhunter: Minnesota IT Recruiter | Minnesota Headhunter, LLC | Blogger | Speaker & Consultant: Recruiter, HR, Career & Social Media | Sports Politics

@RecruiterGuyNW: Yorkshireman. General sports fan. Does a bit in #talentacquisition to pay the bills.

Facebook bio

There are over 2.32 billion people using Facebook each month and, even if you consider it a personal network, it's where people are most active online and therefore most likely to head if they want to see what you are really like.[8] When I hear recruiters complain, stating that they would never use Facebook for recruitment, I despair at their lost opportunity to find the best people for their company or client and wonder why recruiters think people would act the same. Whether you want to or don't want to use Facebook for hiring, create the persona you want them to see, starting with your bio.

The inclusion of your work information is valuable whether you use this network in a professional or personal capacity. Vanessa Raath does this with style 'Happily married & life is great! Making a difference by Sourcing Top Talent & Changing People's Lives' and, importantly, she has also added her job title Head of Talent Acquisition at The iSPartner Group of Companies. If she sends a Message Request to a potential recruit, they see her job title and will understand what she is about from her bio. This leads to better candidate response rates and far less chance of being reported as spam.

LinkedIn headline

One of the most popular links on LinkedIn is 'Who's viewed your profile', which gives people the opportunity to find out who has stopped by their profile and to create new connections. The right combination of profile picture and headline matter when you are trying to gain attention. Though you'll have more success when you explain your intention, if you do send an unexplained invite to connect on LinkedIn, the headline could be the deciding factor between acceptance or rejection.

And is there anything worse than seeing '11 people with the job title recruiter' viewed your profile? What a lost opportunity. Please head to your Settings and under change your 'Profile viewing options' select 'Your name and headline'. Unless you have a safety reason for remaining anonymous, it won't matter if someone knows you have looked at their LinkedIn profile and it may even start an important conversation.

One example of an intriguing headline is from Sophie Theen, who is hiring and developing the team inside 11:FS as Global Head of

HR & Talent. She uses 'Busy shaping a cultural masterpiece here @ 11:FS | Mentor | Speaker | Not a woman but person in Tech'. She supports this statement with her choice of profile and banner pictures.

But beware the buzzword bingo and industry slang! Though you may know what is meant by 'sourcing guru', 'people magnet', 'unicorn hunter', 'search consultant' or for that matter 'talent acquisition', the people you are trying to reach may not. Use words they will understand immediately because building trust takes clarity and clear communication.

A different example of a strong headline is on Yulia Lidovskaia's profile, it simply states 'We are hiring! at Checkout.com'. This is concise and invites the viewer to find out more while also making it clear that she's involved in recruitment.

A successful headline can also be used to demonstrate valuable industry experience, like Andrew Dunne, Recruitment Consultant at First Hand Recruitment, '10 years solving recruitment problems in the Engineering & High Technology markets.' Not only does this capture attention, but it also explains to the reader that he's experienced and likely to be able to help, perfect.

But wait there's more!

I have a friend looking for a position as a remote sourcer and she has found that well under half of the recruiters she has viewed have completed their profiles. She is finding it off-putting, even wondering what they are hiding. When we ourselves make recruitment decisions based on the profiles we look at each and every day, it seems crazy that we don't complete or improve our own.

It seems even crazier in this transparent world when it is second nature to run a search to find an answer, to assume that nobody would look at your profile before they reply to your message or apply to your job. On receipt of an email from a stranger, how many have intrigued you enough to look up the sender? And how many times have you become sceptical when you have found little information?

If you have managed to get a candidate to click into your profile, your job is to hold their attention!

LinkedIn Summary

The first thing people see is your Summary, yet so often it is overlooked in favour of completing the Experience section. But you have to take into consideration how your profile is being read; though we prefer the desktop version, most candidates are likely to see your LinkedIn profile on the mobile or cell app and there are distinct differences between the two.

In the LinkedIn app, only your job title, company and dates are visible in the Experience section and, without scrolling, it is not easy to see that there is more information a tap away. Yet the Summary is mostly expanded and the fairly familiar use of '...' suggests there is more to be seen.

Fewer words show in the Summary depending on the choice of the device too. For example, this is what you see of my Summary on a desktop:

> I am a Candidate Engagement Author & Keynote Speaker & founder
> of DisruptHR London, Bristol, York & Glasgow. The Searchologist
> was founded to teach HR & recruiters social sourcing & recruiting and
> I have successfully delivered training to SMEs and corporates all around
> the world. In 2...

Compared to what you see on the mobile:

> I am a Candidate Engagement Author & Keynote Speaker & founder of
> DisruptHR London, Bristol, York & Glasgow...

Your first 20 or so words now matter more than ever, they need to increase curiosity so that people will click to see more.

While you're tinkering with your Summary, add some rich media. Photos and videos show well on both the desktop and mobile application versions of LinkedIn. This could be anything from your own achievements, to your company's or to something more personal but use these visual aids to reinforce that you are a recruiter worth talking to.

LinkedIn Experience

If you want to add the benefits or your achievements to your profile, you'll find these by asking yourself, 'so what?' A strong example of how to make the most of your experience can be seen in Sjamilla

Van der Tooren's profile: 'Blendle makes journalism accessible for everyone. One place for the best journalism from newspapers and magazines, without any subscription. Want to work at the nicest startup of the Netherlands? –> Check our job openings at [URL] or email me at [email address].'

It's easy to see what Blendle's mission is and the benefit of working there, to be intrigued by the cheek of calling it the nicest startup, and to follow the link to read more. Reading 'one place for the best journalism' could have left you feeling sceptical but because Sjamilla added 'without any subscription' the benefit is clear.

If you can, detail the achievements, challenges, passions, and the opportunities of your company like Technology Recruiter, Almog Greenberg at Zalando, has done, 'From logistics to big brands, to manufacturers; we're building the platform that connects all people and parts of the fashion ecosystem. We aim to set new standards for the industry. We are developing our own solutions to solve complex technical challenges and create new value for everyone that connects with our platform.'

To stand out on the agency side, be inspired by the wording on Debi Easterday's profile, 'Candidate-centric, heart-centric, employer matchmaker. At the centre of everything I do is the awareness that there is a human being at the end of every transaction' and her LinkedIn recommendations support this statement.

Look at your experience. Is it too generic? Is it a list of skills? Are you using it to market yourself and the company? Again, you can add rich media in this section, though preferably different from that in the Summary. Some ideas will be sparked when we discuss post ideas a little further on.

LinkedIn Recommendations

Considering how much we value restaurant and holiday reviews, I am always surprised to hear recruiters' scepticism of LinkedIn Recommendations. It is an opportunity for you to offer reassurance that you will take care of a candidate, that you will provide clarity and certainty during the stressful hiring process, and that you won't waste their time.

As recruiters, we understand that our role is often to support a candidate through the hiring process and recommendations offer reassurance that we will.

For example, Amy Miller starts her LinkedIn profile with 'Recruiter for Microsoft – helping rescue résumés from ATS black holes'. Now compare this with a recommendation from Matt Kincer that not only reminds us of the importance of our job, it reassures the reader.

> I can honestly say that without Amy, I would most certainly not be where I am today. I approached Amy at a time in my life when I was very frustrated and unhappy with the work I had been doing. Amy took it upon herself to help me in a way most wouldn't. Amy is an amazing person and it for that reason I feel comfortable recommending her for whatever she wants to do in life.

By adding recommendations to your profile from people that you have sourced or recruited, you too will be providing valuable reassurance to candidates.

Twitter links and location

As you saw in the earlier examples the bio can include references to other accounts, like your corporate Twitter account, by using the @ symbol and their username but you can make it even easier for people by adding links to your profile. If you're using Twitter for recruitment, you could link to your jobs or career site, or even across to LinkedIn. And if you do link to LinkedIn, be sure to add your Twitter account there too.

Though being quirky about your location may make you a little harder to find you don't have to include your exact location. Mine says 'London | Global Traveller ✈' because I'm so rarely here in London and so often on a plane. Recruiter Steve Levy, who tweets under @LevyRecruits, has written 'At the beach or on the trails', using the location field as an opportunity to share his interests and instead he includes his New York location in his bio.

Instagram links and Highlights

Just like on Twitter you can link to other sites from your (public) Instagram account so use this to direct people to your website, jobs, careers site or other profiles.

In 2018, Instagram also introduced Highlights as a way to save Instagram Stories, which normally disappear in 24 hours, into saved folders. This is another way to enrich your profiles, I've created Highlights for my speaking, 'The #SocialRecruiting Show' and, of course, my dogs. They're easy to rename so get creative.

Facebook featured images and links

Under your Facebook bio, you have the opportunity to represent yourself with five featured photos and nothing tells a story like an image. If you don't set your featured photos, the first thing a visitor to your profile sees are the last six public photos that you're tagged in. So rather than let Facebook choose the order, I've used photos that cover my speaking and training, my charity work, having fun in London and my annual birthday selfie.

Under your featured images, you can direct profile visitors to more information by adding links to your other social media sites or your website. You can also choose to display any Pages that you manage.

Side note: while you are in Facebook, under Privacy Shortcuts, look up your Activity Log and specifically photos you're tagged in and just check there aren't any old unflattering public photos floating around. If there are you can remove the tag or even ask for the photo to be deleted.

Another thing to consider is the visibility of your friends list. If you choose to hide it and send a potential candidate a Message Request, which we will cover later, the recipient will be looking at your profile to see if it is real or fake. If you hide your friends, it may seem fake. If you are concerned for your friends' security, most profiles are visible to a certain extent anyway, and your friends are in control of their own profiles and can completely lock down their visibility to the public.

Banner photos

Banner photos on LinkedIn, Facebook and Twitter are like the icing on the cake. You are probably familiar with using them on Facebook but few recruiters add them to LinkedIn and they're such great conversation starters.

Independent recruiter, Jay Perreault, uses a banner photo of him scuba-diving on both LinkedIn and Twitter @DCTechRecruiter, to stand out in the competitive technical recruitment field by showing off his love of diving. Manager of Talent Acquisition, Sydney Busch, on the other hand, shows off her love of sci-fi and Netflix with a banner photo of different shows on Twitter @RecruiterSydney and LinkedIn. And sourcer Mark Lundgren, shares his passion for his podcast, 'Sourcing Challenge Show', by displaying it in his banner photos on LinkedIn, Facebook and Twitter.

As you can see, there are no hard and fast rules and it is your profile after all but you could use yours to stand out and give someone a reason to start a conversation.

Become known, liked and trusted

You'll remember I opened the chapter talking about our poor reputation. Whether we deserve this negativity or not, you have to back up your great-looking profile with social media actions that show you are in fact a recruiter worth talking to.

In 2013, Copyblogger wrote a great post on this aimed at content marketers, called '30 ways to build the "know, like, and trust" factor that grows an audience'. While aimed at marketers, let me break it down for you and share some examples of how these points can be utilized by recruiters.[9]

Become known

It is important to become known for the right reasons. Unfortunately, all too often on LinkedIn I see recruiters complaining and even bullying each other in an attempt to be popular. And seen by whom, other recruiters? Before you even begin sharing updates and content decide who it is you are wanting to attract and talk to, and do some research so you know where to focus your attention; you want to be where your target candidates are being active.

Mark Lundgren is known for his 'Sourcing Challenge Show', in which he interviews other sourcers, to raise awareness of this fairly new industry specialism, the profile of the guest, and his own knowledge and skills.

As a contractor, it makes sense that he shares it on LinkedIn where recruiters and sourcers are most active. Tej Singh has become known for the interviews with minority founders on his podcast, 'Tej talks – diversity in startups', and because startup founders are on LinkedIn promoting their products and services he promotes it there and on Soundcloud.[10]

When you are hiring developers it makes sense to become known where they are most active. It's true, programmers don't like us much and the majority of recruiters avoid sites like GitHub because they don't understand them. But not Sjamilla Van der Tooren, she not only creates Repositories to become known by those she is seeking to hire, but she also stands out to other startups who may look to hire her. And she doesn't keep it a secret, she wrote a piece for the recruitment community on Sourcecon and then headed over to Medium, where 60 million monthly readers search for tags on tech, startup and programming, and shared the knowledge there too.[11]

Be likeable

In the Copyblogger article, they mention ways to be likeable online that include using your own voice, being real, being nice (that even got an exclamation mark!), inviting two-way conversation, being relevant, visible and generous.

Founder of Thomas Lee Recruitment, Mark Hopkins, is incredibly candidate-centric in all he does and expresses this through his updates, comments and free website downloads. He's also an avid fan of video, sharing vlogs like 'How to stay positive in a job search', which is so moving that I encourage you to go and watch it to remind yourself how important our job is.[12] You can find it on the Thomas Lee Recruitment website or YouTube channel.

He is always supporting others through his kindness and candour. Recently he created an outtake video that besides showing vulnerability and a great ability to laugh at himself, was highly encouraging to other recruiters to start using video.[13] Go watch how Mark Hopkins interacts online, you'll find he's exactly the same offline, which makes him genuinely likeable.

Build trust

In this section, Copyblogger suggests that in your blog or updates you give away your best stuff (tips, support, advice), don't disappoint, be consistently good, don't steal, avoid jargon and pompous language, apologize when you need to, and let your audience choose you.

Have you been letting your audience choose you? Just as we make consumer-based decisions, researching and thinking and making sure we are spending our money wisely, candidates are also researching and considering and deciding if they'll place their career in your hands.

Instagram makes it very easy to show people our complete selves. I am a huge fan, it's far more than a site for selfies, and it's helped me turn many client relationships into genuine friendships through the simple sharing of photos and comments.

Share your interests, your hobbies, your highs and even your lows. Aylin Halil, Global Talent Brand & Attraction Manager at ARM, does this perfectly sharing a mix of everyday moments, work high-lights, conferences and events, books she's reading, travel, food and, of course, gin. You gain personal insights which are far more believable than those found on most staid LinkedIn profiles.

Be sure to take those genuine Instagram moments and share them directly across to Facebook, if relevant, and via your camera roll to LinkedIn. And you will definitely want to use the free web-based service IFTTT to share all of your photos directly to Twitter as images (not links) too! You will find the IFTTT applet here: bit.ly/IFTTT-TI

In a different fashion, South African tech recruiter, Vanessa Raath, uses Twitter brilliantly to build trust with the job seeker community. Tweeting under @Van_Raath, she has increased her own visibility and been active support for job seekers, co-running #JobAdviceSA, a weekly Twitter chat connecting job seekers and recruiters. She also shares updates and articles that are relevant to the community she is building, answers any questions she receives, and is an avid supporter by retweeting those she follows.

When you meet me one day, you will find I am the same online and in person, and I know all the recruiters in this chapter are also easy to know, like and trust due to their actions ringing true both online and offline. It is essential that your online persona matches your real life one or any credibility you have gained with candidates will be lost in a moment. In the next chapter, I will explain how to make your hiring managers' online profiles and presence stand out to people with skills that are in high demand.

Summary

- Candidates are snooping around your social media profiles too so be sure to complete them and look like a recruiter worthy of their valuable time.

- Run an incognito search for yourself on Google to check for things that may be unexpected or need to be removed.

- Make sure that you look friendly and approachable in your profile picture and on LinkedIn, make sure your photo is visible to everyone in the settings.

- Inject some of your interests and hobbies into your profiles so that people have something to talk to you about besides jobs.

- Share updates and rich media that help you become known, liked and trusted.

Has this chapter surprised you? Tweet me @KatrinaMCollier using #RobotProofRecruiter

Notes

1 Statcounter [accessed 11 April 2019] Search engine market share worldwide Mar 2018–Mar 2019, Statcounter [Online] http://gs.statcounter.com/search-engine-market-share (archived at https://perma.cc/A9RU-9TH8)

2 Internet World Stats (2019) [accessed 11 April 2019] Internet users in the world by regions – March 2019, Internet World Stats, March [Online] https://www.internetworldstats.com/stats.htm (archived at https://perma.cc/W2PL-Q6P2)

3 Koutoudis, D (2016) [accessed 11 April 2019] How to rock your LinkedIn profile picture! Linkedsuperpowers blog [Online] https://linkedsuperpowers.com/post/how-rock-your-linkedin-profile-picture (archived at https://perma.cc/SD75-PJUP)

4 Tweet from Katrina Collier [accessed 11 April 2019] Twitter [Online] https://twitter.com/KatrinaMCollier/status/995305805925756928 (archived at https://perma.cc/TMS7-4TKP)

5 Kirwan Institute (2015) [accessed 11 April 2019] Understanding implicit bias, The Ohio State University [Online] http://kirwaninstitute.osu.edu/research/understanding-implicit-bias/ (archived at https://perma.cc/J4LT-GZHJ)

6 LinkedIn User Agreement (2018) [accessed 11 April 2019], LinkedIn, 8 May [Online] https://www.linkedin.com/legal/user-agreement (archived at https://perma.cc/K42P-VQKB)

7 Statista [accessed 11 April 2019] Number of monthly active Instagram users from January 2013 to June 2018 (in millions), Statista [Online] https://www.statista.com/statistics/253577/number-of-monthly-active-instagram-users/ (archived at https://perma.cc/ZS38-JW4G)

8 Facebook Company Info [accessed 11 April 2019], Facebook Newsroom [Online] https://newsroom.fb.com/company-info/ (archived at https://perma.cc/H7Z6-PF8B)

9 El Morshdy, G (2013) [accessed 11 April 2019] 30 ways to build the 'know, like, and trust' factor that grows an audience, Copyblogger [Online] https://www.copyblogger.com/30-know-like-trust-actions/ (archived at https://perma.cc/5V9D-5PRD)

10 Tej Talks Diversity [accessed 11 April 2019] SoundCloud [Online] https://soundcloud.com/tejtalksdiversity (archived at https://perma.cc/57PJ-V4CD)

11 Van der Tooren, S (2018) [accessed 11 April 2019] Budget sourcing 101: Building a talent pool in GitHub, Medium [Online] https://medium.com/@sjamillavdtooren/budget-sourcing-101-building-a-talent-pool-in-github-dcda0e08d517 (archived at https://perma.cc/282X-XZ6F)

12 Thomas Lee Recruitment (2018) [accessed 11 April 2019] How to stay positive in a job search? YouTube, 3 August [Online] https://www.youtube.com/watch?v=BADV4ALznXk (archived at https://perma.cc/EL7Q-BCSL)

13 LinkedIn post from Mark Hopkins [accessed 11 April 2019] LinkedIn [Online] https://www.linkedin.com/feed/update/urn:li:activity:6431184707077046272/ (archived at https://perma.cc/8K5H-QKC8)

What about your hiring managers? 03

The most successful recruiters have strong bonds with their hiring managers. This seems obvious, right? Yet I have had clients so scared to leave the safety of their office only to be blown away by the difference it makes to their hiring when they have got out into the business and formed positive connections with their hiring managers.

The more time you spend cultivating these relationships the easier the recruiting process will be. You'll gain the knowledge to know what they're really looking for, you'll understand the team dynamic, you'll know the projects they are working on and what is exciting or challenging them. Importantly, you will gain their trust and respect, and that is invaluable if you want to deliver the best possible experience for your candidates.

Technical recruiter, Jatinder Bansal, agrees, 'Investing the time to talk to the business; my hiring managers, their managers and beyond allows me to influence correctly – especially when it comes to recognizing skills gaps, making L&D technical upskilling recommendations, and continually improving the technical selection and interview process.' Working in the startup world, where competition for people is fierce, Jatinder knows he needs to keep his managers in the know so they will make good hiring decisions, 'I bring my hiring community loads of market intel and data points around tech stacks and competitor info, which means they really know what is going on outside of their day-to-day work bubble.'

If you have your hiring manager on your side they will be more open to being proactive in the recruitment process, even open to the basics like filling out their social media profiles so they look more interesting when potential applicants are checking them out online.

Hiring manager profiles

How often have you asked in an interview, 'What do you know about us?' only to be disappointed when the interviewee has little to say? In today's online world it does seem crazy that people haven't run a search, especially when our phones are rarely out of reach. But are we even giving them the information they want?

Recently I became acquainted with Simon Halkyard, Resourcing Manager at ASDA, and I sure wish it had been sooner. He's not short of an opinion on how we can do recruitment better and he backs it up with facts and a dose of humour. In the middle of researching for this chapter he asked on LinkedIn, 'If you were applying for a new job would you check out the LinkedIn profile of the person you would report into and the team beforehand?' and though the majority of answers backed up my thinking there were a few surprises.[1]

I was reminded that diligent recruitment agents send the interviewer's LinkedIn profile to their candidates; it makes sense, they want their candidate to have done their research so they are hired. If you work in-house, you will want to influence your hiring managers to complete their LinkedIn profiles at a minimum and preferably, complete all of their profiles on the sites most likely to be used by your industry. For example, they may need to complete their GitHub profile if they recruit developers or their Bēhance profile if they recruit designers.

Recruitment Founder at Maxwell Bond, Steve Jagger, answered Simon's question by explaining that his candidates are looking for commonality, wondering if they can work for the person or team, if they will share values, if it will be beneficial to both the candidate and the company, and if they know someone who can tell them what the company is really like. He went on to add that he sends more than just the hiring manager's LinkedIn profile, 'There are so many social media tools out there like Facebook, Reddit, Twitter, Xing, GitHub, StackOverflow, Bēhance, use all the tools available! Always give yourself the best chance, 7Ps.'

If you translate the 7Ps there is a lot to take into consideration:

1 Product: your job, the project, the challenge, the skills, the knowledge to be gained, etc.

2 Place: online job boards, job posts, billboards, vehicle stickers, newspapers, magazines, etc.

3 Price: the salary or rate, benefits, perks, learning and development opportunity, etc.

4 Promotion: proactive sourcing, headhunting, targeted PPC campaigns, referrals, etc.

5 People: your employees, customers, alumni, the hiring manager, the team, etc.

6 Processes: the hiring process or obstacles to hiring, and the candidate experience.

7 Physical environment: your company, onsite or remote, flexible working, values, culture, etc.

So few recruiters are even taught to sell, even fewer to market themselves, but to stand out in a market where candidates have so much choice and so much distraction, you have to. Your hiring managers have to. Your company has to.

Simon's Talent Acquisition colleague, Peter Tam, added this 'It's like when you view a trailer and are either enticed to see the film or not...' and reinforced it with 'the outside view needs to mirror the reality.' If you are shaking your head like me and thinking 'Exactly!', our scepticism of over-polished content makes people yearn for honest peer-to-peer information. It has to seem real; overly corporate profiles will work against you too, they need grit.

Graeme Coyne, who had recently joined DocuSign, added 'Definitely. I did this only a month ago as I moved roles. I was looking to see the calibre of my teammates and manager based on experience, tenure in the company and the skills they have.' He went on to explain that he was looking at their recommendations, at their experience to determine how much he could learn, what their background was as this explains who they hire and gives more insight into whether the culture was for him.

This is evidence that people will read recommendations, no matter our own scepticism. Adding a rounded view of your hiring managers, by asking them to add recommendations from those they manage, those they work alongside and those they report into, can only help the hiring process.

But this reply, from GDPR Programme Manager Natasha Pye, was my favourite, 'Absolutely and Facebook, I'm interviewing them as much as they are interviewing me, who you work for is so important, it can easily make the difference between loving and hating your job.'

Though the irony of Business Intelligence Manager Gareth Roberts adding 'Snap. Interview stalking. They always seem surprised when I mention about it' was a close second. We spend our days looking at people's profiles, and we regularly send profiles of interviewees to our hiring managers, so why is anyone surprised that people look at us too?

Polish up your hiring managers' profiles

It is definitely a fine line because you want your hiring managers to look interesting to candidates so they will want to come in for an interview but you don't want them to look so great that they are enticed away by other recruiters.

Ashley Bush, University and Employment Brand Recruiter at Tenable, trains her hiring managers on LinkedIn, encouraging them to use a profile picture and add rich media to their Experience section, from the library of pre-approved content. 'It's tricky. We don't want to ask our hiring managers to just be brand advocates for Tenable and we also don't want it to be forced on them. And nor do we want them to market themselves so well that they get poached!'

Working in the cybersecurity industry, some are reluctant to add their photo so she encourages them with, 'You connecting with someone on LinkedIn without a photo is like you going to a networking event with a bag over your head, it just doesn't make any sense. The point is to network and put a face to the name, right?'

Everything mentioned in the last chapter applies to your hiring managers' profiles though, frustratingly, you may find they undo your hard work and guidance when too many recruiters approach them. It is a necessary catch-22 because your future hires are looking at them.

You are encouraging them to add a great profile and banner photo, plenty of information under the summary and experience, rich media demonstrating their passion for the company, anything that shows they would be a great boss to learn from. If they volunteer, ask them to include this information to inspire, and any achievements that reinforce their knowledge and experience.

Just updating your hiring managers' profiles won't be enough, you need to encourage them to engage and by doing so they will build a community of people interested in your company and the work. David Wolstenholme, Founder of BrandMeBetter, agrees that personal brand is so much more than a great profile and it can be used to build a following that makes talent acquisition easier:

> They have such an opportunity to build a community of people aligned to the organization and their team by sharing their stories and personality. They could easily remove barriers to attracting the right people if they were more involved in sharing their purpose and values. But it has to start at the top with your CEO, get them on board and you will be able to differentiate yourself from everyone else vying for your candidate's attention.

If you really want to maximize your talent attraction use peer-to-peer or employee-generated content, which you will learn about in the next chapter. People want to see information from people who understand their role so encourage your hiring managers to share either their own updates or content from their colleagues and peers.

If your leaders speak at events and conferences, you have the opportunity to harness their networks and reach, which will be discussed in more detail in Chapter 6. Make sure your hiring managers share online that they are speaking because it shows off their knowledge and experience and will generate interest in potential recruits. Edosa Odaro, Head of Data at AXA, did this simply by sharing an update that said, 'Delighted to be speaking at this year's #AICongressLDN – looking forward to collaborating, knowledge sharing, and learning from the exciting line up of not just attendees but other speakers too.' Importantly Edosa answered every comment, which ensured he and AXA looked good, and that the visibility of the post was raised further.

Transparent C-suite

If I asked you to name the CEO of Virgin or Tesla, you would probably have no problem naming Richard Branson or Elon Musk, or if I asked you for the name of the COO of Facebook, you would most likely know Sheryl Sandberg. These C-suiters have a brand, people feel like they know them, they have character and they seem accessible because you can see inside their lives on Instagram. But you don't have to be a big-name company to have open senior leaders.

My friend Kelly Hartman adores being Chief People Officer at Flywire, one of the most transparent companies I have come across. In the Inside Flywire section of their blog, you will see a post from their CEO Mike Massaro, talking about Flywire's recent Series D funding round.[2] In the video Mike talks with enthusiasm about the opportunities that the investment creates for FlyMates, the term they use for their people. This transparency not only aids employee engagement and retention, but it also attracts new recruits and Kelly confirmed, 'He attracts loads!'

Mike Massaro does have advice for other CEOs:

> If you are going to be a CEO that wants transparency in your business
> and tells your employees that they can ask you anything, you better mean
> it! Be ready to answer the hard questions like 'how much money do we
> have?', 'why are we doing this?', 'how many shares are outstanding on the
> Cap Table?', etc. If you aren't ready to answer these types of questions,
> you shouldn't make transparency a cornerstone of your culture as it
> won't be authentic.

But if you are ready to be transparent, you will not only attract many new people like Mike does, you will also keep your current employees engaged.

Talent attraction through sharing and mentoring

People like to work with people they'll learn from and grow with. Rather than believe what they hear from recruiters or the hiring manager during an interview, people do their research. In the same way people research for holidays and purchases, candidates are looking for evidence of where they will learn and grow.

If you were hiring for a designer to work at WhatsApp, you could simply send candidates the LinkedIn profile of hiring manager, Charlie Deets, but it isn't especially inspiring considering how creative he is (sorry Charlie). And though he does hint at his other work, the link to his personal website and the amazing stuff he contributes to the product design industry is hidden under Contact Info and not immediately obvious to the less savvy LinkedIn user, which realistically most LinkedIn users are.

Yet, digging deeper you find his personal website and there discover that Charlie co-hosts a micro-podcast about design and technology with Gabriel Valdivia.[3] Episodes tackle tough topics like quitting your job, gaining confidence and how to present design at work, which are valuable to nurturing the next generation of designers. It is the kind of information candidates want to see, especially if they are looking for evidence that they will learn and grow. If Charlie was my hiring manager, I would encourage him to share the podcasts on LinkedIn and, of course, I would share them myself on all of my social networks.

Charlie is also an avid blogger on Medium, writing posts like 'One year designing at WhatsApp: Thoughts on how WhatsApp and Facebook design at scale', a post of lessons learned and differences discovered.[4] In the blog, written for other product designers, he talks about things they would be drawn to, the strong product principles, utility driving engagement compared to engagement driving utility, design tools and skills, and problems encountered.

Importantly, he wraps up the post with enthusiasm and a call to action, 'I also wrote this in the hopes of raising awareness of WhatsApp Design. We are a growing team and looking for more people to help out. If these values or ways of working sound interesting to you, you should check out our open positions, especially our Product Designer role,' because even Facebook and WhatsApp need to work to attract people with these niche skills.

Reinforcing the fact that though recruiters may be overflowing on LinkedIn, the people they may be looking to recruit are active elsewhere. Consider Sarah Kuehnle, Head of Product at Dribbble. She not only uses her own platform, Dribbble, to attract people to her work, she also shares exactly what is involved in her daily work via live video-streaming site Twitch and on her Instagram account. This gives her the opportunity to tap into a daily active audience of 15 million Twitch users and to showcase the job in a unique way, literally looking over her shoulder while she works.

Pablo Stanley, Design Lead at InVision, ensures his LinkedIn profile shows that he shares knowledge and mentors. He has one of the better hiring manager LinkedIn profiles around, with the addition of plenty of rich media and the extension of an open invitation to get in touch. It could do with the addition of a summary and some recommendations but it is great that he clearly refers to his two side hustles, his blog on Medium and his workshops at Sketch Together, that attract people through the sharing of knowledge and through mentoring.

On Medium, where he has over 25,000 subscribers, Pablo writes a comic series called 'The design team' that pokes fun at the tech world and the quirky design culture in the middle of it, while it also educates junior designers.[5] He also creates his own pool of talent as Founder and Mentor at Sketch Together, affordable design and prototype tool workshops. As if this is not enough, he also finds the time to run the 'Late night design show' on YouTube for his 67,000+ subscribers.[6]

Are your hiring managers as enthusiastic about their craft? You may need to go digging to find out but once you know, your job is to maximize it. Share their posts to your own networks, instead of sharing a stream of boring job posts, and ask your hiring manager if they could add a call to action and a link to your jobs, as Charlie Deets has done.

In their own words; give people a voice

There's no denying it, blogging or vlogging is time-consuming! Those who write often and in detail are incredibly dedicated to sharing their ideas but many people end up failing due to a lack of consistency caused by limitations on their time. But you can make it easier for your leaders by giving them space to share their expertise on your own platform; a blog full of many authors.

I'm differentiating this space from traditional employer branding blogs, which I'll talk about in the next chapter because these are your leaders sharing their expertise, experiences and lessons learned in their very own words, and they're doing it for any number of reasons, not just talent attraction.

Zalando SE is Europe's leading online fashion platform, connecting customers, brands and partners in 15 countries, delivering to customers in 17 countries, and hiring people from the incredibly competitive design and technical space.

On Medium, you will find a blog called 'We design', which is a collection of thoughts from their very own design team and it is made up of different series, like 'Zalando design leadership series' and 'Role call'.[7] The transparency of the leaders writing about their roles, responsibilities, opportunities, growth and more is especially appealing. They all end their blogs with a call to action to join the team but they are completely valuable on their own as advice to other designers, setting realistic expectations of life within the role and Zalando, and even to those who will rule themselves out and choose a different path.

Blogging is such a great way to demonstrate your values and culture. In 'Role call with Leonardo Lanzinger', an interview with Zalando's first creative technologist, you hear directly from Leonardo about the creation of this new position and how it came about. It shows that Zalando truly values intrapreneurs and isn't just paying them lip service.

Fearlessly the blog links to Leonardo's GitHub portfolio, which includes his direct email. Could you poach him? You could try, but it is unlikely he would leave a firm that created a job position especially for him. Could your people be poached if you showcase them? Definitely, so look after them.

Talent deselection due to poor candidate experience

People deselect themselves from the hiring process and that's OK if it is for the right reasons. In fact, in later chapters, you will learn about technology that can be used to aid deselection, but you don't want people with the skills you need deselecting because of a poor experience with your company.

Explaining candidate experience, employer branding expert, Audra Knight says, 'Candidate experience is still fairly new for every company and it feels like this is the first year people are taking it seriously. There is so much more to the candidate experience; it is the whole hiring process from too many clicks to apply, to their experience with content and, of course, to how the hiring manager treats them. It's so much more than if the recruiter gets back to them or not!'

Audra's colleague, Ashley Bush, trains the hiring managers on candidate experience. They are under instruction to be respectful of a candidate's time, not to ghost, to give feedback appropriately, etc, and they understand the impact to recruitment of delivering a poor candidate experience.

When I asked Ashley how she wins them over, the eternal struggle, she said, 'They like stats! Facts only. Logic. Show them the numbers of declines, show them the struggles, and show them the disruption caused by changing the interview process part way through. Educate them on the numbers and explain to them that you are trying to save them time and money. Speak their language, stats get buy-in!'

But the impact of not taking care of candidates is now easy to see online and not just on Glassdoor. Feedback on application and interview processes can be found on review site Comparably, on Xing company pages, in Facebook public posts and on company pages, on LinkedIn updates and company pages, on Twitter and even on Google Maps, which is visible to all candidates looking for directions to your company.

Interview feedback

You are the main point of contact for the candidate. Your job is to obtain and deliver feedback from the hiring manager, especially if the candidate has invested time interviewing online, on the phone or in person. During the intake strategy session, which we will discuss in Chapter 5, get your hiring manager to agree to the interview process and a time frame for delivering feedback. If you want to prevent people from deselecting because of how they are treated or how others are treated, it is essential to get good at delivering feedback.

In Chapter 8 you will read about technology that can be used to assist with the interview process but put the human first. As Recruitment Manager Joanne Ward says, 'An applicant who makes it through face-to-face interviews should always, at the very least, be rejected by a phone call or video chat. They've committed a lot of time and effort to your process and this should be reflected in the manner of your rejection. Provide them with honest, constructive interview feedback and specific reasons, and follow up via email if they request it for reflection later'.

Delivering negative feedback is tough, especially when you are attached to the outcome, but because recruiters receive more applications than needed for the role, recruitment is a business of rejection. It is better to deliver negative feedback than to infer another person's time and effort isn't valuable. Plus today, candidates have an outlet for their annoyance, negative interview reviews end up on sites like Glassdoor and will stop you hiring, it will help people deselect.

My hope with this book is to inspire recruiters and their hiring managers to provide closure so that it is not possible to find 27,000 results when running this search **site:glassdoor.com/interview "never heard back" OR "no feedback"** in Google. In the staggeringly high number of results, which are only from the people who took the time to write a review, you will find interview reviews from other recruiters interviewing; it seems recruiters often mistreat their own peers during the interview process.

One of the more memorable ones is for a recruiting coordinator interview at Twitter. It stood out because the interviewee used email tracking software and could see that the recruiters and hiring managers had read her emails and were still not replying. 'I got ghosted! I had a phone interview, two face-to-face interviews and met with five other recruiters and the hiring manager', then she heard nothing. All of that time invested interviewing and not a word of feedback or closure.

Ironically, this past Halloween a sourcer at Twitter, attempting humour, added a post on LinkedIn about candidates ghosting, meaning disappearing in the middle of the hiring process. Hoping to inspire a change of behaviour, I added a screenshot of the aforementioned review to the thread of comments and suggested that if Twitter's recruiters looked after candidates they wouldn't ghost. It was very disappointing that instead of replying with the intention to investigate and improve their processes, the post was simply deleted.

Much of the motivation for writing this book is because I despair that we cannot even look after our industry colleagues. On top of the disrespect exhibited to this interviewee, there is the problem that four people found the interview review helpful. Four potentially great people won't have applied. How many others will have found this review helpful and simply not clicked the box? We don't know.

Not delivering feedback to someone who has invested time in interviewing is poor but imagine how an interviewee would feel after paying for their own flights to attend an interview, after the hiring manager promised in writing to reimburse all expenses, to discover that they won't be reimbursed? The company is refusing to answer correspondence or the phone, and as this was done to a global head of talent acquisition, they knew to write a review online to warn others and hamper the company's future hiring. It is essential that your hiring managers don't make promises they don't intend to keep.

On the bright side

Interview reviews are dynamite! They can show you where your process needs to improve and will definitely tell you what support you and your hiring managers need. Difficult conversations in the workplace don't come naturally to people, and interviews and rejection conversations are right up there in terms of difficulty.

I remember how hard it was to tell someone they did not make the cut, but if you put yourself in their shoes and think about how it would feel to be interviewing over and over, and nobody taking the time or having the kindness to tell you why you are being rejected again and again, it is much harder for the candidate.

Master of difficult conversations and author of *Fire Well,*[8] Sue Ingram, added:

Hiring managers have the opportunity to change lives by giving feedback on things that people cannot see about themselves, both strengths and talents as well as weaknesses. It is a necessary skill for all managers to acquire. Once learnt and practised it is easy and simple to apply and will transform their own career because staff and candidates will clamour to work with a manager who truly develops their talents. A manager who is generous enough to treat everyone, whether a shining star or a rejected candidate, with the same attention, care and professionalism will find it easy to attract and recruit great employees.

Candidates are in charge. They have choice. They can talk to you or not. They can pick your company or not. They can interview or not. They can write a poor or a glowing review. It comes down to you and your hiring manager.

Senior Manager, Global Talent Acquisition at INAP, Michael Crouse recommends you 'Treat everyone like they are your friend. Let them know if they are not selected. They may not like the news but they appreciate the transparency. Last year I made four hires from referrals from rejected candidates, because I was honest and took time to let them know.' How is that for an incentive to get your hiring managers giving you feedback?

There is plenty more that your hiring managers can be doing to help your recruitment process, which ultimately helps them build a successful team. You will hear more about how to involve your hiring managers throughout the book and discover how to gain their buy-in in Chapter 5 when we discuss intake strategy sessions, the most critical yet often overlooked part, to ensure successful recruitment.

Summary

- By proactively sourcing and sharing industry and competitor intel you will become invaluable to your hiring managers.

- By building stronger ties with your hiring managers they will be more likely to share your posts to their networks.

- Encourage your hiring managers to be more relaxed and human on their social media profiles and to showcase their work so candidates can see their interests and values.

- Don't focus energy exclusively on LinkedIn, ask your hiring managers to complete profiles and engage where potential recruits are most likely to be active.

- Encourage your hiring managers to be respectful of every candidate in the process by always delivering clarity and feedback so that candidates don't deselect for the wrong reasons.

What will you do differently? Tweet me @KatrinaMCollier using #RobotProofRecruiter

Notes

1 LinkedIn post from Simon Halkyard [accessed 11 April 2019] LinkedIn [Online] https://www.linkedin.com/feed/update/urn:li:activity: 6424986112380542976/ (archived at https://perma.cc/RRE8-9PU6)

2 Massaro, M (2018) [accessed 11 April 2019] Recent series D funding round, Flywire, 8 August [Online] https://www.flywire.com/currentcy/ inside-flywire/mike-massaro-ceo-temasek-investment-100m/ (archived at https://perma.cc/TD6S-B2VM)

3 Bread Time podcast [accessed 11 April 2019] Bread Time [Online] https://breadtime.simplecast.fm/ (archived at https://perma.cc/MG6H-KCWF)

4 Deets, C (2017) [accessed 11 April 2019] One year designing at WhatsApp, Medium [Online] https://medium.com/facebook-design/ one-year-designing-at-whatsapp-c20b4c46bae6 (archived at https://perma.cc/N43H-QESV)

5 Pablo Stanley [accessed 11 April 2019] The Design Team, Medium [Online] https://thedesignteam.io/@pablostanley (archived at https://perma.cc/WC7G-B9YK)

6 Sketch Together YouTube channel [accessed 11 April 2019] YouTube [Online] https://www.youtube.com/channel/UCZHkx_OyRXHb1D3XTqOidRw/f (archived at https://perma.cc/4PDF-CZRV)

7 We Design blog [accessed 11 April 2019] Medium [Online] https:// medium.com/zalando-design (archived at https://perma.cc/Z552-DBCW)

8 Ingram, S (2015) *Fire Well: How to fire staff so they thank you*, Rethink Press Ltd, Great Britain

Show you are a 04 company worth talking to

Reputation is an important factor when it comes to attracting, recruiting and retaining employees. In Ranstad US's 2018 survey, 86 per cent of respondents said they would not apply for or continue to work for a company that has a bad reputation with former employees or the general public, and 65 per cent would likely leave if their employers were being negatively portrayed in the news or on social media because of a crisis or negative business practices.[1]

That is a staggering figure! Eighty-six per cent of people would not apply to or stay at a company that has a bad reputation, which they can easily see online. Unlike reviews about the candidate experience, which are only separated out on Glassdoor, Comparably and Indeed's Q&A section, reviews from employees are more prominent on Glassdoor, Indeed, Comparably, Jobcase, Fairygodboss, RateMyEmployer.ca, TheJobCrowd, CareerBliss, Vault, InHerSight, LookBeforeYouLeap, Kununu and even Yelp. People will write their reviews where they want to, which means you need to monitor them all, especially now that Google for Jobs makes them all the more prominent.

Disruptive Google for Jobs

In 2015, a developer wrote a post on LinkedIn that explains the problem with job searching quite aptly, 'The majority of agencies swamp job boards and ads to the point where *real* job ads are hard to find.' The developer went on to explain that most jobs are generic, because the agency doesn't have a role in mind, that they really are only gathering CVs so they can use them to open a door at a company. In his experience, the developer finds most recruiters only know 'keywords rather than have any understanding of the profession or geography, so about 90% of the roles they match you to are completely inappropriate.' This is far from a pleasant experience for a job seeker.

Unfortunately recruiters now also swamp LinkedIn so much so that the developer states eight times on his profile 'recruiters do not contact me', but I will come back to that in Chapter 7.

Google for Jobs has been introduced to make the job-seeking experience smoother. Instead of active job seekers trawling through countless job boards, which were dominated by the job board aggregators and those who paid the most to be in the top three results, they can now see tidy results.

To provide an example, I have run a search on Google for 'recruiter jobs london', which can be seen in Figure 4.1.

In my results, the very first job was for Industrial Light & Magic. In one easy roll down the job description, I faced review rankings from Glassdoor, Indeed and PayScale, and could see the likely salary via LinkedIn. With ease the job seeker can also see where a role has been posted and choose how they would like to apply. Which would you choose, a job board, LinkedIn or the company's website?

Job seekers can also filter further by Category, Title, Location, Date posted, Type and Employer, and in quite a game-changing move, they can also filter out staffing firms under Company type. This creates even more opportunity for companies who take the time to improve the quality of their job postings, have a great employer brand and deliver an exceptional candidate experience.

Another change impacting agency recruiters is that Google requires the location and salary to be included or the post is unlikely to be among the Google for Jobs results. Transparency is key and this goes against the thinking of a lot of staffing firms who are still trying to hold on to their little black books of contacts. Instead they need to build closer ties with their clients through value-added service and aim for exclusivity of jobs.

There are also technical considerations to make when posting jobs on your website, like ensuring your jobs will be indexed and improving your search engine optimization (SEO), so I recommend you have

Figure 4.1 Google for Jobs results

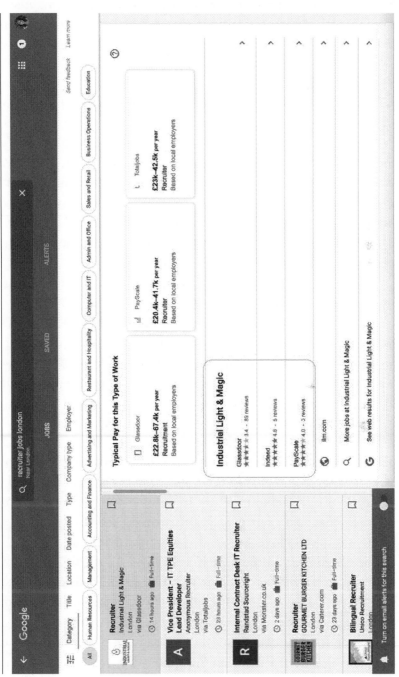

a look at the 'Google for Jobs playbook for recruiters' from Firefish Software, which you can download at bit.ly/FirefishG4J. Also consider using Jobiak or GJtraffic to ensure your jobs are posted directly to Google for Jobs.

Employee and interview reviews

People want to be heard. That is why consumers write reviews when they are disgruntled. It is why we go to Twitter when customer service isn't helping us. Whether we like it or not, company review sites give people the opportunity to have their say in a way that is often not possible in the office. They also make up for exit interviews because few people will be truly honest about their reasons for leaving in case they jeopardize receiving a reference.

That is why there are over 40 million reviews on Glassdoor and a staggering 72 million plus on Indeed.[2]

Having heard every objection under the sun from recruiters saying that reviews don't matter, that candidates don't look at them and even an indignant 'How very dare they!', and even if you don't believe it when Glassdoor says that job seekers read four to seven company reviews, Google for Jobs is placing them front and centre.[3] It's better to deal with them than repel the people you do want to recruit.

Research carried out by Indeed in April 2018 found that nearly 75 per cent of respondents said seeing responses from employers to negative reviews would change their minds. Thirty-six per cent said their perceptions of the employer would become much more positive and 36.2 per cent said their perceptions would become somewhat more positive if the employer responded to a negative review online.[4]

The first thing you must do is 'claim your company' or 'claim this page' which is as easy as clicking the links provided, using your corporate email address and confirming that you represent HR/personnel, recruiting, marketing, PR, or are an executive of the company. On Glassdoor, for example, this gives you basic employer branding tools, company-specific analytics and the opportunity to respond to reviews.

Reward Gateway takes its reviews seriously, on their Glassdoor page you will find that their CEO Doug Butler, writes responses to each and every review, the complimentary ones and the tough ones. Each reply is respectful, appreciative of the time given, genuine, long and sincere.

Cleverly, Doug Butler starts each review off with 'Hi it's Doug', which not only adds a human touch, it means when the anonymous reviewer receives the email telling them that there is a reply, they know who wrote it. They are offered the opportunity to discuss the matter further – offline – and each reviewer is thanked for their time. They will definitely feel heard, even if Doug has disagreed with them.

Balancing out negative reviews

In Glassdoor's FAQ section the first question they answer is the common misconception 'Isn't Glassdoor just a site for disgruntled former employees to vent or rant?' Glassdoor state 'No. In fact, our surveys show that 70 per cent of employees on Glassdoor say they are "OK" or "Satisfied" with their job and company. Meanwhile, the average company rating is 3.4 (on a scale of 1–5).'

Thinking of consumer experiences, it's well known that people will tell far more people about a bad experience than they will a good one. The last time you made a purchase or looked for a holiday, did you see silly reviews like a product receiving a one-star rating because the packaging was damaged or a resort receiving a one-star rating because the pool was colder than they expected? Thankfully, most people can see when people are being extreme and venting unceremoniously but that doesn't mean these reviews should be ignored.

Whether you have claimed ownership of your company on Glassdoor or not, people can write reviews about the employee and candidate experience. If these are negative then people researching your company can find these off-putting and 'deselect' or remove themselves from the application process. That could be a great hire you are missing by not taking these sites seriously.

If you find there are many reviews with the same common thread, your company has such a great opportunity to improve. This information is dynamite. Current employees don't usually go straight to review sites to vent, they have usually tried speaking with their manager or HR and not found help or support. There is also the freedom that comes from being able to speak anonymously, it's safer. Ever wanted to express an opinion at work and not been able to for fear of losing your job or the consequences? Hence the continuing rise of review sites.

But if there are a few reviews that are extreme and truly don't represent who you are as an organization, it doesn't hurt to balance these out, authentically. Not by the addition of several HR employee reviews all on the same day, and definitely not by sending a mass email to your employees asking for good reviews! You are after genuine reviews. Encourage your employees to write genuinely how they feel, remember it's dynamite feedback that you will never get in an annual appraisal or exit interview.

CASE STUDY   Employer branding at Tenable

Audra Knight and her team are responsible for employer branding at Tenable. She explained how they balance their reviews, 'We never ask people to write a good review, that would not be authentic. Instead we ask people to let us know how they are getting on and, importantly, we let them know that we will listen and take action when possible.' She expanded on this, to say that they ask new starters to share their thoughts on the recruitment process and their first six months at Tenable, and then added 'Sometimes it's about opportunity, for example we had an internal company hackathon and everyone was having a great time and feeling valued. At the end of the event, I got up and explained what Glassdoor was and asked if they'd be happy to write a review. We received eight honest five-star reviews! There are so many happy people at our company that just don't think to write a review.'

Quick wins for review site company pages

Indeed's research found that an inadequate online presence provokes automatic distrust in 70 per cent of job seekers. They also asked respondents to rank their five most important considerations when researching a company, the research they do before submitting an application. You can use the review sites and social channels to share the information they want, genuine insights on:

1 The stability of the company.

2 Insights around benefits and perks, flexibility and salary ranges for relevant roles.

3 Information about growth opportunities.

4 Company management.

5 The company's mission and vision.

If you work in a big corporate you may feel that the battle to win over corporate marketing or communications isn't worth the energy but anything that eases your talent acquisition is worth doing, and I bet you don't really want to repel 70 per cent of job seekers.

Take the time to explain to your corporate marketing why it is important to improve, monitor and respond to activity on review sites and to share the information people want. In this age of transparency it is every employee's responsibility to recruit but you will be the one they look at if you are not filling roles so don't let bureaucracy hinder your efforts. If you are lucky enough to have a dedicated employer branding specialist, like Audra, be so thankful! You can work with them on any pages that may have been missed and collaborate on content and engagement.

Some of the following are free to do and some will be paid depending on the site. I'm all about using review sites for free as I think you can invest your employer branding spend better in other places but do what feels right for your company and make sure you measure the results.

- Claim your company page and decide who will be responsible for responding to people.
- Add a banner or header image that genuinely represents life inside your company.
- Be recognizable by adding your logo.
- Link to your social feeds, giving people the option to follow you on their favourite site.

- Add videos and photos that are a true representation of life inside, ie ditch the stock photos!
- Complete the 'why work for us?' remembering it's about them not you.
- Share your latest news and value-adding company updates.

For ideas have a look at Facebook's page on Indeed.com, who have an enhanced paid version that is yet to be rolled out beyond the US, and Tenable's page on Comparably. For inspiration on Glassdoor, check out Reward Gateway's premium page and Zillow Group's free page, to compare the difference and to see how they both handle reviews and share content and photos.

Having seen so many responses to both good and bad reviews from executives at Zillow, I had to ask their Senior Researcher, Kay Kelison, if it has a positive impact on recruitment, 'Yes! When I speak to candidates and ask what they have heard about Zillow, they usually mention Glassdoor. It's great, our VPs and CEO actually answer reviews, they genuinely care how our past, present and future employees feel about Zillow.'

Final thought, cross-collaboration between review sites is delivering an even better picture than ever before. Under reviews on the US version of Indeed, for example, you will see scores for diversity from Comparably, and ratings from women via Fairygodboss and InHerSight so it is no longer enough to state you are diverse or have a great inclusive company culture, you need to show it.

Employee advocacy

Employee advocacy is the promotion of an organization by its employees and, according to LinkedIn, companies with a successful employee advocacy programme are 58 per cent more likely to attract and 20 per cent more likely to retain top talent.[5] Employee advocacy could be its own book and because I think like a recruiter, the following are inspirational ideas that you could implement with the help of your marketers or do yourself.

Compelling human stories

The internet has been disruptive in its creation of this transparent search-engine-led world! It is no longer enough to tell us how great your company is, people want to see it from your employees. Reviews are only one part, people also want to see your people living the values you say you have, showing what it is like inside and why you are unique from all the others vying for their attention.

True, it can be difficult. I have walked into offices that due to the nature of their business must appear incredibly formal online but you then go behind the scenes to discover they are anything but. The atmosphere is relaxed, colourful, even playful, and the staff are not dressed in the corporate attire you'd expect. But these companies are the exception to the norm and most companies can show what they are like inside, without giving away trade secrets.

When I interviewed Bennett Sung, Head of Marketing at AllyO, an AI recruitment technology company, about human stories he explained:

> Persuading candidates to come and work for you is one of the most complex story tells that anyone has to engage with. Unlike products, which have a tangible list of features, selling your values, mission, culture, team, manager (your employment brand), is much more experiential and personally different for each candidate. This storytelling requires finding a way for a candidate to virtually experience the employment brand and that could be via a wide range of channels including hiring manager videos, employee videos, reputation sites, and so on.

It takes more than beanbags, food, gyms and indoor slides to create a working environment that is engaged and inclusive too so you need to do more than share photos of your funky office. If you really want to attract and retain great, diverse talent, invest in the profoundly uncool things that employees actually want like great workplace benefits, like paternity and maternity leave, health insurance, flexible working hours, remote working and so on, and then be sure to let people know about it.

Diversity and inclusion

You have most likely seen many posts on LinkedIn, Twitter and Facebook showing companies attending and supporting their city's

LGBT community's annual Pride parade, and though this is wonderful and shows how far we have come, true inclusivity is something else altogether. Working for a company that genuinely lets you bring your whole self to work is still rare and for it to be believed, people need to hear from your employees.

Over on ThoughtWorks' website, under Insights, you will find a tab for Career Hacks. I love that it is placed front and centre with Cloud, IoT, Security, Transformation, Experience Design, Retail and Financial Services, content that is aimed at their customers. Sure you will also find it tucked away in their Careers site but its prominence in the blog says a lot about its importance to ThoughtWorks. The posts are written by many different employees across the organization, they tackle tough sensitive topics openly and honestly, and appear to be written for clients, employees, industry peers and potential recruits.

'Technology changed my life' by ThoughtWorks' Technologist, Effy Elden, is a powerful story. Effy discusses transphobia, mental illness and suicide with such rawness that you cannot help but feel emotional and applaud her courage.[6] She says that technology helped her become a person and ends her post with

> I'm passionate about technology because I've seen first-hand how it can change lives, create friends & relationships, and form amazing communities. I hope that my work as a technologist can help bring people together. It's why I work for ThoughtWorks, somewhere where I feel like I can truly be myself and still contribute to making the world a better place.

Letting your employees share their stories gives them a voice and lets the reader hear from real, diverse individuals.

You will also find posts on their Women in Leadership Development programme and information on how they have adapted their offices for disabled workers; the posts feel like they have been written to inspire other companies, not just to attract new recruits, which sets them apart from other companies.

In the diversity section of Netflix's careers site, there are detailed workforce demographics showing ethnicity and gender across the company. For inspiration, it is worth listening to some of their videos for ideas of what you could be sharing. You may need to go to

'WeAreNetflix' on YouTube to find '#SheRules: Episode 1 Anna', but it is worth the time to watch Anna speak so genuinely and movingly.[7] At no point does she mention her disability, though it's clear to see how accessible and inclusive Netflix has made her feel! Amazing and, if your firm is like this, easy to emulate.

Flexible and remote working

Mercer's 2018 Global Talent Trends study, of 800 business executives, 1,800 HR leaders, and over 5,000 employees across 21 industries and 44 countries around the world, found that 51 per cent of employees wish their company offered more flexible work options.[8] Plus recent research from the UK's Advisory, Conciliation and Arbitration Service (ACAS) found flexible work arrangements can actually improve the effectiveness of both individuals and teams, with 91 per cent of HR professionals reporting that employees were more engaged and satisfied when working remotely or flexibly.[9]

If you need more reasons to offer remote working, a 2017 survey by FlexJobs found that there are many benefits to employers:[10]

- 79 per cent of respondents said they would be more loyal, which is great for retention.
- 73 per cent said remote work is conducive to strong working relationships.
- 29 per cent of respondents even said that they would take a 10 per cent or 20 per cent cut in pay, and 22 per cent would even forfeit vacation time.
- 97 per cent of respondents are interested in being flexible in the long term as people try to balance work and life.
- Flexible working also helps attract well-educated professionals with solid experience who come from diverse backgrounds.

If you are lucky enough to work for a company that understands that flexible working improves engagement and productivity, share your advantage. It doesn't need to be complicated either. Managing Partner, Talent Acquisition at GroupM, Michael Wright, knows he has a competitive advantage so has been sharing supporting photographs and posts like this:[11]

> Do you work for a company who have a stated policy on home-working? We fully support flexible working arrangements that benefit the individual, our clients and the agencies. Everyone is entitled to have a conversation with their manager about working in a more agile, flexible manner. This includes both the occasional, ad-hoc requests and requests to work more flexibly on a regular, continuous basis. #Lifeworks.

Another company embracing remote working is Buffer and because one of their core values is transparency, you can read all about it on their Open blog. Be inspired by their Buffer Values blog, which demonstrates how they live each value daily, and hear from Courtney Seiter who shares '40 lessons from 4 years of remote work'. If your company's leaders need persuading, Buffer even offers a guide to the types of remote working available and, essentially, the technology and tools you will need in place to make this work effectively.

As a member of 'Generation X' who has been working remotely for over nine years and is writing this chapter sitting in Victoria Falls, Zambia, I am biased towards remote or flexible working. Many of my generation also yearn for this freedom and flexibility so please don't think it's just for the Millennials or even for everyone. It's not, some people hate it. But if your company still refuses to allow the people who want it to have it, you may lose them, and you will miss out on hiring extraordinary people from talent pools such as return-to-workers, job sharers, people with disabilities, and more. Remember people can see how many jobs are out there, they are no longer fearful to change jobs to get what they want.

Career paths and change

One of the best ways to retain staff is to keep them feeling engaged and like they are growing. That can be by being able to see clear paths ahead or by being able to change careers along the way. The hype will tell you this is only what Millennials want, but it's what all people want. I am on career number four but I left full-time employment because I wasn't challenged; could your employees be feeling the same, unaware they could move to a new team? People are attracted to firms that make it possible to grow and evolve, so if yours can do that, show it.

In a Question & Answer blog on GrouponPeople, Aria Srinvasan talks about her move from finance to product management, the passion she feels for the products she is creating and Groupon.[12] Possibly unintentionally, the post also highlights gender and minority diversity. On the blog it is also easy to find posts like Ashley Homampour from Risk Operations, who talks about her career path, her move from Chicago to Ireland and the evolution of the company over her seven years as an employee.[13] None of these are expensive to emulate, who in your company could you interview in a similar manner?

Over on H-E-B's career site, you will see one of the best examples of career paths around! They are proud to offer 'One company, multiple careers' and 'Design your career', and the video contains employees sharing their stories from starting on day one to where they are now. There's no doubting that they love and are thrilled to have grown their careers within the company. One of those featured, Cesar Carter, even states he plans to be with them for life! That's retention.

Events

Hosting your own events is an excellent way to show off the inside of your company and to give people the opportunity to meet your employees. Compare The Market (CTM) like many in the technical space struggle recruiting data scientists, so they hosted the London Data Science Workshop's Meetup. This gave CTM's data scientists the opportunity to share their expertise and to speak to industry peers in a collaborative and relaxed environment about the work they are doing and challenges they are looking to solve.

If you don't have space in your office to host an event, you could approach a relevant Meetup group about other sponsorship options or even start your own group. Meetups work well when they are led by your hiring managers so that those attending feel they are coming to learn not to be jumped on by a recruiter!

If sponsoring isn't possible, you could ask the owner of the Meetup how they feel about you attending. I recommend you sit back and learn, taking the time to become known and trusted, before hitting anyone with 'I'm a recruiter!'

And what about agencies?

If you are an agency recruiter reading this, you may be feeling left out. But as your candidates look at the companies you are recruiting for it made sense to show you what they could be doing first. As a consultant, you can encourage your client to share more employee stories and interesting insights or you can share the information that will help your candidates make a better decision. Of course, as an agency you also also need to look worthy of a person's time!

James Whitelock, MD of ThinkinCircles, specializes in digital strategies for recruiters and shared this advice:

> Most staffing companies either live in a state of blissful ignorance or stubborn arrogance when it comes to what their clients and candidates think about them and the messages that they are inadvertently sending through their branding, marketing and tone into the world. They may be the hippest company, where every day is dress down, but their website uses stock photos of people in grey suits shaking hands over a boardroom table. It's just disingenuous. Modern audiences respect and expect transparency; it's OK to have a relaxed working environment, the key is to tell people and let them in.

In the same way companies do, you need to be showing what it is genuinely like inside your agency so that you can build trust with your clients and your candidates alike.

One of the best examples of getting it right and one of the most social recruitment agencies I know is aptly named, Recruiting Social. They are easily identifiable on many social networks and huge contributors to both the recruitment industry and to job seekers. Individually, they definitely look like recruiters worthy of someone's valuable time; have a look at their Recruiting Partner Angela Bortolussi, @ABortolusssi on Twitter and Instagram, and you will see that she looks completely approachable and knowledgeable, and is clearly living their mission 'to make recruiting about people'.

As a company, they definitely embrace James Whitelock's preference for authenticity on their website! Not a stock photo to be seen and complete transparency. They share that fewer than 5 per cent of their hires come from job boards, which is impressive, the number of positions they have filled since they opened in 2012, and that they give 10 per cent of their profit to charity.

Where most agencies hope their clients won't try to source from the 4 billion people on the internet, Recruiting Social clearly explain how they recruit and write detailed articles explaining what they teach their recruiters on day one.[14] The information shared could enable a company to go out and find people themselves but they know that this information is already available online and rather than be afraid, they know that their service is second to few.

Nothing negates misguided stereotypes like an agency giving back to the community. TPP Recruitment offers free services to their not-for-profit clients, including mentoring, free use of the boardroom and employee volunteering. They regularly hold events to raise money for their charity sector clients, employees run in marathons, hold bake offs and participate in charity Tuesdays. This helps TPP Recruitment to build a better bond with and a deeper understanding of their clients. Instead of only posting jobs, their recruiters talk about their experiences volunteering on social media and easily stand out to candidates and potential clients alike.

It can be easier for smaller agencies to be free on social media but KForce, who has 50 offices across the US, sets a fine example of a corporate understanding their clients and sharing valuable information. Established in 1962 there is little they don't know about helping job seekers and they share their advice in detailed articles. In their Knowledge Centre, under Thought Leadership, you will find so much valuable information in the '2019 Job search guide' and there is also advice on how to tweet your way to a new job.

Delving below the surface, you will find they have over 1,300 reviews on Indeed and a solid rating of 3.8 out of 5, and similarly on Glassdoor there are over 1,400 reviews giving them 3.7 out of 5, showing their flexible working policy and staff recognition. These are positive insights for a client debating who they will work with.

Corporate hashtags

A great way to open the door to your company is by using a hashtag that all your employees know about and can use to share insights into their work life. Your employees share photos and videos on their own social media profiles as usual and, if they choose to, add your corporate hashtag. If the post is public, you can find it easily and even repost it onto your corporate channels. If your team is spread over multiple locations this not only creates an easy way to gather content to share, it also gives current employees more understanding of what is going on in other offices.

Though it's great to see the contribution KForce makes to the community on their website, importantly people can see real posts from real employees via their corporate hashtag, #KForceFamily, on Instagram and Twitter that add credibility. KForce's employees are using their own photos to show their efforts and giving permission for the photo to be shared by using the corporate hashtag and publishing publicly.

Others who get it right, due to their authentic employee photos, can be found under some more of my favourite hashtags: #IWorkForDell, #WeAreCisco, #Epamers, #AdobeLife, #LifeAtATT, #RGfun, #LifeAtSky and #LifeAtCA.

Employee advocacy overkill

There is a fine line between employees authentically sharing insights into the company and employee ambassadors being so 'happy' that people become sceptical or worse.

In August 2018, TechCrunch wrote an article titled 'What is this weird Twitter army of Amazon drones cheerfully defending warehouse work?' after a Twitter user called out the exceptional number of similar 'Amazon FC Ambassador' accounts responding to negative tweets. The problem is that they all communicate positive messages about how great it is to work in the warehouse, in an incredibly similar fashion. People are sceptical, feeling that these have come from the communications team and not real warehouse employees. Worse, there are now a number of fake ambassador accounts active on Twitter.

To avoid this lack of authenticity, keep your content real and let employees use their own voices. Don't press employees to use branded banner pictures or wording on their social media accounts, let them be natural. And be sure to implement a social media policy that's easy to understand and consider investing in some employee advocacy training.

Remove barriers to hire

Now you know how to look worthy of a person's time and confidence, have begun sharing great peer-to-peer content and your company has polished up its reviews, it is a good time to remove any barriers that could stop someone from applying to your job or coming in for an interview.

It makes sense to do this before we discuss successful intake strategy sessions and irresistible messaging because there is little worse than attracting the attention of a great potential employee and losing them due to an easily fixable hitch.

Career site considerations

You have heard about different kinds of content to share on your blog, your career site or on social media. But there are also technical considerations to make, specific to your career site or pages, which will ensure a smooth candidate experience. These include:

- For better navigation use subcategories by department or location: H-E-B Careers URL is careers.heb.com and they create ease by listing their technical roles in the subcategory found here: careers.heb.com/careers/technology/

- Avoid confusing potential employees by only stating 'send us your CV' – be sure to add your jobs.

- If you have added your jobs: allow people to search for 'all' locations not just specific locations.

- Avoid iframes: iframes are an HTML document embedded inside another HTML document on a page. Not only are these not crawled by search engines, which is even more important now with Google for Jobs, they can cause all sorts of navigation issues for candidates.

- Avoid putting all your job descriptions on one page with one URL. You'll find individual URLs more useful for both sharing of your jobs and SEO.

- Include an opt-in to your talent community on every page; give people the opportunity to engage with your career content, learn more about your company and apply when they are ready.

- Check your career site regularly for broken links.

For more information on the design, content, functionality, marketing, search engine optimization and legal considerations of launching a new careers site, download That Little Agency's free guide: bit.ly/TLA-CareerSite

Audit your application process

Successful ecommerce companies would never accept a high percentage of shopping cart abandonment because of the cost to their business. Yet few companies put thought into their job application process or are aware of how many people they lose during the application process. Adding analytics to your website will give you valuable insight into visitor behaviour but you could also walk the process yourself.

As 30 per cent of job applicants refuse to spend more than 15 minutes on a job application, it's time to make sure yours isn't stopping people in their tracks.[15] Pretend you are a candidate and walk through your entire application process. As over 50 per cent of internet searches happen on a mobile phone, start there.[16]

Is it easy to find your jobs from the home page or are they tucked away? Can people search your jobs easily when they find them? Can an applicant attach their CV to the application on their mobile? Are there too many steps? Is there a lot of duplication that wastes time and is difficult on a cell?

Repeat this process on a tablet and then on the desktop; check the process via Internet Explorer, Chrome, Firefox and Safari. Look for any steps or errors that can be removed or fixed. If giving the option to apply using a social network or a job board profile, check it works too.

It's natural to want certainty and clarity so did you receive an acknowledgement confirming your successful application? If you do, is it generic and off-putting or is it appreciative of your efforts and from a real human? Is there an indication of the process and recruitment time frame or a feeling that your CV just disappeared into a black hole?

In this candidate-driven market, where people with the skills your company needs are in high demand, it is essential to address any matters that arose now.

Inclusive applications and interviews

Ninety-three per cent of people with a disability don't use a wheelchair so though accessibility to your office could be key to the individual, disabled talent is a highly-skilled and diverse group of potential employees that you could be recruiting from.

This means that other forms of accessibility are also important; for example, ensuring that your website content, including your job descriptions, is accessible to everyone. Consider adding an audio option and ensure that you are using fonts and colours that are easily legible for people with dyslexia. Ensure that any interview tests will be OK for people with neuro-disabilities and if you are asking candidates to deliver a presentation, be sure to accept a range of formats.

Check your job descriptions in case you are also ruling people out without meaning to. For example, ensure that you are not asking for a full driving licence or a clean background check when it's not required for the role. Check you are not ruling out applicants who have a wealth of relevant experience because your job specification asks for a degree that the role doesn't need. Also watch for bias in the wording that can rule out people based on gender; I'll discuss tools for avoiding this a little later.

Consider the accessibility of your office; it is stressful enough attending interview, let alone getting lost on the way or needing a helping hand to get inside. To create ease let people know about the parking or public transport options. Simply adding a phone number and detailed directions to your website's contact page can make a huge difference to all interviewees.

For more information, not-for-profit social enterprise, Evenbreak, helps inclusive employers attract more talented disabled people and you will find a wealth of helpful information in their employer portal: bestpractice.evenbreak.co.uk

Unrealistic hiring manager expectations

Nothing is a bigger obstacle to hiring than managers with unrealistic expectations of the marketplace or when they want A+ candidates but are only offering B– roles.

To hiring managers, recruitment is a very small part of their responsibilities so it is your job to know the market and know when their expectations are unrealistic. The more information you share with them about the state of the market and industry trends the easier this will be. In the next chapter, will talk more about this and improving intake sessions.

Summary

- Google for Jobs has been a game changer and will present your company reviews and salary bands to candidates.

- Ensure your job descriptions are detailed, including locations and salary, and polish up your reviews on the many different review sites.

- Share compelling human stories that demonstrate life inside your company; remember people want genuine information from their peers not over-polished PR.

- Walk through your recruitment process and simplify it by removing unnecessary obstacles to the application and/or interview.

What changes have you made? Tweet me @KatrinaMCollier using #RobotProofRecruiter

Notes

1 Business Insider (2018) [accessed 12 April 2019] Your best employees are leaving. But is it personal or practical? Markets Insider, 28 August [Online] https://markets.businessinsider.com/news/stocks/your-best-employees-are-leaving-but-is-it-personal-or-practical-1027490284 (archived at https://perma.cc/96YM-CTK4)

2 Christoi, R (2018) [accessed 12 April 2019] Two giants under one umbrella: Indeed and Glassdoor by the numbers, KRT Marketing blog, 10 May [Online] https://www.krtmarketing.com/blog/glassdoor-acquisition/ (archived at https://perma.cc/JJC9-UW5U)

3 Glassdoor [accessed12 April 2019] Glassdoor for Employers [Online] https://www.glassdoor.co.uk/employers/what-we-do/respond-to-reviews/ (archived at https://perma.cc/2797-U34X)

4 Wolfe, P (2018) [accessed 12 April 2019] Report: An inadequate online presence provokes 'automatic' distrust in 70% of job seekers – here's what to do about it, Indeed blog, 15 May [Online] http://blog.indeed.com/2018/05/15/jobseeker-transparency-report/ (archived at https://perma.cc/K4WE-69BY)

5 Levinson, K (2018) [accessed 12 April 2019] What is employee advocacy and how do marketers win with it? LinkedIn Marketing Solutions Blog, 13 March [Online] https://business.linkedin.com/marketing-solutions/blog/linkedin-elevate/2017/what-is-employee-advocacy–what-is-it-for–why-does-it-matter- (archived at https://perma.cc/VQ6S-BZTX)

6 Elden, E (2018) [accessed 12 April 2019] Technology changed my life, ThoughtWorks Insights, 17 August [Online] https://www.thoughtworks.com/insights/blog/technology-changed-my-life (archived at https://perma.cc/9XW3-PQQV)

7 WeAreNetflix (2018) [accessed 12 April 2019] #SheRules Episode 1: Anna, YouTube, 7 March [Online] https://www.youtube.com/watch?v=3Gb6EyDQIUI (archived at https://perma.cc/QET5-NBPA)

8 Mercer [accessed 12 April 2019] Global talent trends 2019, Mercer, Our Thinking [Online] https://www.mercer.com/our-thinking/career/global-talent-hr-trends.html (archived at https://perma.cc/A7PR-UXK4)

9 Clarke, S and Holdsworth, L (2017) [accessed 12 April 2019] Flexibility in the workplace: Implications of flexible work arrangements for individuals, teams and organisations, ACAS Research Paper [Online] http://www.acas.org.uk/media/pdf/o/7/Flexibility-in-the-Workplace.pdf (archived at https://perma.cc/PB93-DYY9)

10 Reynolds, BW (2017) [accessed 12 April 2019] 2017 Annual survey finds workers are more productive at home, and more, Flexjobs, 21 August [Online] https://www.flexjobs.com/blog/post/productive-working-remotely-top-companies-hiring/ (archived at https://perma.cc/E5CH-TZG5)

11 LinkedIn post from Michael Wright [accessed 12 April 2019] LinkedIn [Online] https://www.linkedin.com/feed/update/urn:li:activity:6438447073317654528/ (archived at https://perma.cc/H2S5-NC58)

12 Interview with Aria Srinivasan [accessed 12 April 2019] Groupon People [Online] http://people.groupon.com/2018/aria-srinivasan-product-manager-for-groupon-in-san-francisco/ (archived at https://perma.cc/M4KR-6UZM)

13 Interview with Ashley Homampour [accessed 12 April 2019] Groupon People [Online] http://people.groupon.com/2018/womengroupon-ashley-from-risk-operations-in-dublin/ (archived at https://perma.cc/PHT3-4N2U)

14 Recruiting Social (2018) [accessed 12 April 2019] Sourcing passive candidates: What we teach our recruiters on day #1, Recruiting Social, 3 August [Online] https://recruitingsocial.com/2018/08/sourcing-passive-candidates/ (archived at https://perma.cc/NH9J-SXNY)

15 Gittens, J (2018) [accessed 12 April 2019] Google for Jobs is here already. But are your jobs all ready for Google? Ruutly, Medium [Online] https://medium.com/ruutly/google-for-jobs-is-here-but-are-your-jobs-for-google-ee3783f2b15 (archived at https://perma.cc/539C-85C7)

16 Statista [accessed 12 April 2019] Percentages of mobile device website traffic worldwide from 1st quarter 2015 to 4th quarter 2018, Statista [Online] https://www.statista.com/statistics/277125/share-of-website-traffic-coming-from-mobile-devices/17 (archived at https://perma.cc/3XYZ-77BE)

Get your intake right

05

Successful recruitment starts at your meeting with the hiring manager discussing the new role. Yet recruiters and sourcers regularly struggle to give the intake strategy session enough attention and set themselves up to fail.

When I reflect on my recruitment agency days, it still seems crazy that my ability to get the information I needed was so limited. I was heavily reliant on the job specification and rarely given access to the hiring manager, no matter how hard I tried. But I was recruiting in a time when there was less competition for people's attention and definitely less interruption. Without stepping up my game I would fail in today's candidate-driven market!

In this chapter you will discover all the information you need to get from your hiring manager or client, and how to gain their trust and time, so that you can grab the attention of people with highly sought-after skills and stand out from all the other recruiters vying for their attention.

Overcoming fear

'But surely working from the job description is OK?' No, it's definitely not OK.

Because recruitment is only a small part of your managers' responsibilities, they will often try to 'save time' by hastily compiling a new job requirement or using an outdated job specification. This leads to hiring managers wasting time interviewing unsuitable candidates and blaming you for it! Of course, they could have hired successfully by giving you more time and information upfront, delivering a better experience for the interviewees and improving future hiring by reducing poor online interview reviews.

Working off a job description alone is also not OK because changing jobs is a scary process through which most people need more information and support. Though some may debate that a permanent job is not permanent anymore, those that prefer full-time employment would tell you differently. They like the security that comes with a regular salary, the comfort of knowing that they can pay their bills and meet their commitments. They don't like uncertainty and are harder to entice to a new job opportunity.

Take a moment and put yourself in their shoes. Think about how you would feel about changing jobs and the concerns this would raise. What is the company really like to work for? Will you like the people? Will they like you? What if you go from bad to worse? What if you don't perform well during probation and lose your job, what then? What if you can't meet your commitments, support your children, pay your mortgage or rent? What will happen then?

Candidates also have more general fears to which you need to pay attention, such as the fear that recruiters are incompetent and could even mar a candidate's reputation.

Expanding on the conversation I was having with Ondřej Procházka, Recruiter at Facebook, in Chapter 1, 'Candidates fear incompetency from a recruiter far more than anything else because it might lead to everyone wasting their time or even botching their chances of getting the job! This leads to people ignoring messages from recruiters and even circumventing them altogether.'

Ondřej shared five areas where he has seen recruiters and sourcers go wrong in the past, especially in the talent-scarce world of technical recruitment:

1 They don't understand the role of the candidate and therefore which role suits them best.

2 They don't understand the candidate's current level or scope of work and engage without having a suitable opportunity for them.

3 They have not researched and engage without knowing that their offer cannot possibly match the candidate's current compensation at their level, company and/or position.

4 They set the wrong interview loop that does not play to the candidate's strength or they even choose the wrong interviewers.

5 They are unable to represent the candidate properly in a quorum when hiring decisions are finalized.

Yet with some research, the right questioning in the intake strategy session and proper conversations with candidates, these can easily be overcome.

You must get your hiring managers on side!

In Chapter 3 I mentioned the importance of getting your hiring managers on side so that they can attract recruits with their improved social media profiles and footprints. Securing their trust and respect will also help you gain their time at the beginning of the recruitment process and that will save both of you time later and, importantly for improved candidate experience, the potential recruit's time.

Creating a better working relationship may involve a difficult conversation. Tangie Pettis, Talent Acquisition Manager at Aspen Dental, a dental practice management corporation in the US, suggests you let your hiring manager know that you are there to find them the right person and ask them what their expectations are.[1] 'But be prepared to listen without interrupting them! Ask them for some recommendations on how the two of you could work better together. And be sure to come to the table with ideas to present as well' and then, of course, be ready to deliver.

You are there to deliver excellent service and it's not (usually) personal, you don't know the pressure your hiring manager is under, yet. As Tangie also recommends, 'try and remove your emotion from the situation'; remember the poor reputation of recruiters, it's possible your hiring manager needs time to trust you. And remember, manners maketh the (hu)man! Often forgotten in our modern fast-paced world of work, but a please and a thank you are always appreciated.

Sometimes you will even have to bring in an outsider to create better working relationships. When Aylin Halil was at BGL Group, she invited me in to facilitate a session between the sourcers and the hiring managers with the aim of creating greater collaboration, transparency and efficiencies. It gave the opportunity for the hiring managers to air their concerns about the talent acquisition process and the session also raised unexpected issues that could then be resolved.

Even though the hiring managers were willing to confess that they receive multiple job offers each week, they had little understanding of the hiring marketplace and didn't realize that investing valuable time with the recruiters and sourcers upfront could save so much time down the line. The result according to Aylin was that 'By getting the hiring managers working closely with the recruiters and sourcers we were able to intrinsically understand the human they wanted in their team. You can't automate that!'

Your job as a recruiter or a sourcer is to understand your industry and its recruitment landscape. The more facts and data you can provide, the better you will partner with your internal hiring managers or clients, and the easier it will be to obtain the information you need to stand out.

There were over 4 billion people using the internet in 2018; generating 187 million emails, 18 million texts, 38 million WhatsApp messages, every single minute.[2, 3] As you will discover in the next chapters, it takes work to create a message or a job advertisement that gets attention, but it is easier when you share the information you gain during the intake strategy session and make the job advertisement or message more enticing than a list of skills and duties.

Intake strategy session

When industry veteran Steve Levy was on 'The #SocialRecruiting Show' he shared the hiring successes he has had because he has ensured that two key elements were part of any intake strategy session: preparation and questions that answer 'What is the problem we're hoping to solve?'

Preparation is key

The more information you take with you into the meeting the easier it will be to gain your hiring manager's trust. Steve suggests you go in with a dossier that includes past job titles, LinkedIn profiles, internal documents that you have access to, and an understanding of what has been delivered and accomplished, and then ask 'You seem to like this professional standpoint, do you agree?' Because it is an open question, you will receive a detailed response and not just a list of requirements.

Include the team in your dossier. Steve takes along the team's résumés, their social footprints, information on the groups they belong to, the conferences they attend or speak at, the blogs they write and the things they do, and then asks 'Is it something like this?' When challenged if this created bias, he countered with 'We're not recruiting people like us. We are recruiting people to solve problems. The whole thing is performance based.' He's right, it is about finding someone who has complementary skills to the team, who can also solve the problem.

Other information you could gather includes:

- Information from ukdataservice.ac.uk or datausa.io can give you an understanding of the industries, housing costs, demographics, unemployment rates and more in your location.

- Information from sites like Glassdoor, LinkedIn, Payscale, Salary. com, Indeed and niche sites like IT Jobs Watch, that give you an indication of salary bandings in your location.

- Software like Gapsquare FairPay can conduct pay transparency, gender and ethnicity pay gap analysis on your current employees to ensure the compensation for the role is fair.

- Cost-of-living comparisons between cities or countries on sites like numbeo.com or expatistan.com.

- If you plan to attract people from abroad, especially in technology, look at relocate.me, a platform listing people looking to relocate.

- If you plan to establish in a new European country, consider the European Recruitment Dashboard, which provides detailed insight into the local labour market and culture.[4]

- If budget permits, talent intelligence sites like TalentNeuron from Gartner can provide in-depth supply and demand statistics that will help you partner better with the business.

- Intel on your direct competitors: on top of being a potential source of people, check out their online reputation, their hiring process, their culture and be armed with their compensation packages.

- News and information from sites like BuzzSumo or Google Alerts using keywords to deliver competitor intelligence directly to your inbox.

What is the problem we're hoping to solve?

Now you are heading into your strategy session as prepared as you can be, it's time to find out what this new employee or contractor will be doing. As Steve said on the show, 'We don't hire people to take pay cheques, we hire them to solve a problem! Six months from now, what will they have accomplished that tells you hiring them was the right thing to do?'

You will find hiring managers who struggle to answer this question but if they can't describe it for you now, how will they know what they're looking for? Imagine the time this will waste and how this could impact your company's candidate experience reputation. When people with highly sought-after skills are hard to find and get the attention of, you cannot risk going to market without an answer to this question.

Steve suggests trying another tack to get around this, by asking questions like:

- What problems are keeping you up at night?
- What tasks or deliverables are you trying to get done?
- What kinds of problems will you be solving in 12 months' time?
- What will their targets be for the next 6 or 12 months?
- Why would a [job title] leave [competitor] to come and work for us?
- What would they be doing here that they wouldn't be doing at [competitor]?
- What will tell you at the end of six months that hiring this person was the right decision?

The information you collect in the intake strategy session becomes a performance document for use to close your hiring manager on their requirements and to use in job advertisements/posts and candidate conversations.

This is the moment to ask your hiring manager 'If I find someone who can take those deliverables off your table, will you interview them on my recommendation?' I'll confess when I heard Steve suggest this, I thought it was audacious but if the hiring manager says no, that gives you the opportunity to delve deeper, probe into what you are missing or uncover other concerns that may have been missed.

Hiring for skills

When my sister was returning to employment, after successfully running her own event management company for 20+ years, she would regularly fall at the first obstacle, the requirement for a degree. Instead of a piece of paper, she has the skills and experience that come from running corporate events for two decades. It was depressing, she is dynamic and extremely well connected, employers should have been lining up to hire her skills and knowledge.

Lucky for Caryn, I could teach her how to circumnavigate applicant tracking systems but few job seekers are in this position. How many potential recruits do you lose because the hiring manager has asked for a specific job title, degree or length of service that you know isn't needed for the role? If you challenge your hiring managers, you will be able to broaden your search.

When Derek Murphy-Johnson, Talent Acquisition Manager at KinderCare Education, was on 'The #SocialRecruiting Show', he shared an example of recruiting for skills over experience. They were looking for a project manager for their centre operations, people that liaise between the field and corporate. Instead of looking for job titles and length of service, they looked at the skills required to do the role, namely great communication skills, proactive, organized and able to influence. This opened up a bigger pool of people because they realized that district store managers, in charge of multiple stores and people, have these skills and could easily transfer into a head office role.

Derek went on to say 'It's how someone gets the work done, focus on the skills that get the job done. Sure, if you are hiring a physician, you will definitely want to know they have the right training and qualifications but look at talent holistically, search for the skills the person needs to carry out the role, not just specific job titles.' This will also open up your hiring potential to people making a career pivot from within or outside of your company, who could bring a whole new perspective to the role.

Where will this new opportunity take new recruits?

Most people don't like to be acquired or thought of as a resource or capital. Humans like to learn and develop. Most people like to work in organizations where they can thrive and make an impact. Will they be able to do that in yours? What is the next logical step from this position? Can you offer career change, a new direction within your company? Ask your hiring manager during the strategy session.

If you know what your company can offer or the potential next career steps, you can have a much more open conversation with candidates. Which is more enticing, 'where do you want to go in your career?' or 'want a job?'

Recruiting personas

Initially the idea of using recruiting personas – fictionalized and generalized representations of the ideal candidates – felt too uncomfortable to me, too marketing focused, even too fluffy. Yet by using them, you gain the characteristics of your candidate and you could even end up changing the direction of your sourcing to open up a new pool of potential recruits.

Recruiting personas delve into the human characteristics of the individual you are looking to hire. Their psychology, how they spend their time outside of work, their behaviour and their interests.

To uncover these characteristics, I asked Recruitment Marketer, Katrina Kibben, to share the questions she uses. She suggests you ask your hiring manager and anyone currently working in the role the following:

- Describe the person who was most successful in this role.
- What is the first app you open on your phone in the morning?
- Do you prefer to communicate via text or email or another way?
- How do you spend free time?
- Where do you get your industry news? Any favourite blogs or tweeters?
- What conferences or events do you attend?
- If you were job hunting, what websites would you use? Where else would you look?

Jérémy Goillot from Spendesk used the interests of his employees when he was looking to hire. Realizing that many of his colleagues love the TV shows *Mr Robot* and *Silicon Valley,* and because Spendesk wants to hire people from other startups who also love technology and growth, he used this information and sponsored the subtitles on both shows.

This is just one idea and not necessarily the cheapest but the information you gather will not only help you recruit, it can be used to produce relevant employer brand content that will help you stand out from your competitors, especially if your company is new and unknown.

If you are time poor or wanting to reach a wider group, this is a great time to use tech to help you be more human. Use free survey tools like Google Forms or SurveyMonkey, or more aesthetically pleasing Typeform, to gather responses and be sure to share the results so that the team feel more involved in the hiring process.

Candidate persona resources

- Great toolkit for staffing agencies from Firefish Software: bit.ly/FSPersonas
- The wealth of insight from Katrina Kibben at threeearsmedia.com

---

Implement a service level agreement (SLA)

If you want to counteract the recent rise in ghosting, where candidates drop out of the recruitment process unannounced and become uncontactable, you need to have firm service level agreements in place with your hiring manager and anyone involved in the decision-making process. A service level agreement (SLA) is a commitment between a service provider (you) and a client (your hiring manager). They usually include things like quality, availability, timeliness and responsibilities, and they are mutually agreed between both parties. The best time to agree to them is during the intake strategy session. In this candidate-driven market they are crucial to hiring success and improved candidate experience.

In your SLA, you will want to specify:

- What it is you are both trying to achieve.
- The type of service they would like, from hands-off to silver service.
- The impact to the business if you meet or miss your agreed SLA.
- Your expectations of each other: clarifying elements like who sends candidate outreach, schedules interviews, delivers feedback, etc.
- How the search will be conducted: sourcing, advertising, referrals, etc.
- How many CVs the manager would like and how they would like to receive them.
- The mutually agreed timeline for the search, review and feedback.
- Who is in the interview process and what the role of the recruiter is in it.
- Who owns the candidate relationship.

SLAs won't work if your working relationship with the hiring manager is fractured but by providing transparency, clarity and certainty, you will have a greater basis to improve the relationship and gain their commitment to a better recruitment experience.

Collaborate continually

Recruiting isn't a solo sport. In fact, recruiters and sourcers may be the doorway to the company but you are far from alone in the hiring process. Think about who else is involved in the journey; the person who signs off the headcount, the team they'll join, the receptionist who greets them for the interview, the interview panel, HR who issue the contract, and more.

They can all contribute to the information you need for the role and the soft or hard skills they feel would be a bonus. Imagine what the team can tell you about the role that the hiring manager may have not thought of. Speaking to the business will save you so much time in the long run and provide a better candidate experience, which is essential when there are so many places where disgruntled candidates can express their opinion of the process.

Collaborating continually is something Sourcing Leader, Maisha Cannon, swears by.[5, 6] She doesn't sit in a silo, instead, she collaborates with her hiring managers looking for the nuances of the role, 'I host internal sourcing parties and recruit alongside my hiring managers. Talking to or shadowing people who are working in the role helps me go beyond the job description and construct a realistic picture of it too.'

Maisha also recommends that during the interview process you meet with your hiring manager for a debrief so you can review your research and uncover profiles together, in real time, and make adjustments as needed. 'We examine why the people who looked good on paper haven't advanced through the interview process, and update the job description, rethinking the must-haves we defined in the initial strategy session.' This also works well counteracting those hiring managers who always want to interview one more person 'just in case' because they will know they have seen the best people available.

Narrowing the talent pool

In the last chapter, in the context of showing you are a company worth talking to, I talked about the barriers that stop people physically applying or interviewing, and how you can lose applicants by including requirements you don't need, like a clean driver's licence or a degree. There are also a number of other ways you can restrict your talent pool, which you need to be aware of and take steps to avoid.

Bias

What's in a name? This was something that Australian, Ahmad Imam, decided to find out six years ago after being rejected from over 20 job applications his skills were perfectly suited to. Privately schooled, degree educated, intelligent and, most importantly, perfect for the opportunities, it was baffling.

After a comment from a friend, he resubmitted his CV to the exact same jobs but this time using the name Adam Smith. The very next day he received four calls and so began his journey through an elongated five-month interview process as Adam Smith. Eventually, though he had to come clean! Thankfully, though appalled, the company was happy to have an open conversation about the situation.

The company wanted diversity but the bias came from assumptions made by the recruitment consultant. Different types of biases are ingrained within all of us; the key is being aware of them and taking steps to remedy them when needed. Agency recruiters are paid on results so they will send you the person most likely to be hired and they may make an assumption from looking at your existing employees that your company doesn't want diversity.

Ahmad recommends that you spell it out, 'We as a business have to have open conversations, with hiring managers and recruiters, telling them exactly what we are after, that we do want to have diversity and for this reason. We simply have to have these uncomfortable conversations. That's the only way we can move forward.'

There are so many other biases too around age, gender, disability, mental health, ex-offenders – it's time to take action. Look to companies who are leading by example, like ThoughtWorks mentioned in the last chapter, who share openly articles for their employees, clients and future recruits to see, voluntarily written by their own employees, which demonstrate true diversity and inclusion, and the challenges they overcame.

Diversity and inclusion training is a great starting point but change takes work. As Co-Founder of Awaken, Michelle Kim, advises in her article on the effectiveness of unconscious bias training, 'Guiding people to sit in their discomfort and tension while asking questions they've been too afraid to ask and say things they've been too scared to say is the only way we create real change. Because we cannot un-learn what we are too afraid to acknowledge.'[7]

Remote and flexible working

You will remember I discussed flexible and remote working in Chapter 4. Refusing to offer it could be reducing your opportunity to hire the perfect person. With the amount of technology available today, is it absolutely necessary for your new employee to work in the office all the time? If a company like the digital design platform InVision can be valued at $1 billion and have 700 employees without any physical offices, do your working policies need a rethink?

After my friend Joanne Ward started working for a new company, she discovered that they were fundamentally opposed to people working from home. She suffers from rheumatoid arthritis and fibromyalgia, both invisible conditions that result in chronic pain among other symptoms. Initially, all was well but over time the commute into London took its toll. As a recruiter, she could easily have worked remotely, even some of the time. Knowing about the policy though, she feared asking for the flexibility she needed and instead looked for a new opportunity. Joanne now works remotely 80 per cent of the time for a company that sees her incredible talent and not her inability to be physically present in the office every day.

There are countless other types of invisible conditions that can at times be debilitating, which your current and future employees will have, and possibly not disclose due to the fear of stigmatization or discrimination. By being flexible and inclusive to all your employees' needs, you'll be better placed to compete in a candidate-driven market and you will attract grateful employees who will stay, reducing costly retention issues.

Helpful resources

- Pauline Yau is on a journey to discover what's stopping most organizations from measuring people on their output instead of the amount of time they are on their laptop or in the office and is discussing it with guests on her podcast, 'The flexible movement'.

- Abodoo aims to fix the issue around sourcing great remote workers and bias by matching people based on experience, not their location.
- FlexJobs puts the candidate first and won't work with every employer but if you are invited to join you will have access to their free candidate database and unlimited job postings.

Disabled workers

Over 1 billion people have some form of disability, that is around 15 in every 100 people.[8] While certain jobs may have, for example, specific physical demands and requirements, this is not likely to be the case for many/the majority of the jobs you are recruiting for.

I had the honour of hearing Jane Hatton from Evenbreak speak recently. Her social enterprise, run by disabled people, helps other disabled people find work. Jane has written a really informative and invaluable book, *A Dozen Brilliant Reasons to Employ Disabled People*,[9] and she challenges you and your company to consider the following feedback from companies that accept disabled candidates:

- Can be more productive than non-disabled colleagues: someone with poor coordination using dictation software can be quicker and more accurate than those typing manually, or someone who is deaf or autistic can be less distracted by unproductive office chatter.

- Can avoid workplace accidents: Jane herself has a particularly fragile neck and makes absolutely certain that she doesn't risk further damage from a fall, inside or outside of work.

- Better retention: when a disabled employee feels valued and supported, they are much less likely to take the risk of moving to a new employer where this may not be the case.

- Some organizations have reported 30 per cent less sickness absence from disabled employees who are used to dealing with their disability and/or side effects of medications.

- To navigate a world designed for non-disabled people, they have tenacity, resilience, creative problem solving, planning skills and more. The disability itself can create skills: attention to detail and spotting patterns for people with autism, or immense creativity for people with dyslexia and/or some mental health conditions.

- Employing disabled people gives you the internal intelligence to ensure you cater for disabled customers, which gives you access to the 'purple pound', the spending power of disabled people and their families, estimated at £249 billion per annum in the UK in 2018.

Here in the UK, the Department for Work and Pensions provides a Disability Confident scheme, which provides guidance and resources to help a company become more inclusive. Employers learn what sort of workplace adjustments may need to be made to support inclusivity, and how to help people realize their potential and contribute fully to the success of their teams. Check if your government also provides guidance.

Generational typecasting

You won't need to look far to hear my DisruptHR London talk on the negative impact of buying into generational buzzword bingo. Ignoring one generation in favour of another impacts employee morale, retention and future hiring. We are all individuals, with individual needs and wants; every age group has its pluses and minuses.

As a Generation X, who however has more Millennial traits than the average Millennial according to Pew Research, I can understand that if you are a company full of 20-something-year-olds, it may appear to make sense to hire a younger person but I wonder what you will miss. Did you see the movie *The Intern*? I know it's a Warner Bros feel-good movie but each generation was able to help the other both personally and professionally and there are real-world examples.

A great example of this can be seen at Melanie Silverman's company, GLL, which is responsible for 141 swimming pools across the UK. Struggling to recruit lifeguards, she looked at the current employees and realized that the older lifeguards were fit if not fitter than their younger lifeguards. Lifeguards need to be good swimmers, able to take control and be vigilant, and those skills are not exclusive to the young. By looking beyond stereotypes and looking at the data, GLL now employs 40 lifeguards over the age of 50. They found the people they needed to fill their vacancies and save lives.

Job share

During the intake strategy session ask if job share is an option. From a retention and new employee attraction standpoint, there are many advantages to employers who offer job sharing, including double the expertise, increased productivity, seamless holiday and sickness cover, succession planning, increased motivation and better relationships with colleagues.

There can be disadvantages too. You are dealing with two employees and it's possible that the working relationship could fail, and you could have extra expense depending on how you structure hours and benefits. You could also have to battle with leaders who insist it's two heads, not one!

Back in my early recruitment agency days, my mentor and director fell pregnant and the company, being anything but progressive, managed her out. It was dreadful to witness and bad for morale. So you can imagine my delight to hear that Jacqui Barratt, the CEO and Founder of Salt, a 180-strong recruitment agency with eight offices around the world, fully embraces modern day working practices.

I asked Jacqui for her top piece of advice for your company or clients considering offering job sharing.

> Great communication is key between the two people job sharing and with the organization. It is essential that everyone feels that there is a seamless transition during the changeover and that's why handover is critical. A key benefit we saw in job sharing is that the two individuals bring more to the table than one person can. Unexpectedly we found that each played to the other's strengths, allowing the other to shine and fill any gaps. Another benefit was the appeal that two individuals have to different clients and candidates ensuring a diverse and happy customer base – two heads are better than one.

If you can offer job share, have a look at Further&More, Ginibee or DuoMe, they can help you with the structure of the job share, to source internal and external candidates, and can even provide coaching to ensure it works.

Return-to-workers

Employing return-to-workers takes a distinct mindset shift. It is easy to think that people with a gap have lost their knowledge rather than thinking of what they gained during their absence. Think of the multitasking and logistics skills that come from becoming a new parent or a primary carer, or the resilience that comes from overcoming an illness or accident. In this candidate-driven market could more emphasis be placed on the valuable life skills that are gained during an absence rather than the time and mentoring they will need to catch up?

In 2016 research by PwC and Women Returners found that two-thirds of women will return to a lower-level role or be under-employed in a part-time role, meaning they are working below their potential.[10] Not only is this lost opportunity for the employer, but it will also impact morale, retention and productivity.

In research conducted by KPMG for Vodafone, it was found that there are circa 96 million skilled women aged between 30 and 54 on career breaks worldwide, and an estimated 55 million are experienced at the middle-manager level and above.[11] To tap into this potential and increase the proportion of women in management and leadership roles, Vodafone created their ReConnect programme.

Vodafone's ReConnect programme:

- Targets people on career breaks (which you could do on niche job boards, in women's forums, your alumni, or even through Facebook and Instagram targeted pay-per-click advertising).

- Training and induction programmes to update professional skills and ready women for re-entry into the workplace.

- Unconscious bias training for hiring managers.

- Employment terms that include flexible working options and/or a phased return to work.

Another idea is returnships, which were started in the US by Goldman Sachs in 2008, then brought to the UK in 2014 by Credit Suisse, Morgan Stanley and Deutsche Bank. They are typically three to six months long, aiming to refresh technology skills, boost confidence and prepare the returner for the corporate landscape, often with the help of a mentor.

Twenty-three companies offered returnships in the UK last year and around 90 per cent of those on placements are women.[12] Often, the higher up the career ladder these women have climbed, the more of a lifeline they need after taking time off.

According to Peterson Institute for International Economics, companies with diverse leadership are 15 per cent more likely to outperform industry averages. With the pressure to balance up gender diversity, could you emulate Vodafone's programme or introduce a returnship?

Women Returners provides consultancy, coaching and a network organization that focuses exclusively on enabling talented professionals to return to work after an extended career break. In their Employers section, they have useful best practice guides to support your company embrace this pool of talented professionals.

Veterans

Research from Deloitte found that those companies who have employed veterans found:[13]

- They are particularly strong in areas relating to communication, planning and time management, teamworking, leading and inspiring others, and being able to pick up specialist knowledge and solve problems.
- They perform well in areas where 33 per cent surveyed have skills gaps: strategic management, managing and motivating staff, teamworking, positive attitude and listening skills.
- 79 per cent agree they take fewer days off sick, and that includes the nearly three-quarters of medically discharged service leavers who are employed.
- Employing veterans is as much a means of improving organizational productivity and performance as it is a means of meeting the obligations of social responsibility.

However, the research also found that there are still negative perceptions and stereotyping when it comes to hiring ex-forces personnel. In my experience, many recruiters struggle to see the transferable skills on the CV and can overlook the opportunity to recruit a talented individual. I was also shocked to see a tweet on Veteran's Day that said 'Managers need to be trained in questions to avoid like "did you kill anyone?" and to ask questions like "tell me about skills and experience you acquired in the military" ', so there is no denying we have work to do but there is help available.

Start with your country's military transitions services as they usually have advice for hiring vets. In the UK, you will find help at the British Forces Resettlement Services and the Career Transition Partnership (CTP). In the US there is advice at Military.com and Hiring Our Heroes, and also look at Career Spark, who can help you open the untapped pool of people who are military spouses.

Refugees

Research from Tent Partnership for Refugees found that refugees tend to stay with their employers longer and will help recruit other refugee employees.[14] Looking at the current Syrian refugee crisis, 38 per cent of Syrian refugees are degree educated but struggle to find work due to lack of understanding of the job market, language barriers, and because employers make the incorrect assumption that there will be extra costs and administration involved in hiring a refugee.

UK charity Breaking Barriers has developed alternative routes, including placements, apprenticeships or permanent job opportunities, to help refugees who often have language barriers and gaps in their CVs but can also be highly skilled. They provide English language training with the aim of helping the 120,000 refugees with employment rights to gain employment, bringing language skills, diversity, loyalty and wealth of experience to employers. Similarly, in the US, your company will find help and support from Tent.org, and in Australia there is the Friendly Nation Initiative, fni.org.au.

Ex-offenders

It may or not have been a scam when the ex-offender knocked on my door this week and I ended up purchasing dog grooming gloves but he did get me thinking. He was polite, bright and genuinely wanting to make a fresh start. He doesn't want to return to prison and is grateful to be in London away from the gangs of his home town. He is looking for a break so he can use the skills he has learned in prison, which include plastering, bricklaying and personal training, and to get out of the halfway house and on with his life.

Could your organization employ an ex-offender?

Could you be like Timpson who boldly state on their website 'We consider anyone for our vacancies as long as they are able to do the job. This includes ex-offenders and other marginalized groups. We recruit exclusively on personality and expect all of our colleagues to be happy, confident and chatty individuals'? [15] Could you be like Greyston Bakery, who believe so passionately in hiring 'anyone willing to work, no questions asked' that they have even trademarked Open Hiring™?

I highly recommend watching Greyston Bakery's video on Open Hiring™. Hearing 'you invest to bring people in rather than spending to screen them out' gave me goosebumps, what a change that makes from what we as recruiters do every day! They have learned a lot since they started hiring this way in 1987, including that they had a rise in applications from people who are vested in social responsibility and that employees appreciate that the company is giving someone a second chance, and this increases morale.

Here in the UK, for example, 50 per cent of criminal convictions are driving offences and only 8 per cent of those sentenced each year actually go to prison.[16] Yet 75 per cent of employers admit to discriminating against people who tick the 'do you have a criminal offence' checkbox in the application process![17] Could your company join the Ban The Box campaign?[18] Not only will you increase the diversity of your pipeline, but you will also increase retention and could increase your business's reputation and credentials.

Search the internet for 'ex offenders charities' and you will find many initiatives like The Clink Charity, which through its own restaurants places ex-prisoners in the hospitality industry, or Unlock, which offers training for recruiters, or you could provide work experience as an employer champion for Switchback, a London-based prison rehabilitation charity. You will also find help via specialist recruitment agencies like BlueSky and Working Chance.

On top of opening up a whole new place to recruit from, if you give an ex-offender a chance, you will employ someone who doesn't want to fall back into what they did before and who will feel loyal to you for giving them a chance. You will also find it helps society by reducing reoffending and unemployment costs, and it will boost employee morale as your people will see it as a great thing to do, it will make them proud to be part of your company.

Summary

- To recruit people successfully, especially those in demand, gain their attention and allay their fears with the understanding of the role you gain during the intake strategy session.
- Your job is to partner with your hiring managers by being prepared and setting an SLA that you are both prepared to be accountable to.
- It's OK to query your hiring manager's specifications, especially if unconscious bias is reducing your ability to recruit diverse employees that represent society and improve productivity.
- There are plenty of resources and charities available to help you widen your talent pool.

What will you be doing differently? Tweet me @KatrinaMCollier using #RobotProofRecruiter

Notes

1 Pettis, T (2017) [accessed 12 April 2019] Do you want fries with that shake? Oops! I mean intake! SourceCon, 2 October [Online] https://www.sourcecon.com/do-you-want-fries-with-that-shake-oops-i-mean-intake/ (archived at https://perma.cc/83BX-LN35)

2 Internet World Stats (2019) [accessed 12 April 2019] Internet users in the world by regions – March 2019, Internet World Stats, March [Online] https://www.internetworldstats.com/stats.htm (archived at https://perma.cc/3HTR-WXGQ)

3 Desjardins, J (2018) [accessed 12 April 2019] What happens in an internet minute in 2018? Visual Capitalist, Technology, 14 May [Online] https://www.visualcapitalist.com/internet-minute-2018/ (archived at https://perma.cc/7936-S62K)

4 European Recruitment Dashboard [accessed 12 April 2019] Intelligence Group [Online] https://intelligence-group.nl/en/solutions/recruitment/european-recruitment-dashboard (archived at https://perma.cc/S8LH-5VPP)

5 Recruiting Social (2017) [accessed 12 April 2019] Influencing Hiring Managers: Q&A with Maisha Cannon, Recruiting Social, 8 March [Online] https://recruitingsocial.com/2017/03/recruiters-influencing-hiring-managers/ (archived at https://perma.cc/VE5C-SBF7)

6 Pettis, T (2017) [accessed 12 April 2019] Flashbacks and fast forwards with Maisha Cannon, SourceCon, 16 October [Online] https://www.sourcecon.com/flashbacks-and-fast-forwards-with-maisha-cannon/ (archived at https://perma.cc/3GJH-RBSE)

7 Kim, M (2018) [accessed 12 April 2019] But really, is unconscious bias training effective or ineffective?, Awaken, Medium [Online] https://medium.com/awaken-blog/but-really-is-unconscious-bias-training-effective-or-ineffective-666e15b74fd1 (archived at https://perma.cc/YL9A-AJAV)

8 World Health Organization (2018) Disability and health, World Health Organization, 16 January [Online] http://www.who.int/en/news-room/fact-sheets/detail/disability-and-health (archived at https://perma.cc/TCK6-AJMN)

9 Hatton, J (2017) *A Dozen Brilliant Reasons to Employ Disabled People*, Elite Publishing Academy, Great Britain

10 PwC [accessed 12 April 2019] Women returners, PwC Insights [Online] https://www.pwc.co.uk/services/economics-policy/insights/women-returners.html (archived at https://perma.cc/FS6U-852Q)

11 Where Women Work [accessed 12 April 2019] Vodafone's ReConnect Programme for women returners, Where Women Work [Online] https://www.wherewomenwork.com/Career/698/Vodafone-ReConnect-womenreturners (archived at https://perma.cc/47PT-VCG7)

12 Hoyle, A (2017) [accessed 12 April 2019] Move over millennials: the rise of the 'returnship' for middle-aged mums, *The Telegraph*, 23 January [Online] https://www.telegraph.co.uk/women/work/move-millienials-rise-returnship-middle-aged-mums/ (archived at https://perma.cc/J6B8-BGS3)

13 Veterans Work (2016) [accessed 12 April 2019] Veterans work: Recognising the potential of ex-service personnel, Veterans Work [Online] https://www.veteranswork.org.uk/wp-content/uploads/2017/10/J10136_Veterans_work_brochure-web.pdf (archived at https://perma.cc/ADE4-N5SR)

14 Dyssegaard Kallick, D and Roldan, C (2018) [accessed 12 April 2019] Refugees as employees: Good retention, strong recruitment, Tent, May [Online] https://www.tent.org/resources/good-retention-strong-recruitment/ (archived at https://perma.cc/F6GG-HKNW)

15 Timpson [accessed 12 April 2019] Working at Timpson [Online] https://www.timpson.co.uk/about/careers-at-timpson (archived at https://perma.cc/V25V-LTNJ)

16 Hill, J (2018) [accessed 12 April 2019] Why wouldn't you employ an ex-offender?, People Management, 2 October [Online] https://www.peoplemanagement.co.uk/voices/comment/why-wouldnt-employ-ex-offender-jacob-hill (archived at https://perma.cc/G8K6-LZ38)

17 Marsh, R (2018) [accessed 12 April 2019] Exploring the myths behind employing ex-offenders, RG Foundation, 30 August [Online] https://www.rg-foundation.org/blog/exploring-the-myths-in-employing-ex-offenders (archived at https://perma.cc/Q7EG-5WBB)

18 Business in the Community [accessed 12 April 2019] Ex offenders: Ban the Box and employment, Business in the Community [Online] https://www.bitc.org.uk/campaigns-programmes/employment-diversity/employment/exoffenders/whybanthebox (archived at https://perma.cc/PC54-V37F)

Human-first job posts and advertisements

06

There are many ways that people will come into contact with your company. They could be your clients or people known to your employees. They could read about you in the press, on social media, or see your advertisements for your products and services. They may come actively looking for you or you may approach them, for your company's offering or for employment.

Though we hope people will look at our career site pages first, analysis by CareerBuilder of over 5,000 corporate career sites found that 92.5 per cent of people go to your job pages first.[1] Yet this is often the area we put little time or energy into and worse, we can even send candidates to clunky applicant tracking systems or databases.

This chapter will look at two areas that impact your hiring success, job posts and advertisements. It makes sense to talk about these before we improve your direct messaging because this is where you lead a potential candidate when you have gained their attention.

By job advertisement I mean the information that you place about the role on a job board or the page on the career site, website or applicant tracking system (ATS). I don't mean the job description, which is too often produced with little thought by hiring managers, rarely follows the advice in Chapter 4, and is the worst thing to use as the advertisement! Your job advertisement competes for attention against others online and this is exacerbated by the job boards and sites like LinkedIn highlighting 'similar jobs' so, as will be explained, it needs to do more than list the role requirements.

The job advertisement is often where you send the people who read your messages so they can discover more. It is where people will go when they see your update or come across your job from traditional advertising methods like billboards, posters and other signs.

By job post, I mean an update, image or video usually found in a social media news feed, which aims to grab a potential candidate's attention and send them to the job advertisement. It has mere seconds to gain someone's attention and evoke a reaction. Preferably it will lead to a well-thought-through series of steps that you have tested to ensure it will lead to a successful application or show of interest.

Job posts

One of the best job posts I have seen was a video that mimicked Adele's song 'Hello', created by a digital agency to promote their own vacancies. It was timely and fun, but I'll never forget the feeling of disappointment when they sent me from this vibrant video to a lengthy and dull LinkedIn job advertisement. The agency didn't focus on the candidate's journey and many would have dropped off at this point instead of completing their application. To maximize the return on your time and creativity, be sure to walk through the entire journey from post to the completed application.

At the time of writing it was OK to use movie clips, for example, under the definition of 'fair usage' when used as 'caricature, parody or pastiche' as it was in this instance.[2,3] However, with changes coming to European Union copyright laws, often referred to as Article 13, it will no longer be OK to use movie clips or memes, even in parody, and LinkedIn, Facebook, Twitter, YouTube and similar sites will be forced to remove them or face fines. YouTube has been vocal in its protest of the changes and you will find more here: youtube.com/saveyourinternet

Job post mistakes

I will never forget the horror I felt when I saw a job post on LinkedIn that used a sexualized image of a woman from the film *The Secretary*. By the time this post appeared in my feed, it had received 416 comments of complaint from men and women alike. Instead of removing the post at the first complaint, the recruiter argued and this led to articles appearing in newspapers from the USA to Russia, which still mar the reputation of the agency today.

The post stated that the role was in Mayfair, one of the wealthiest and most prestigious areas of London, UK. Ignoring the shock that this was placed on LinkedIn, the implication on gender and the fact that the recruiter was probably breaching copyright, I was stunned that a recruiter, particularly a female one, would think using an image from a movie about sadomasochism would be the best way to represent their client.

In his post, 'What's wrong with this advert?',[4] Director of Ariadne Associates, Simon Jones, pointed out that it does 'Contravene the Equality Act.[5] It is illegal to advertise for someone of a particular sex (with some very clear exceptions) or age, yet this advert visually implies that only young women can be secretaries. As the client, you would be held liable together with the agency if an individual decided to make a claim.' That is worth emphasizing – as the client, you could be held liable!

It is great to get creative and stand out but it must be for the right reasons. Be sure to think about potential implications and if you are at all hesitant to post, seek advice. If someone complains, delete or amend your post immediately, don't wait until someone takes a screenshot and it is used in the press across the world.

Evoking emotion

What sets us apart from the robots is our empathy, creativity and emotions. Facebook and Slack realized early that we like to share our emotions in more ways than just a thumbs-up so they gave us reactions to use that match our emotion. And it's addictive, think about the last LinkedIn comment you wanted to respond to with a sad or angry face but could only like. Should we be using more emojis in our posts to gain attention? They are scarce on LinkedIn so it could be an easy way to stand out and they are as essential in posts on Facebook, Twitter and Instagram as the right hashtags.

One of the most emotive job posts I've seen is from GLL College[6] posted on Instagram (see Figure 6.1). From the happy smiles to the warmth evoked at the thought of a hug, to the reassurance of an interview, to the flexibility of the hours, right through to the timeliness of the post at the end of school holidays, it is a well-thought-through job post. And if you are wondering, they have similarly emotive job posts for the dads too.

Of course, a campaign can deliver the wrong emotion, as evidenced by the one Capita produced for The British Army.[7] Aiming to appeal to Millennials, it evoked the anger of serving soldiers who were soon sharing less than complimentary edited versions of the posters.

The images are confusing and polarizing; is the Army mocking the generational typecasting labels and seeing strengths they want to re-cruit, or insulting a generation of people who would be most unlikely to self-identify as a 'me me me Millennial', a 'phone zombie' or 'a selfie-addict'?[8] It is too unclear. The lesson here is to sanity-check your campaign, be it an expensive outsourced one or your own, to ensure it produces the right message and emotion.

A respected senior talent acquisition leader and Millennial shared confidentially, 'It really fails to address the so what. You need me, so what? So what is in it for me? So what skills will you give me? So what are you doing about the crisis of homeless veterans? etc.' He makes a valid point and when you look at the example from GLL College again, its 'so what?' couldn't be clearer.

Colour and emotion

Marketers have known for years that different colours evoke dif-ferent emotions but it's not something recruiters usually think about. Jan Tegze, Senior Recruitment Manager and author of *Full Stack Recruiter* thinks it's something we need to consider and in

Figure 6.1 Job post on Instagram

SOURCE Reproduced with permission from GLL College

his article, 'How to use the psychology of color in recruitment',[9] he explains that:

- Yellow inspires warmth, optimism, brightness, happiness.
- Blue makes people think about strength, reliability, trust and dependability.
- Green inspires peace, health, liveliness and natural growth.
- Orange is a colour that screams confidence, freshness, friendliness and joy.
- Red represents boldness, excitement and a youthful spirit.
- Purple is the colour of creativity, wisdom and imagination.
- Grey is a neutral colour that inspires calm, tolerance and equilibrium.

Jan goes on to say that '93% of shoppers place visual appeal above sound, smell, and texture when buying a product.' So surely if the colour is so important in our buying decisions we should take it more seriously when sharing our posts.

Testing Jan's theory, I scanned Twitter for a job post that stood out among the noise and stopped at one from a company called Seargin that included the Apple logo with two bites, instead of the usual one. The blue, the visual and the play on words, 'hungry developers wanted' certainly grabbed my attention.

I clicked through to learn more; Seargin is a specialized IT company experienced in providing onsite or outsourced services, who claim that when they commit, they deliver. It makes sense then that both their brand colour and this post are in blue, to instil reliability, trust and dependability.

Job videos

2018 saw the rise of video due to LinkedIn adding video-sharing capability to posts. Those who have uploaded their videos directly to LinkedIn have found that their posts have gained great reach in comparison to sharing a link to a site like YouTube or Vimeo. But do your research – if your candidates are not active on LinkedIn, invest your energy where they are active. The easiest way to find out is to ask your employees where they are active, online and offline.

Interestingly, research from Lighthouse Research Advisory[10] in 2017 found that:

- Candidates prefer to see videos of hiring managers 2.5 times more than company overviews and 10 times more often than an HR/ recruiter message.

- 46 per cent would be more likely to consider the job and 30 per cent more likely to respond to a recruiter or apply if it included a welcome video from the hiring manager.

- 55 per cent of job seekers find an employee-generated video more credible than a company video.

Backing up this research, Maury Hanigan shared that one of SparcStart's clients 'found that the job postings that included a video from the hiring manager had a 60% increase in conversion.'

A great time to capture your hiring manager on video is during your intake strategy session, asking questions that keep it focused on the benefits to the candidate. Employer branding expert Audra Knight suggests you 'Wait until your hiring manager lights up about the role and then dig deeper, that's the information you want in your video, the stuff they are excited to share with the candidate.' And for third-party recruiters, Maury added, 'Staffing firms can also use hiring manager videos in their outreach, simply omit the company name and keep the discussion on the opportunity within the role.'

Recruiter, phone, go

In Chapter 2, I mentioned Mark Hopkins whose authentic, helpful and emotive videos have given kudos to his agency, Thomas Lee Recruitment. He uses his phone, good lighting and a neutral background. On YouTube, you can see how his videos have improved over time while the content has remained helpful and believable.

A few things to consider when creating your own direct-to-camera job video:

- Landscape: save portrait for Snapchat and Instagram Stories and use landscape for LinkedIn, Facebook, Twitter and your Instagram feed.

- Camera angle: there seems to be a trend for men to shoot video upwards at an unflattering angle and for women to do the opposite, which can be too revealing. For better results, try shooting straight on and investing in a stabilizing selfie stick.

- Microphone: for better sound quality, I use the inexpensive Boya omnidirectional condenser microphone, which plugs into my phone, laptop or DSLR.

- Lighting: you don't have to invest in expensive lighting kits, consider instead using a selfie stick with light or creating your own with a lamp and greaseproof paper.

- Video motion: 'The Running Recruiter' is making a great name for himself but remember your audience. I cannot watch his videos because I suffer motion sickness, which means his videos are losing their impact and reach.

- Energy: it is easy to avoid creating an awkward job video, like the ones where the recruiter is standing in front of the logo speaking in a monotone. From creating many direct-to-camera videos over the years I have learned to shake my body out before I hit record and then I aim my voice and energy at the ceiling thinking I am speaking to a room full of people.

- Change your tone of voice and facial expressions: video doesn't pick up nuances as well as our own eyes, be more expressive and be aware that what you are thinking will show on your face and in your voice.

Two videos, two different vibes

On LinkedIn I found a job video from a US staffing agency looking for truck drivers and one from UK courier company, Yodel, looking for delivery drivers. Though I appreciate that it is easier for a company to create a video from an employee for their industry peers, by comparing the two videos you will see how to create a more engaging video.

In the staffing agency's video there are stock images of 15 men and 1 woman and though that does reflect the industry, only 6 per cent of US truck drivers are female, the subliminal message is 'we hire men'.

According to free online tool Gender Decoder the wording, as I suspected, will also deter women. You could also use Textio or TapRecruit to assess the gender neutrality of your wording. Women tend only to apply for roles they are a 100 per cent fit for and the overuse of 'must' through the video is a deterrent. For example, it describes how 'You **must** have frequent communication with management. You **must** report any and all issues that may arise. To be considered for this position, you **must** have your CDL A or CDL B license. You **must** have a clean driving record.'

Within the video, there is a click to apply button but unfortunately, it sends you to Indeed where you are confronted with a one-star review and have to start the search all over again.

At Yodel Opportunities you will see two videos for employed drivers, from Danny and Penny, who both talk about what it is like and what you can expect. Though asked similar questions their responses are personal reflecting their own values.

'My name is Penny Wiggin and I am a Delivery Driver for Yodel. The best thing about working for Yodel, for me, is the freedom of being my own boss on the road and I really enjoy being out and about and meeting different people. I do feel satisfied, I do feel tired as well, but I do feel satisfied.' She goes on to explain her day, the pace, the laughs, the training opportunities and suggests you need to be fit. The use of the word 'feel' naturally attracts female applicants. To apply you stay within Yodel's career site and can be assisted by their job-matching bot, which is something that I'll come back to later on in this chapter.

As an agency, you will need to be more creative in your creation of peer-to-peer content but it's not impossible and it will set you apart from your competition, especially when you are now competing against your own clients for the attention of candidates.

Company videos that inspire

Not forgetting that candidates prefer hiring manager videos over company overviews, the two following examples are great because they use real employees and convey their culture with authenticity. The first has had over 1.6 million views and for a country shy of 5 million people, that's impressive.

'Freeze! NZ Police's most entertaining recruitment video, yet!' uses over 70 real cops, the police band, police cats, helicopters and stunts that aims to encourage a range of New Zealanders to join their team.[11] It has a strong call to action, it is diverse, explains what they are looking for and what you will gain if you join. It captures the essence of New Zealanders with local humour; the outtakes at the end are an authentic bonus.

It's rare to see a video from the CEO that is anything other than over-polished by PR, which is why SodaStream's 'Join the revolution' video stands out.[12] Their CEO, Daniel Birnbaum, not only conveys his passion for their product and what they are looking for, he shows his capacity to laugh at himself and shares insight into their culture. Their 'Island of peace' video about diversity and inclusivity is extremely moving and well worth watching too.

Video resources

- Skill Scout have an excellent job video recipe and a wealth of information on their blog that will help you to show the job and capture behind-the-scenes footage.

- VideoMyJob helps you to create, edit and share branded video job ads from your mobile and includes a teleprompter to help you remember important points.

- Jobviddy can help you create your branding, job advert and chatbot videos to keep your career site visitors engaged and in your talent pipeline.

- Lumen5 transforms articles into videos ready for sharing on social media.

- ClickIQ and Vonq offer technology that can help you place your job video or post in the right media channel to ensure you receive the maximum return on investment.

Creative non-social media job post ideas and hacks

We can over-complicate our job posts and opt for something complex when maybe a sign on the side of a bus or van is enough to attract new drivers, for example.

One of my favourite campaigns was by Ikea in Australia searching for staff to run a new megastore.[13] They created a career instructions flyer and inserted it into customers' flat pack purchases, it led to 4,285 applicants and 280 careers assembled with no media spend.

Risking some strange looks, sourcer David Sankar captured and shared online a photo of a cleverly placed advertisement in Dublin airport toilets. Right above the urinals, it hits a captive audience and targets expat engineers, with a clear and simple message. It worked too, the recruitment agency responsible received many applications in a field where people with relevant skills are in short supply.

Sometimes though, the people with the skills you need are so scarce that you do need to go above and beyond to attract and hold their attention. Marketers call this guerilla marketing, where your aim is to raise brand awareness among large audiences, without interrupting them. In other words, you want to make your job or employer branding do some of the following:

- Be difficult to ignore.
- Use things people pass by every day to do something unexpected.
- Make people do something involuntarily.
- Create shock and awe.
- Use your audience to create your content by asking them to share stories, for example.

Rename your WiFi or device

If you are recruiting tech for high-growth startups and able to work remotely say, in the coffee shop near your competition, you could copy what Willem Wijnans does and rename your device with something that attracts attention.[14] His device is called 'Do you code Java-Script? Come see the guy with the long hair ;)' and the name will be seen by anyone looking to log onto the WiFi within his vicinity. You could do this with your work WiFi too, renaming it 'we are hiring'.

Laptop stickers

Reddit is renowned for having only spent $500 on advertising, using all of that on stickers.[15] They used the stickers to build a sense of community and allegiance to the brand. It worked, whether we use Reddit or not, their logo is well known.

If you commute, travel or work remotely, laptop stickers can be great conversation starters. Talent Expert Eva Balúchová's laptop is covered in technology stickers and even one saying 'Are you a developer?', which has led to a great conversation on a train and a CV sent to her client!

While my inner introvert shuddered, Talent Manager, Teddy Dimitrova, shared that she started a great chat at the airport over a sticker, 'I pointed at his laptop and said, "I was at React conference this year as well! Did you go to... talk?"' She added that attending tech conferences has proved beneficial for headhunting developers. She attends to listen and learn and to talk with the exhibitors so she can share anything useful she discovers with her tech team.

Source code

The Guardian was one of the first to use its Page Source as a way to attract digital recruits. By right-clicking at TheGuardian.com and selecting View Page Source you will see 'we are hiring' and a link to their digital development jobs. It's a simple and effective way to capture the attention of curious technical professionals. Tapping into that curiosity, Tenable.com's call to action, for anyone looking at the source code, is more persuasive because it makes the reader feel special with the words 'If you're looking at this, we want to hire you.'

Conference hashtags

In Chapter 2 I mentioned being baffled by recruiters missing out on opportunities because they are using conference hashtags at events, but not attracting followers because they have not filled out their Twitter and Instagram bios. Many people have incomplete bios, some even intentionally to remain anonymous; by searching for updates that use a particular conference hashtag you have the opportunity to find and interact with people that you would have missed if you were only looking for complete bios.

You can find people by manually searching for those using a specific conference or event hashtag or save time by using Zapier or

IFTTT to save hashtag mentions to a Google spreadsheet. You can then go through these accounts and create a quality prospect list, especially useful if you are attending.

Take advantage of the notification they receive that you have followed their account by ensuring that your bio is filled out and that your last post was about your available job or insight into your company. On Twitter, you can pin your post to your profile so it is always the first thing someone sees.

Three things to avoid:

1 Rather than create more recruiter spam or noise, don't use hacks to automatically follow or comment when someone uses a certain hashtag. I see it happen when I use #London on Instagram, for example, and two seconds later I am followed by 10 random accounts and receive comments like 'well done' when I have just posted about train cancellations.

2 Don't use the hashtag or tag conference speakers in your job posts if you don't have the permission of the event organizer or speaker. This is akin to taking your printed job description and forcing it into their hand, you wouldn't do that in real life so avoid doing it online.

3 Don't follow and unfollow over and over to gain attention. There will be valid reasons that they are not following you back. The account that does this to me uses a company name and only sells in their posts, and this attention-seeking tactic makes me think poorly of their product.

Conference presentations

When you find yourself in front of a room of your target audience you are in a prime position to gain interest but also in the awkward position of not wanting to be blatant and annoy the organizers.

On Codility's 'Creating a competitive candidate experience' webinar, their CTO Wojtek Erbetowski shared that he adds links to assessments at the end of his presentations that have encouraged developers to participate and, of course, to get their CVs.[16] In the past, I have used Leaddigits to share free gifts during presentations, all the attendees did was text a number, add their email to the reply, and the freebie was on its way.

Could your employees do similar when speaking at events in front of your target recruits? Unlike handing out swag and hoping someone gets in touch, you will be gaining valuable contact details which can be used to strengthen the relationship and in your talent pipeline.

Geolocation and filters

A lot like creating a WiFi name that refers to your jobs, your location on Facebook or Instagram could also be renamed to attract the attention of people when they go to check in at your location. As they search they could see, for example, 'Company name – want to work for us?' rather than just your company name. You could also create a job-related Facebook Frame or Snapchat filter for your location or event. It is also possible to target promoted posts at specific locations and demographics, effectively giving you the opportunity to place your opportunity in the feeds of conference attendees.

Product placement

Sometimes it takes audacity. My client was so desperate for nurses that she visited the nearby hospital, popped into the staff room and put posters up on the back of the toilet doors! But Michael Wright, Managing Partner – Talent Acquisition at GroupM, has taken the idea to a whole new level with fewer potential repercussions.

You'll remember I mentioned GroupM in Chapter 4 when discussing flexible and remote working and promised to share the recruitment campaign that went with the LinkedIn posts.

Knowing that GroupM is the only media agency group with a stated policy on home and flexible working and with the insight to target Labor Day, when people in the US have their minds on family, family time, vacation, etc, Michael bought media space in the lifts of three buildings that house their largest competitors in New York City. Using a creative video that subtly highlighted the flexible benefits offered, the video ran all day in the elevators. Because the offices are in shared premises, the employees saw them while using the elevator and there was little the companies could do about it.

Taking it further, to target all employees, not just the ones in these three buildings, they used the device IDs of the mobile phones, seeing who was frequently in the buildings during the working day and targeted them with a programmatic display, the adverts that seem to 'follow' you around. That allowed GroupM to hit all of the buildings of their competitors and gain millions of ad views or impressions for an investment of under $10,000. All traffic led to a simple and friendly Typeform landing page.

Michael Wright shared that 'It exceeded benchmarks on both mobile and desktop for click-through rate and it was a great success in terms of lifting the visibility of GroupM. The objective was less about driving applications, though we received 55 via our landing page, and more about grinding the gears of our competitors, like serving Pepsi at a Coca-Cola conference.'

Of course, you'll want to make sure your lifts don't have the ability to play videos before implementing a similar strategy so your competitors cannot reciprocate.

Job advertisements

If you saw an advertisement for 'carbonated water, sucrose caramel, phosphoric acid, natural flavours and caffeine', would you buy a can of Coke? This is why Coca-Cola doesn't advertise its products the way we advertise our jobs and instead invests in campaigns that tell us that 'nothing can ever bring us down when we taste the feeling'.

This being said, there is much recruiters can learn from traditional media and that section could be a book in itself so, for the sake of brevity, here are the some of the biggest mistakes to avoid:

- Job titles that don't explain the role or aren't industry norms. Developers are as likely to search for 'rockstar OR ninja job' as a recruiter is to search for a 'hot job'. Make it realistic and searchable or all your efforts will have been for nothing.

- The use of I. Listen to advertising, it's all about what you will get from the product or service. Make the reader feel like you are talking directly to them by using you, your and yours.

- Passive voice. You will gain more applications with an active voice because you are providing certainty. For example, 'You will join the team involved with x and be working on y.'

- Euphemisms! If you saw 'self-starter' would you answer honestly with 'No, I prefer to be told what to do' if you do? Make sure the requirements can be objectively self-assessed.

- Discriminatory statements. Though writing 'If you get sick a lot, have drama in your life, or have other commitments that get in the way of your work, then please do not apply,' would seem an honest way to explain the importance of an executive assistant, there are less abrasive ways to explain that you need reliability and dedication.

- Too many must-haves. If the must-have requirement is not a deal breaker move it to the nice-to-haves and keep must-haves to fewer than five to attract more potential candidates and female applicants.

- Duties are too generic. Use the information gained in the intake strategy session to share the problem they will be solving and what the future could hold.

To create irresistible job descriptions the following specialists and resources are worth your time:

- Copywriting by a recruiter for recruiters, Mitch Sullivan: fasttrackrecruitment.com

- Covering everything from the history of job descriptions to whether we should eliminate them is this resource from Ongig: ongig.com/job-descriptions

- Great recruitment marketing advice from Three Ears Media: katrinakibben.com

- The blog from augmented writing platform Textio covers a wide range of related topics: textio.ai

- A surprising list of words that will attract applicants in one city and detract in another: bit.ly/hiringwords

- ZipRecruiter discusses the impact of gender bias through the words you use: bit.ly/BiasWords

- Ph.Creative's free tool, Job Page Grader, will analyse your job advertisement and give you clear steps to improve it: jobpagegrader. com

- Tris Revill increases job applications by ensuring the relevant top search terms per industry found at indeed.co.uk/jobtrends/ category-trends are included in the title and description.

The application experience

A Talent Board survey found that 61 per cent of people who had a positive candidate experience would actively encourage their colleagues to apply, while the 27 per cent of respondents who had a negative experience said they would warn people against applying.[17] Candidate experience impacts a company's bottom line and Talent Board have created an interactive calculator to help you work the impact out – you will find it here: thetalentboard.org/candidate-experience-resentment-calculator/

In Chapter 4, I suggested that you audit your application process to improve the flow for candidates, ensuring that it is easy to find and apply for your jobs on a mobile, tablet and the desktop. I also recommended checking your process is inclusive by, for example, using better fonts, adding audio options and removing unnecessary requirements.

With candidate experience so important to future recruitment and the bottom line, here are some examples of companies who have made changes to provide certainty, clear communication, ease and a feeling that candidates matter.

Job pages

Traditionally recruiters and marketers have focused on career pages, social media posts and employer branding videos, when it would be better to invest time improving job pages, which is proven to be more impactful in converting visitors to your job advertisement into applicants.

By creating a candidate persona, in discussion with the tech support team, Tenable's employer branding team discovered that many of the tech support team like the later shift hours because they like

Figure 6.2 Photo of the team on each job page

We 🖤 clean, simple code (and fun times)

We're a small team of smart, friendly people who collaborate closely and take pride in delivering amazing software and providing extraordinary customer support. You'll help shape what we work on and how we do it. You won't be micro-managed or stuck in a rut. We work hard on challenging problems and have a good time doing it.

We believe focusing on automation, testing and code quality enables us to move faster than our competitors whilst delivering better software.

gaming. This was incorporated into a targeted job landing page used for organic and paid social media posts.

The image and wording are also gaming specific, 'The world of global cybersecurity never sleeps. But that doesn't mean our people can't enjoy their working life. In fact, our shift patterns accommodate colleagues who prefer to stay up gaming at night, or simply want to savour a couple of hours extra sleep in the morning.' It goes on to explain the importance of the role and the perk that there are games in the break rooms.

When the candidate selects one of the jobs they arrive at a page that is dedicated to them and the individual role. The page includes a video offering tips on applying from the tech support team. Rather than use the same generic video on each page, great care has been taken to use a video from the appropriate technical team, no matter location, and the video thumbnail is so specific to the role it entices you to hit play.

Even if your job pages are on an applicant tracking system it is possible to include rich media as FundApps has done (see Figure 6.2). Further down the page are clear statements on diversity, which are also reflected in genuine photos of FundAppers. The hyperlink takes you to employee bios and LinkedIn profiles giving hesitant applicants the opportunity to gain more insight into the culture.

Side note: while researching this section I noticed too many unintentionally negative subliminal messages on career sites. For example, one company showed a very diverse employee team on their About page but showed a lack of diversity on their Career page. Another implied that women held lesser roles, just by where they had placed the links to individual departments. Check your pages objectively to ensure that they are a true representation of your company.

How to apply

Technology and mobile devices have given us so much certainty that it has become an expectation. From satellite navigation guiding us to our destinations on time to the freedom to contact someone for help wherever we are to the ability to jump online to find an answer, we have clarity. So it makes sense that job seekers want the same level of transparency from your application process.

Booking.com have an entire section dedicated to 'how we hire' including application tips and career videos to explore, but it is the clear steps outlined in their 'route to hire' that stand out because it provides such clarity. It looks a lot like a London Tube map and gives a potential applicant all they need to know about the recruitment life cycle.

Groupe Renault also provides clear steps and advice on its How Do We Recruit page. There is a promise of speed and closure with statements like 'Whatever the result of the interview, our recruiter contacts you quickly, either to make you an offer or to tell you why you haven't been selected. It's feedback that's never easy to hear, but it's helpful for future interviews' and this is reflected in their positive Glassdoor and Indeed reviews.

Ease candidate communication

Nobody likes to feel that they are not heard or that their application has disappeared into a black hole and with today's technology it is easy to engage with visitors to your website.

Groupe Renault has a section where you can contact Renault Insiders, employees who can answer questions on opportunities and careers. It's fully interactive, even helping people find the right person to speak to.

FundApps have implemented HubSpot conversations and when you arrive on their career page, you receive a friendly greeting from Pat and Rohan (Figure 6.3). To ease the pressure of answering questions live, you could use the chatbot builder to create bots to direct candidates and provide answers to common questions.

On Zalando's and Yodel's career sites you will find chatbots that provide answers to common questions and provide direction. When I asked Zalando's bot, created by Jobpal, if I needed to be able to speak German, not only did I receive a reply, I gained insight into the broad range of nationalities and a potential employee perk, language lessons. In Yodel's case the bot, created by Meet & Engage, pre-screens and even rejects candidates, which provides clarity and closure. On the right of the image (Figure 6.4), you will see that I was ruled out because I replied stating that I cannot lift packages to 30 kilos.

Figure 6.3   The chat box on FundApps

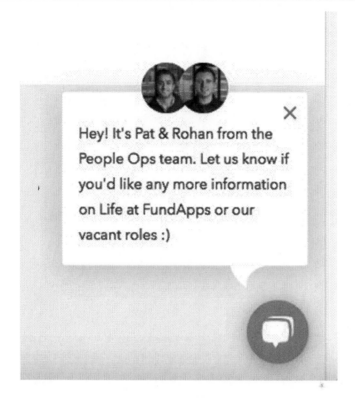

Yodel's Ben Gledhill shared the results from 1,500 candidate chatbot screens. As Figure 6.5 shows, unsurprisingly, most candidate activity took place in the evening when recruiters are unavailable. Impressed with the results Ben shared, 'Proper candidate experience means working around their lives, not ours.'

Ditch the CV/résumé?
If we are really serious about improving candidate experience, reducing bias and increasing diversity, wouldn't it make sense to ditch the CV and instead test for capability?

Finding herself stretched too thin and in need of a large number of testers, Talent Acquisition Manager and writer at Recruiter Notes, Noa Ferber, decided to ditch the CV and try something new.[18] In discussion with her team, they created a process to remove the CV and

Figure 6.4 Conversations with Zalando and Yodel's chatbots

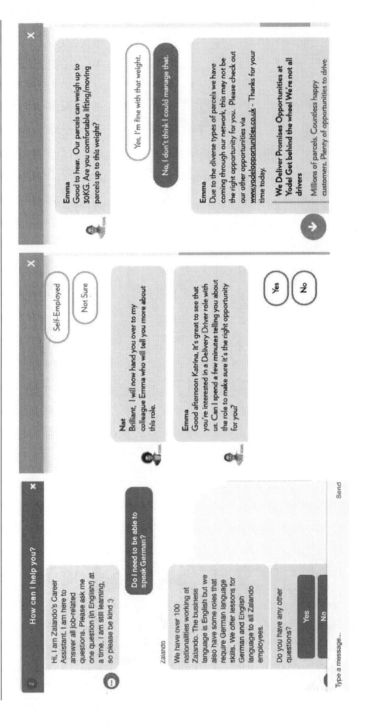

Figure 6.5 Graph of Yodel's chatbot results

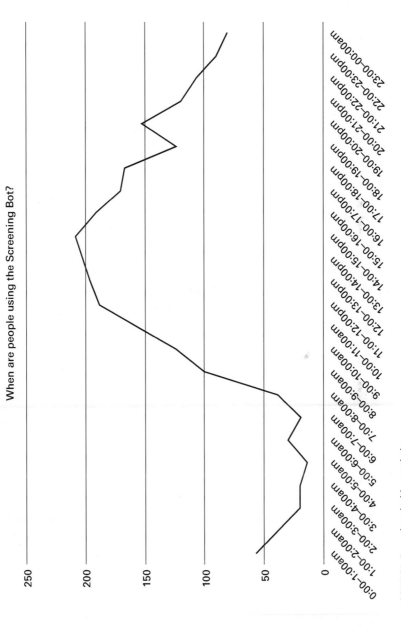

When are people using the Screening Bot?

SOURCE Reproduced with permission

a way to assess applicants before discussing it with the hiring managers and taking it live. 'We found that the process only works for roles where you have defined and clear screening criteria. For example, specific technical skills, specific professional knowledge, etc. The tool you are using should be as automatic and as easy to use as possible.'

Noa recommends these steps to ensure you run a smooth CV-free campaign:

1 Make sure your screening criteria are clearly defined.

2 Decide on the process and the tools that you will need.

3 Communicate the process to managers and stakeholders, and address their concerns.

4 Create a candidate application landing page with something mobile friendly like Typeform.

5 Create the social media campaign, choose your sourcing channels and take it live.

6 Collect data: monitor, test and candidate-funnel results and compare these to your regular application process, and ask candidates and managers for their feedback.

From an initial campaign, this is now a regular part of Noa's hiring process because it provides a better candidate experience by removing long application forms, it provides fairness and diversity by eliminating class, age and gender bias, and it is a fast and efficient process for recruiters and managers.

There are many tools available to help assess both soft and technical skills. I will share more on this in Chapter 8, but if you want to implement a pre-screening assessment you will definitely want to raise this idea during the intake strategy session as the success of your campaign will depend on the quality and suitability of your test, and that will need the right hiring manager input to deliver a great outcome.

Whether you choose to continue using CVs in your application or not, your job posts and job advertisements will always be a crucial part of your talent attraction and will be an integral part of your robot-proof messaging, which we will discuss in the next chapter.

Summary

- Your job post and job description need to work hard to stand out in the noise created by 4 billion people using the internet.

- Get creative with your job posts through colour, images and video to evoke emotion and action, and think about where you place them – offline works too.

- Take advantage of your proximity to your target recruits at events and conferences with WiFi names or invitations to quizzes and competitions.

- Consider improving the candidate experience by using screening tests instead of CVs or chatbots to screen and guide on career sites.

What has been your biggest takeaway? Tweet me @KatrinaMCollier using #RobotProofRecruiter

Notes

1 Lighthouse [accessed 12 April 2019] The ROI of video in the candidate experience, Lighthouse Research and Advisory [Online] http://lhra.io/blog/roi-video-candidate-experience/ (archived at https://perma.cc/EFX5-UQ6F)

2 British Library [accessed 12 April 2019] Fair use copyright explained, British Library Business and IP centre [Online] https://www.bl.uk/business-and-ip-centre/articles/fair-use-copyright-explained (archived at https://perma.cc/2FPR-YXD3)

3 Legislation.gov.uk [accessed 12 April 2019] The Copyright and Rights in performances (Quotation and Parody) Regulations 2014 [Online] http://www.legislation.gov.uk/ukdsi/2014/9780111116029 (archived at https://perma.cc/R6BA-9RNB)

4 Jones, S (2015) [accessed 12 April 2019] What's wrong with this advert? Ariadne Associates, 4 March [Online] https://ariadne-associates.co.uk/2015/03/04/whats-wrong-with-this-advert/ (archived at https://perma.cc/3MWE-E9NJ)

5 Equality and Human Rights Commission (2016) [accessed 12 April 2019] Unlawful adverts jeopardise job opportunities says Commission, Equality and Human Rights Commission [Online] https://www.equalityhumanrights.com/en/our-work/news/ unlawful-adverts-jeopardise-job-opportunities-says-commission (archived at https://perma.cc/3MWE-E9NJ)

6 Instagram post by GLL college [accessed 12 April 2019] Instagram, 3 September 2018 [Online] https://www.instagram.com/p/ BnRRgFuAUW0/ (archived at https://perma.cc/3WQQ-G23Z)

7 *Daily Mail* (2019) [accessed 12 April 2019] 'Any f*****, we're desperate!': Furious soldiers take aim at Army's new £1.5m recruitment drive calling on snowflakes and phone zombies, *Mail*Online, 4 January [Online] https://www.dailymail.co.uk/news/ article-6557031/Soldiers-aim-Armys-new-recruitment-drive-calling- Snowflakes-sign-up.html (archived at https://perma.cc/QV8X-DVB8)

8 Sadler, C (2019) [accessed 12 April 2019] 'Your army needs you': army recruitment campaign, Forces Network, 3 January [Online] https:// www.forces.net/news/your-army-needs-you-army-unveils-latest- recruitment-campaign (archived at https://perma.cc/DLB6-D9FU)

9 Tegze, J (2018) [accessed 12 April 2019] The psychology of color in recruitment, SourceCon, 5 June [Online] https://www.sourcecon. com/the-psychology-of-color-in-recruitment/ (archived at https:// perma.cc/3NFB-RT8S)

10 Lighthouse [accessed 12 April 2019] The videos job candidates actually want to see (not your branding video), Lighthouse Research and Advisory [Online] http://lhra.io/blog/videos-job- candidates-actually-want-see-not-branding-video-new-research/ (archived at https://perma.cc/3QQ2-ETNB)

11 NZPoliceRecruitment (2017) [accessed 12 April 2019] Freeze! NZ Police's most entertaining recruitment video, yet! YouTube, 25 November [Online] https://www.youtube.com/watch?v= f9psILoYmCc (archived at https://perma.cc/VSV9-WZF4)

12 SodaStream (2018) [accessed 12 April 2019] SodaStream's join the revolution, YouTube, 31 January [Online] https://www.youtube. com/watch?v=b5FoXLxpFPk (archived at https://perma. cc/43AP-ZG6G)

13 adsoftheworldvideos (2011) IKEA: career instructions, YouTube, 22 December [Online] https://www.youtube.com/watch?v= qwmXRAGDHeo (archived at https://perma.cc/L96Q-YQ6Y)

14 Wijnans, W (2018) [accessed 12 April 2019] What's the greatest recruiting hack you've ever seen? Quora, 12 November [Online] https://www.quora.com/Whats-the-greatest-recruiting-hack-youve-ever-seen/answer/Willem-Wijnans (archived at https:// perma.cc/5J8B-A47P)

15 Ohanian, A (2012) [accessed 12 April 2019] How Reddit built its empire on 500 bucks, stickers, and giving people what they want, Fast Company, 28 June [Online] https://www.fastcompany.com/1841389/how-reddit-built-its-empire-500-bucks-stickers-and-giving-people-what-they-want (archived at https://perma.cc/HZ5W-G7A5)

16 Codility [accessed 12 April 2019] Creating a competitive candidate experience: Strategies for candidate-focused tech hiring teams, webinar, Codility [Online]https://www.codility.com/resources/webinars/creating-a-competitive-candidate-experience (archived at https://perma.cc/6WPB-QZVX)

17 TalentBoard [accessed 12 April 2019] 2018 Talent Board North American candidate experience awards research report, TalentBoard [Online] https://www.thetalentboard.org/cande-awards/cande-research-reports/ (archived at https://perma.cc/6ZY3-HSBF)

18 Recruiter notes home page [accessed 12 April 2019] Recruiter notes [Online] https://www.recruiternotes.com/

Robot-proof messaging

07

TL;DR

It is amazing that too long; didn't read (TL;DR) is now a part of our vocabulary and cited in respected dictionaries. That's how often we are interrupted by emails, notifications, messages, calls and texts, that we can struggle to read articles that are of interest. That's the impact of technology.

As a recruiter or sourcer, you are in a fight for attention not a war for talent. If you haven't read what has come before this page, you won't be able to compete. You will lose the fight for attention. If you want to win, read and apply the advice in the previous chapters and then improve your messaging.

Robot-proof first contact

According to Jobvite's 2018 Recruiting Benchmark Report, every passive candidate you recruit is worth more than 18 candidates applying through external job boards because they are usually more suitable to the opportunity and the culture, and sourcing is 1.5 times more efficient than referrals.[1] Your success depends on the impression you make when you first get in touch, whether that is by email, InMail, phone, text, message or carrier pigeon.

Time-poor recruiters want templates and shortcuts to copy and paste but if that worked your InMail response rate would be 100 per cent. In a market where there are more jobs than people to fill them, effective candidate engagement needs more than a great message or call. As you will discover, direct contact is the easiest step to fix but alone it is not enough to secure a response or an application.

Personalized outreach is easy to implement and it will evoke a response but if you and your company still don't look worthy of a person's time, you won't get a return for your time. And if you don't take the candidate on an easy and enticing journey, you won't secure an application.

With the plethora of resources available to assist you it is easy to find people and their contact information, in fact, it is too easy. You are up against all of the other recruiters who also want attention but use the tools to spam. In this section, I will show you how to use the tools to start conversations to ensure that you are not perceived as yet another robot recruiter about to waste their valuable time.

Sourcing resources

- Read the SourceCon blog and attend SourceCon or SOSU conferences and events.
- Listen to Mark Lundgren's interviews on his 'Sourcing Challenge Show'.
- Look for interviews and content by Ronnie Bratcher, Glen Cathey, Maisha Cannon, Iker Jusue, Steve Levy, Aaron Lintz, Balazs Paroczay, Katharine Robinson, Irina Shamaeva, Jim Stroud and Derek Zeller.
- Read both of Jan Tegze's *Full Stack Recruiter* books.
- Join Ryan Leary's Secret Sourcing group on Facebook and look out for Dean Da Costa's posts about tools.
- On Facebook, join Susanna Frazier's Sourcers Who Code group, Tris Revill's Growth Hacking Recruiters group and Mark Lundgren's Storytelling Recruiter group.
- Every Friday, join Glenn Martin and me as we interview sourcers and recruiters on 'The #SocialRecruiting Show', or listen to the podcast replay.

Email basics

I am old school, I would rather you called someone before sending an email but usually when I say that, recruiters and sourcers stare at me in horror. I believe that if someone answers your call they are giving you permission to speak but let's argue that point later and focus on your email.

Subject line

As important as headlines in a newspaper, subject lines must evoke curiosity so people will continue reading. Though to you, it may seem important to state that your role is urgent, hot or an opportunity, it probably isn't to the recipient. Unless the recipient is an actor in *Star Wars*, a master of ninjutsu or in a rock band, it is also best to avoid using Jedi, ninja and rockstar.

Recruiter Angie Verros was impressed when she received a scouting email with the subject line 'I'm on the hunt, I'm after you'. Vying for Angie's attention, the recruiter had not only taken the time to read her profiles, they also created a subject line using song words from her favourite band, Duran Duran. To find more about a person try looking for a Twitter account under 'See contact info' on LinkedIn or searching their name in Google or Facebook.

Search Katrina Collier and you will easily see my dogs, so a subject line of 'Dogs are welcome at [company]' would definitely get my attention. Audra Knight's Twitter bio says she is an ice-hockey nut so you could try 'Get your skates on' and for Glenn Martin, whose bio states that he is always in denim, you could try injecting some humour with 'No double denim!' Corny though they may seem, the recipient will know you have done more than scan LinkedIn. Adding their name or an emoji will also increase the likelihood of your email being opened.

Hi or hey?

Controversially, I find emails from strangers that commence with 'Hey' rude and 'Hey Katrina' too familiar. It could be a cultural thing or it could be a generational thing. But by doing some research on the person's social accounts and blogs you can ensure that you start your cold email off well or it may be easier to play it safe and use 'Hi [first name]'.

You could try a tool like Crystal Knows which suggests you use 'Hey Mark' for Danish sourcer Mark Lundgren and to use 'Hello Kim' for Dutch sourcer Kim Lokenberg. I am not convinced it has taken into account cultural differences, which is why you must also use your knowledge of local customs. For example, Mark advises never to use anything less formal than 'Sehr geehrte Frau' or 'Sehr geehrter Herr' when emailing someone in Germany.

Crystal Knows initially suggests you address me with 'Hi Katrina' but further on it suggests you use a template that starts with 'Hey Katrina, We just…' This is one of the reasons I have concerns about advice that is provided by vendors – have they even had input from recruiters or sourcers? It is a good question to ask as you vet new suppliers.

First name

If you have just used their name in the email address there is no excuse for not starting an email with their name. Please use their first name. Please spell it correctly. Please don't call them by their surname in error. Recruiter Glenn Martin shared, 'So many people spell my name incorrectly, I receive Dear Martin, Hello Glen, Dear Mr Glen and more!' It is hard to undo how you make someone feel, especially a stranger.

I am amazed how often strangers shorten my name and again it's too familiar. I recommend using their name as it appears on LinkedIn and looking at how they reply to your message before shortening. For example, starting with 'Hi Catherine' and only replying with 'Hi Cathy', if they use it themselves in their reply.

Signing off

Be courteous and transparent. Remember you want to look like a recruiter worth talking to, so please include an email signature with your full name, job title, phone number, and links to your website and social media profiles. Make it easy for people to discover more.

Engaging email content

You don't really know if they are perfect for your job. You don't know what they are looking for next. You don't know their future career plans. Your job is to get their attention and to find out more.

Conversation starters

Conversation starters make magic. They get you the right attention. They are snippets of information that you use to either show that you have done your research, for example by directly referencing a blog they wrote or a tweet they shared, or to use to tailor your conversation to the recipient, for example mentioning child care benefits to a parent.

People tend to share different information on different social networks so be curious and look in more than one place. For example, you would have to look hard at my LinkedIn profile to find the word dogs, yet in my bios on other networks, it is easy to spot. My pictures on Instagram and Facebook tell you more about my interests and hobbies. These are all public pieces of information that can be used to start a conversation. To a parent, you probably wouldn't want to lead with 'I saw on Facebook that your children are called Ben and Audra', but you could talk about your flexible hours or work from home policy knowing that this is likely to pique their interest.

Chrome extensions are small software programs that customize the Google Chrome browsing experience and they are useful for finding a person's other social media accounts. But what you may find is that one will work on one network and not on another. For example, on LinkedIn a tool may not reveal any other social networks yet under 'See contact info' you will find a Twitter account, then on Twitter, the tools will show connections to Facebook, Instagram and even back to LinkedIn, so it pays to be curious and not just reliant on the extensions.

Tools often disappear too and many, due to the nature of what they do, can also get you in hot water with social networks. For example, I love that the Chrome extension Discovrly connects the dots between social networks but, if you use it on LinkedIn you are breaching Clause 8.2p of your User Agreement because it does 'Overlay or otherwise modify the Services or their appearance'. To save time managing extensions, I use the Chrome extension Extensity and to avoid breaching my LinkedIn user agreement, I turn Discovrly on when I am on other networks and off when I head back into LinkedIn.

For quickly finding other social media accounts, my favourite Chrome extensions include AmazingHiring, Prophet, Connectifier

Social Links and Discoverly (not for LinkedIn), and I have been known to use Hiretual and Lusha, but I also look at their websites, personal and company, and for blogs. Because many people use the same profile picture across social networks, I also run image searches on Google, Bing or Yandex.

Now is a great time to consider using a tool like Hello Talent. It is a place to store profiles of people you find online before you have spoken to them because unless you have spoken to the potential recruit they technically shouldn't be in your applicant tracking system or database. Hello Talent allows you to create pools of public social profiles, add notes and tags, and share profiles with hiring managers. Unlike projects in LinkedIn Recruiter, you are not reliant on a person having a profile on LinkedIn and it is distinctly more cost effective.

'What if I find nothing?' Tris Revill asked me that on our DBR Live, his video chat show for recruiters, and it is fair, not all people are active on social media but you still need to show you have done your research. So you could:

- Look for shared connections, one you know well enough to mention or contact them for a referral or maybe some advice on the best way to catch their attention.

- Run a search for their name in the News section of Google, Bing or DuckDuckGo as each one will show different results.

- Look for relevant employees or ex-employees of the candidate's current company and see if their profiles reveal something interesting you could use.

- Look to see if their current company is in the news and whether that could be used, positively, to start a conversation.

- If none of that works, hopefully they have some volunteer experience or recommendations to draw from to show that you did, in fact, read their profile.

The power of you, your, yours

Response rates drop by 80 per cent when you use phrases like 'I came across your profile on LinkedIn' because candidates receive this exact wording from many different recruiters, recruiters who were initially recommended to use it by LinkedIn and latterly by sourcing tool providers.[2] But if you get specific about their achievements or mention something unique, you will see a 20 per cent increase in response rates.

Imagine opening with 'Your blog post about [topic] caught the [name of hiring manager]'s attention because you mentioned [add a point], and we wondered if you would be the right person to help us with [from the intake] problem. The experience you gained at [company] could prove useful for solving this. You will also find we [insert a unique benefit]. May I tell you more?' This stands out from the copy and paste template messages.

I've kept it short and specific and switched the focus from the role to the candidate by using the word you. If you want to ensure they feel special, don't reduce your chance of getting a reply by 50 per cent by asking them to pass it on or refer someone else at this point. However, you could use Steve Levy's trick for adding value and include 'One more thing – if anyone you know needs career assistance, I'll help them any way I can.' It works because it offers your help instead of demanding their help.

Length

Advice varies about the ideal message but if you keep it intriguing, make it about them, personalize it, sound genuine by writing how you speak, share something you have in common from your research, short or long, you should receive a positive response and the opportunity to speak further.

Writing tools and further reading

- Respondable from Boomerang App: the free version will tell you as you write how likely it is that you will receive a response, analysing subject length, word and question count, and reading level. The premium offering uses machine learning to analyse positivity, subjectivity and even the politeness of your message.

- Grammarly: is a free tool that can help you communicate more effectively by making your messages and social media posts clear, error-free and impactful.

- TextExpander: lets you insert snippets of text or even images as you type a keyboard shortcut or abbreviation to save you time.
- Written by a developer in 2015 and more relevant today: bit.ly/ ihaterecruiters
- An experiment in recruiter spam by Panic At Recruitment: bit.ly/recspam
- Sjamilla Van der Tooren's findings from interviewing 40 developers: bit.ly/ sjamilla

Ways to really stand out

Hiring manager messages

According to LinkedIn, 56 per cent of people are more likely to respond if the hiring manager gets in touch.[3] This is something sourcer Sjamilla Van der Tooren has found very effective but if she can't get the hiring manager to make the actual outreach she definitely gets input from the team when recruiting for a technical role. 'I meet with one person every week to review profiles because they might see something that I overlooked, I'm not a developer. I learn what they like and why then translate that into my approach. It has resulted in a 93% response rate.'

If your hiring manager is resistant to making contact directly, perhaps because of concerns about the time involved, at a minimum encourage them to share a job post to their connections. Be wary of using your hiring manager's social media accounts on their behalf. Though this would seem a simple solution, assuming they trust you enough, it can breach the terms and conditions of the sites.

Personalized videos

Sourcer Mark Lundgren is a huge advocate for using video in emails, especially after it increased his response rates from 30 per cent to 70 per cent. 'Video in email shows them who you are, plus you can easily ask hiring managers and other colleagues to help record the messages. Having potential future colleagues contact a candidate in such a personal way can be quite effective because it provides an immediate view into what it's like to work with that person or team.' His favourite tool is Lemlist because of its ability to add personalized images and videos at scale, its tracking features and because it saves time.

Loom is another great tool that lets you record screen and camera, the screen only or the camera only, right from the Chrome extension. Imagine sending a personalized message that shows the recipient exactly what you read on their profiles that made you get in touch. Loom gives you a simple link to share, which you can use to hyperlink the image of the video in your email.

My clients have had great success sourcing on Facebook and making the first contact with a video message via Messenger. As discussed in Chapter 2, this only works if your profile is complete, including bio and job title, and you use your own legitimate profile. It is best to record the video on your phone beforehand in portrait mode, introducing yourself and explaining why you are getting in touch – ensuring it is all about the recipient – and then uploading it so you don't have to worry about mistakes. The recipient will receive an alert for a Message Request and can watch your video before they accept. It is more enticing than a toneless text-based message, you will know if they accept your message and it is free to send.

Phone sourcing

Using the phone to make contact is how I learned to recruit. Past candidates still tell me that I improved their life or changed their career so I find calling someone about a job exciting.

My phone rings so rarely these days that it is almost a thrill to hear it ring, and by answering I am giving you permission to speak but use my time wisely. If you call people, remember they may be in an open plan office and it may not be the best time to speak. Say who you are, and definitely use a conversation starter to show you don't plan to waste their time. You will have more success if you display your number and, if you are phoning abroad, you could try using an app like onoff that lets you use local numbers.

Many disagree with phone sourcing but I would argue that it is the fastest way to get a response and that it gives you the opportunity to share your understanding of the role and passion for your company through your tone of voice, which doesn't happen using email, InMail or text. If you want to gain confidence in phone sourcing, I recommend connecting with phone sourcer Maureen Sharib.

Texts and messages

Research conducted by Essendex in 2018 found that the global open rate for SMS is 94 per cent and research by Emarsys found that response rates from SMS are 209 per cent higher than from phone calls, Facebook or email.[4, 5] In Jobvite's 2018 Recruiter Nation survey of 808 American recruiters, 43 per cent stated they had used text to message new or current candidates, receiving 88 per cent positive feedback from job seekers and only 4 per cent negative.[6]

As with email, it is all about the approach: identify yourself, show you have done your research, and be polite and relevant. Because you can see when someone has read your message, WhatsApp is popular to use but make sure your profile is complete and professional. To avoid getting off on the wrong foot, check the timing of your message; their phone is likely to ping so make sure you are not sending your message too late or too early.

The magic is in the follow-up

There are 2,264 emails in my inbox, all marked as read. Sixty need my attention and are flagged for follow up but as they have dropped off my screen, as more emails have piled in on top, they have been forgotten. My inbox won't be the only one managed in this poor way; full of important emails that are being neglected for another day.

Unless you happen to email a candidate at exactly the moment they want to hear from you and at exactly the moment they have time to read it, it is likely to get parked to one side. Recruiters like to think that their email is incredibly important but to a passive candidate it usually isn't.

The most successful recruiters and sourcers follow up their prospects. They don't send one email and start searching again, they follow up multiple times. This is backed up by research from Recruiterflow that found that only 10 per cent of candidates replied to the first email but by the fourth 60 per cent had replied.[7]

Here you will discover multiple ways that you can follow up without being annoying and ideas for staying in touch that reinforce the human connection.

Immediate follow-up

Invitation to connect

If you have just sent someone an email you could also invite them to connect on LinkedIn or one of the other professional social networks. Of course, you could use this as a method of making the first contact but, if they have turned off their email notifications, that means you will be waiting for them to log in and see it.

I receive hundreds of connection requests from recruiters and very few include the courtesy of an explanation. This is the number one complaint I hear from people outside of our industry too.

If this was played out in real life, it would be like a stranger at a conference walking up to you, attempting to pull you away and then demanding your contact details. Because that's what they are giving you when they connect, their information. And contrary to what recruiters have been led to believe, not everyone joins sites like LinkedIn to get a job. So stand out from the people who don't explain what they want and use the 300 characters to add a personal note that includes one of the conversation starters you found earlier.

Choose your words wisely though so you stand out for all the right reasons. Here are some invitations I have received that are great examples of words to avoid:

- Leaving a bad taste with a hollow compliment before hitting me up for help: 'Saw you are in the 30 HR tech influencers to watch in 2019 – so I thought why not approach you as I'm looking for a new career challenge.'

- Leaving me wondering still: from a stranger 'Would love to connect with you on LinkedIn.'

- Sounding desperate: 'I found your profile interesting and would be happy to belong to your network. Please accept my invite.'

- Unintentionally cryptic: 'I'd love to connect, and send you a coffee huggg. It's my more memorable way to say hi.' It was a play on his company's name but it left me confused.

- Sounding like everyone else: 'I came across your profile and would like to connect.'

You could simply state: 'As explained in my email [first name], you caught my attention because of [reason] and [reason]. Can we connect?' This will let them know that you sent them an email, in case the spam filters caught it, and that you have actually looked at their profiles.

Twitter follow-up

Twitter has more monthly active users than LinkedIn and though it receives negative press, Twitter is now consistently turning a profit and those who do use it actively remain loyal. Interestingly, video consumption has increased 220 times in 2018 outperforming gifs, images and links, so be sure to share your job and branding videos on Twitter too.[8]

Twitter makes it really easy to engage and re-engage with people to become known, liked and trusted, so if your candidate is actively using Twitter, it is definitely worth following them there. They will receive a notification, so make sure your profile is complete (see Chapter 3) and you are sharing valuable content, not just your jobs. You then have the opportunity to comment, retweet or favourite but don't overdo it, you want to occasionally appear on their radar, not give them a reason to block you.

Please also remember that many people use Twitter to get vocal when their complaints are not being resolved, so ensure your career and corporate accounts are also replying to and following up with people. To ensure your reputation stays rosy, you could also use a tool like Twilert or MyTweetAlerts to help monitor your accounts and mentions too.

Twitter lists

Within Twitter you can place people into lists. These are great for helping you stay organized and on top of the updates from people you really want to stay in touch with. On a profile, click the '...' symbol and you will find the option to add or remove them from a list.

When creating a new list, you can create a private or public list. Private lists can only be seen by you and the Twitter user won't know that they have been added to it. Public lists are visible to anyone on your profile and the Twitter user will receive a notification that they have been added to it. In the past, I received a notification that I had been added to a list called Prospects, which promptly led me to block the user to avoid their spam, so choose your list name wisely.

If you are recruiting for a specific role and hope to draw more attention to it, I recommend:

1 sharing it in a creative job tweet, perhaps a short video with the hiring manager;

2 adding industry-related hashtags, which you can research at Hashtagify;

3 pinning it to the top of your profile so it is the first thing someone sees; and

4 interacting with the people on the list who would find it interesting.

By interacting, I mean commenting or retweeting, hoping you will entice them to look at your profile. I definitely don't mean tweeting something like '@KatrinaMCollier want this job? [link]' which is the equivalent, in real life, of shoving your job requirement into their hand without so much as a hello. To understand how to use Twitter better for hiring, have a look at this resource: bit.ly/TwitterSocRec

Instagram follow

One billion people use Instagram; 35 per cent of adults online are using Instagram, 500 million each day.[9] I have found it an excellent site for keeping in touch with clients and industry peers because I see more about their lives and with greater ease than on other sites. Like Twitter, you have an opportunity to show your worth by following, liking and commenting on photos and stories.

Some of the Chrome extensions will reveal Instagram accounts, or you may see a link to Instagram in their Twitter feed, especially if they are not using the IFTTT hack shared in Chapter 2 that automatically sends the photo to Twitter as an image, or you could try searching for them by name. Like Twitter, to improve your chances of being followed back, complete your bio and share valuable and authentic updates.

Follow on other sites

Facebook is brilliant for recruiting and though many will be OK receiving your message via the platform, few will be willing to add you, a stranger, as a friend. But there are countless other sites where you could connect or follow someone, including Xing, Viadeo, WeChat, Weibo and Reddit.

For creatives, look to see if they have a portfolio on Behance or Dribbble that you or the hiring manager could follow or comment on. It may be more challenging for a non-technical recruiter but one of your technical team could follow and engage with potential candidates on Kaggle, dev.to, StackOverflow or GitHub. To really stand out, look to see if they have their own blog or if they write on Medium or Tumblr, and subscribe, comment or share their posts.

Email follow-up to a voicemail

If you have just left a message on someone's voicemail, it's a great time to send them an email too because not everyone listens to their voicemail or has a pen handy to write down your number.

Keep it simple with a subject line like 'just left you a message' or 'tried to call you just now' and a quick summary 'Further to my message, your [insert a conversation starter] and [insert another one to show you did your research], caught our attention, and it would be great to discover more. Is there a better time to speak?' Sign off with your full email signature so they have your email address and contact details and they can reply or investigate further with ease.

Follow-up sequence

Using an applicant tracking system with a nurturing system, a technology that allows you to send a series of emails, can help you create email campaigns with three to five touchpoints that operate automatically. This is how sourcer Denis Dinkevich uses Lever Nurture to do this:

1 'First message: I use a subject line like "[candidate name] >> [company name]?" and I record a personalized video message on Loom that is around one minute long, add in a few links to the job or career site, and I include a strong call to action.

2 Three working days later: forward the original email if I have not received a reply.

3 If I still haven't received a reply five days later, I send a follow-up letter with additional calls to action and sharing some unique points related to working in the role, and I set this to be delivered on the weekend.

4 I try one more time after seven working days and then snooze it for two' months when I may repeat it.'

Tracking software

Not all recruiters have the luxury of a database or an applicant tracking system but that doesn't mean you can't get creative in your follow-up or track your emails. Tools like Yesware and SalesHandy can track whether your email is opened, whether they click on links and even if they open an attachment. They can also help you create automatic follow-ups and campaigns.

> My aim is for you to be creative and to rarely copy and paste. The ideas here won't suit all styles of recruiter or company. Use them as inspiration to find your own style, one that suits the recipient too.

Second email

On Twitter, under #recruiterspam or #recruiterfail, you will find people sharing how they would and would not like to be treated and approached. In this case, how not to approach, 'Hi [name], I haven't been able to reach you but my gut feeling tells me I should go on trying.' Perhaps the sender was trying to be funny but the recipient was unimpressed. It is hard to know what to say. You want a reply but you also want to look professional.

As Denis suggested, I would send a follow-up a few days later, forwarding the last email, and keeping it short and sweet. Something as simple as 'Curious to hear your thoughts; is there a good time to speak, [name]? Would love to tell you more about [insert perk or project that should interest them].'

Third email

Now you are entering nag territory so why not embrace that and even inject some humour, if that suits your style. You could try something similar to this but using your own personality and with consideration of the recipient.

> Hi [name],
>
> At the risk of being a nag | bugging you | being blocked | being too needy [choose one] I'm following up | moving this to the top of your inbox | putting this at the top of the pile again [choose one that matches your company and personality].
>
> On [social site] I can see you are busy with [specific detail]. Would love to chat briefly, would it be better if we spoke on the phone | had a coffee [choose one]?
>
> [Email signature]

With so many other paths available to get someone's attention, this could be the time to stop and try a different tack.

Follow-up etiquette

Should you keep following up by email?

CEO & Founder of Firefish Software, Wendy McDougall, showed me a thread of emails from a vendor who was trying to attract her attention. Each time they chased, they forwarded the previous email and by the time she showed me, the thread was eight emails long. Shaking my head in disbelief, I wondered why they hadn't tried another tack because by not replying, Wendy was showing them that either she wasn't interested or this wasn't her preferred communication channel.

There are so many different options available to you and it is better to try something different than to use the one method that you prefer. Running my own business, I have to be available on whatever channel my clients decide to use, and I have discussed business proposals via WhatsApp, iMessage, Messenger, Instagram Messaging, Twitter DM and even old-fashioned phone calls. In case email isn't your candidate's preferred communication channel, try something else.

Watch for passive aggressive

Passive-aggressive behaviour is when someone expresses hostility indirectly. For example, one day I walked out of Waterloo Station and was so intently looking at the numbers on the front of the bus that I didn't see the queue of people. As I got on board the lady who found my behaviour so deplorable could have communicated clearly and pointed it out to me. Instead, she tutted and huffed until eventually, I snapped 'What?' to which she went into a tirade about the queue. It still makes me laugh but it also shows how important it is to use clear communication.

In an email, it happens when the sender thinks that they deserve a response so uses high priority for a low priority email or they suggest that you are making a mistake if you don't reply by using something like 'This is the best opportunity I've seen in the last ten years.'

In follow-up, it would appear as something like 'I haven't heard from you since I sent my email over a week ago. I assume you're not interested, but just in case you are, I thought I'd check in.' The use of 'I assume you're not interested but just in case you are' is what makes it, possibly unintentionally, passive aggressive.

Stolen from sales and used in recruitment, this is one I regularly hear complaints about:

> **Is this the end?**
>
> Hi [name],
>
> I'm in the process of clearing out my sales pipeline and I thought I should let you know that you're on my delete list.
>
> If you're no longer interested, do I have permission to permanently close your file?
>
> If you are still interested, what would you like to do as a next step?
>
> Thanks for your help.
>
> [Email signature]

'You're on my delete list' and 'permanently close your file' are the passive-aggressive triggers; even 'thanks for your help' seems insincere. It is so easy to change, to deliver a similar result, to:

> **Is this the end?**
>
> Hi [name],
>
> In a final run through my pipeline, can you help?
>
> If you would like me to stop clogging up your inbox, please tell me.
>
> If you are interested, what would you like to do as a next step?
>
> Kind regards,
>
> [Email signature]

Other common phrases that you may want to avoid using include 'touch base', which topped Glassdoor's survey of most annoying office buzzwords and 'Not sure if you saw my last email', 'Per my last email', 'Any updates on this?' and 'Reattaching for convenience', which topped Adobe's 2018 Consumer Email Survey.[10, 11]

#FightSpam

If you are looking for advice and recruiters passionate about reducing the amount of recruiter spam being sent, join the #FightSpam group on Facebook.

Value-add follow-up

Nothing beats the personal touch; a comment on a post, an answer to a question or receiving unexpected appreciation. If it is genuine we know and you start to become known, liked and trusted. When you are yet to properly connect with someone this can be a great tack.

Privately, you could send someone a message sharing an article and say something along the lines of 'I saw this and thought of you because...' inserting reasons that show you have researched and know your stuff. Publicly, you could write 'This is a great post about [topic] because of [two reasons], would be really keen to hear what you think of this, [name]?' but only do this if it will be relevant to the person. When it happens to me and it is irrelevant, I end up thinking worse of the person, and I definitely don't reply.

Your aim, obviously, is to get people into conversation with you first, but if not, into the pool of people who are keen to keep in touch and discover more. Specsavers have mastered this with the creation of the Green Club. For free, all eye-care professionals gain access to an online library of clinical articles, training modules and case studies, video content and webinars on clinical and retail topics, are kept up to date on news, and are invited to the annual Specsavers Clinical Conference. This is the perfect way to keep industry specialists engaged and to stay on their radar.

Tech to engage your talent pool

At every opportunity encourage potential recruits to join your talent pool and you can easily keep them interested and discovering more. No longer should your database be a black hole; it should instead be used as a tool to share peer-to-peer content and keep interested people posted on the latest news.

The modern applicant tracking and recruitment software providers, like Clinch Talent, Phenom People, Workable, Lever, Talemetry,

Yello, Firefish Software and others, will give you a platform that helps you engage regularly with people who have shown interest in your company or jobs. Keep them engaged with all of that great content you are producing already to give insight into your brand and your latest news.

Is it worth the effort?

In answer, Shane Gray from Clinch said 'The interesting thing is pretty much any content other than just sharing jobs works. We see clients who share regular company news like an initial public offering (IPO) or a new office opening go on to generate hires from those emails. The really great part is that the apply-to-hire ratio is so much better than the fresh traffic from the job boards, by a factor of 8 to 12.'

Wendy McDougall, from Firefish Software, shared how their staffing agency clients get value. 'Talent pools are filled with the types of candidates that are placed the most often, so they deserve your utmost attention and the best value you can offer. Share relevant market information on the supply-and-demand for their skill sets, success stories of similar candidates you've previously placed and changed their career for the better, or tips on what projects they could be getting involved in to keep their skill set smoking hot. With an approach like this, you're going to be the first recruiter they call when the time is right for them to move.'

Pipeline tracking

Emulating market software providers who have been tracking actions of consumers for years, and sitting on top of the ATS, Candidate. ID allows you to track all candidate activity across your website, careers site and landing pages, as well as engagement with your emails and text messages. Using in-depth automation rules this allows you to more easily nurture wider datasets into pipelines, rather than focusing on people who interact with specific vacancies.

Curious to know what content Candidate.ID know work, I asked their Client Success Director, Billy McDiarmid. 'If you are lucky enough to have an employer branding team, then a schedule of blogs, video and infographics tailored to the candidate persona should be created. But if you don't have that resource, then take a look at what content your marketing team generates already as this can normally be easily reworked into a schedule that prospective applicants will love consuming.'

This is definitely a time to use technology to strengthen your bond with potential candidates and those who have opted into your talent pool, through the sharing of value-adding and insightful peer-to-peer content. Just be sure to keep it more interesting than a feed of your latest jobs!

Summary

- You get one chance to make a first impression with your candidate outreach so ensure each email or message is personalized and relevant.
- Manners maketh the human; be conscious of how you address your potential candidate and sign off with full transparency.
- To stand out, use video and SMS messaging to engage candidates.
- Follow-up, follow-up, follow-up. People are busy, they need reminding, courteously.
- Get creative when you follow up; don't just keep emailing, try another method.
- Make the technology work for you; use your ATS or database to share content that will keep people interested in you and your company.

How have you changed your messaging? Tweet me @KatrinaMCollier using #RobotProofRecruiter

Notes

1 Shetelboim, R (2018) [accessed 12 April 2019] 2018 Recruiting Benchmark report: How do you stack up?, Jobvite blog 20 March [Online] https://www.jobvite.com/jobvite-news-and-reports/2018-recruiting-benchmark-report-how-do-you-stack-up/ (archived at https://perma.cc/6CAL-7PRK)

2 Textio [accessed 12 April 2019] The secret language of sourcing, Textio [Online] https://hello.textio.com/the-secret-language-of-sourcing (archived at https://perma.cc/VV8F-D8E2)

3 LinkedIn [accessed 12 April 2019] Inside the mind of today's candidate: 13 insights that will make you a smarter recruiter, LinkedIn Talent Solutions [Online] https://business.linkedin.com/content/dam/me/business/en-us/talent-solutions/resources/pdfs/inside-the-mind-of-todays-candidate.pdf (archived at https://perma.cc/Q25W-JA99)

4 Esendex (2018) [accessed 12 April 2019] What is the open rate for SMS in 2018? Esendex Blog, 19 March [Online] https://www.esendex.co.uk/blog/post/what-is-the-open-rate-for-sms-in-2018/ (archived at https://perma.cc/N23W-9HLX)

5 Wotten, K (2017) [accessed 12 April 2019] 18 Mobile stats to consider for your 2018 marketing strategy, The Mobile Experience Company, 20 December [Online] https://www.mobilexco.com/blog/18-stats-to-help-you-plan-your-mobile-marketing-strategy-in-2018 (archived at https://perma.cc/6RWH-PSFS)

6 Jobvite [accessed 12 April 2019] 11th Annual Recruiter Nation Survey, The tipping point: A new chapter in recruiting, Jobvite [Online] http://web.jobvite.com/FY18_Website_2018RecruiterNation_LP.html (archived at https://perma.cc/M9W7-HKL8)

7 Recruiterflow [accessed 12 April 2019] Sourcing benchmarks – a report, Recruiterflow Blog [Online] https://recruiterflow.com/blog/sourcing-benchmarks-report/ (archived at https://perma.cc/YB83-GLC5)

8 Neil Patel [accessed 12 April 2019] Is Twitter worth your time? Here's what new 2018 data says about Twitter for Marketing, Neil Patel Blog [Online] https://neilpatel.com/blog/is-twitter-worth-your-time/ (archived at https://perma.cc/TD26-8LMT)

9 Clarke, T (2019) [accessed 12 April 2019] 22+ Instagram stats that marketers can't ignore this year, Hootsuite, 5 March [Online] https://blog.hootsuite.com/instagram-statistics/ (archived at https://perma.cc/UVJ9-HZ23)

10 Glassdoor (2018) [accessed 12 April 2019] Most annoying UK office jargon REVEALED IN NEW Glassdoor survey, Glassdoor, 11 July

[Online] https://www.glassdoor.com/about-us/most-annoying-uk-office-jargon-revealed-in-new-glassdoor-survey/ (archived at https://perma.cc/GUH9-5CYT)

11 Adobe (2018) [accessed 12 April 2019] 2018 Adobe consumer email survey, LinkedIn Learning, 17 August [Online] https://www.slideshare.net/adobe/2018-adobe-consumer-email-survey (archived at https://perma.cc/8G6R-676A)

Applications and pain-free interviews

08

From the moment someone applies, your job is to retain the attention of those people who have the skills that your organization needs to be successful and to treat with respect and kindness those who haven't made the cut and let them know swiftly.

Recruitment is a business of rejection and often time-poor recruiters are under such pressure to fill roles that they forget the hopes and dreams of the human behind every single CV and application. Even though to us a job applicant isn't a candidate until we are speaking to them and they are in consideration for a role, with the plethora of places available for people to vent their displeasure at inhumane treatment, managing applicants or candidates poorly could impair your future hiring.

Co-Founder of Talent Board and The Candidate Experience Awards, Gerry Crispin defines a candidate as 'anyone who expresses an interest in your position not just those who make it to interview' and he shared from their extensive research the five factors that account for 80 per cent of the variance in how your candidates will rate their experience.

1 Set and deliver on expectations for each stage of the journey from application to onboarding or rejection.

2 Actively listen from the point when a prospect becomes aware of you and considers applying, right through to questions they might have while waiting for your decision.

3 Demonstrate fairness intentionally; share why you believe your process offers everyone the same chance to compete and, if not, why you support giving a specific group added opportunity.

4 Be accountable for the measurable rating candidates give about your process.

5 Ensure each and every person who expressed interest in your position has closure.

In this chapter, you will hear how you can use technology effectively to make everything from the moment of application through to the end of interviewing more human. It's less about how to conduct an interview and more about how to use technology to support you in listening, setting expectations, giving closure and delivering a fair process.

Candidate ghosting

Transparency caused by the internet, a tight labour market and poor recruiter behaviour has led to the rise in candidates disappearing during the recruitment process or even accepting an offer and not starting the job. If recruiters had spent years delivering exceptional candidate experience, instead of using technology to avoid replying to or delivering feedback to people, then there would be greater candidate loyalty today.

Run this search on Google **site:glassdoor.com/interview "never heard back" OR "still waiting"** or type this into a search on Twitter **"never heard back" AND interview**; the results are sobering.

Not everyone will make it through to interview and though it may not be possible to answer every single application personally, it is possible to send an email of rejection that sympathizes with their possible feelings of disappointment and gives closure. Though an email of rejection is acceptable for an application, it is not best practice for people who have spent hours preparing for, travelling to and interviewing at your company, they deserve a call and feedback.

If you really want to keep people in your interview process through to onboarding, implement renowned recruiter Stacy Zapar's Friday

Feedback Blitz. 'Every Friday, I block out 3 to 5 pm to send a quick email, call or text to each candidate active in the interview pipeline and let them know their status, even if there's no real news to share. It sends them into the weekend feeling updated and confident, and it allows me to update my ATS so I can go into my weekend having wrapped everything up and ready to truly enjoy it.'

Recruiters must remember that we are playing with people's lives and livelihoods. We are not selling an inert product that doesn't care how it is treated. We are selling people on a new role or career in your company or with your client, and these people will never forget how you made them feel. Let's make them feel special.

The application

In Chapter 4, I recommended that you give your application process an audit to ensure you were a company worthy of someone's time. I referred to the ease of finding your jobs from the home page or on a mobile phone, ensuring each role has its own URL for ease of sharing, and made suggestions for ensuring that your job descriptions are accessible to diverse applicants. In this section, you will hear a few more considerations to ensure a smooth application process, essential if you are an unknown brand.

Employer brand and recruitment marketing expert, Tracey Parsons from Parsons Strategic Consulting, is working with a healthcare company to redesign their talent experience and interviewed a group of candidates who were not selected by the company. Surprisingly, she found that candidates will endure almost any burden to secure a job if that company aligns with their values and mission.

When analysing their data, she found that the company had a 20 per cent conversion rate from a site visit to an application, above the industry norm of 11 per cent. It seems that 'Candidates will go through whatever process we throw at them if they believe in the values of the company, but this is your opportunity to back up your employer brand promise with an application process and candidate experience that validates who you say you are.'

Few companies have an employer brand that is strong enough to carry people, especially those with skills that are in high demand, from interest to a completed application if the process is unduly cumbersome. It also makes little sense to let technology undo all the hard work you did gaining the person's interest in the first place.

A word on serial applicants

Serial applicants apply to every job you advertise. Debating with an industry friend, whether they deserve the same closure as other applicants, he was adamant that the answer was no. He sounded vexed when sharing that three people in his company's database had applied for 125 roles each. Knowing he works for a household name company, I asked how many people were in the database before pointing out that three in a few million wasn't many. My reasoning wasn't especially appreciated, but I wanted to put it in perspective. I understand his point of view but I also wonder if serial applicants realize the damage they are doing to their reputation.

Many recruiters fear that by making their application process easier they will receive even more serial applicants and you may, but you will also create ease for those people with highly sought-after skills, who can pick and choose their opportunity, to step into your hiring process.

Account creation

Creating an account should be an option for applicants, not a forced requirement. Equating it to online shopping, even people who regularly visit an eCommerce site may not want to commit to creating an account. In 2009, when Amazon moved the option to create an account to after the transaction, sales increased by 45 per cent, which equated to $300 million that year alone.[1] The choice to create an account should fall at the end of the application process and not be a deterrent at the beginning.

If forced to create an account, under no circumstances should candidates have to answer security questions that leave them vulnerable if your applicant tracking system (ATS) or database is hacked.

During research, I came across an ATS that asked for three things I use to access my PayPal account, namely my mother's maiden name, the name of my first pet and my father's middle name, none of which should be necessary to access a simple job application. When you are implementing your system ensure that ease of application and a smooth candidate experience remain your top priority.

Résumés and text boxes

Are you asking people to fill out information twice? One of the easiest ways to deter an application is to ask people to copy the information from their résumés into boxes; not only is it time-consuming for the applicant, it's pointless. Modern ATS and databases use parsing technology that allows recruiters to electronically gather, store and organize the information contained in résumés or applications, so it is easy to search this data later even if it is in a Word or PDF attachment. If a box must remain, consider making it optional.

You could consider removing free text boxes altogether but that does depend on your industry and the roles. Some applicants won't have a CV so will need the ability to add their experience manually or, perhaps, to apply using a social media profile.

Generation Z

Though I don't believe in generational typecasting, Generation Z has got different expectations of technology because those born after 1995 are used to having easy access to technology via their devices. Due to their age, even the eldest are likely to have limited work experience and unlikely to have enough experience to have a detailed CV.

At the Jobg8 Job Board Summit, Todor Madzharov from Job Today shared the lessons they had learned from acquiring 5 million millennial job seekers. Realizing the obstacle a lack of CV caused job seekers, they added a seamless process to let people input information that transformed into a CV they could use immediately. Testing it, I created my CV (see Figure 8.1) and was ready to apply for a job in under five minutes.

Figure 8.1 My Job Today profile

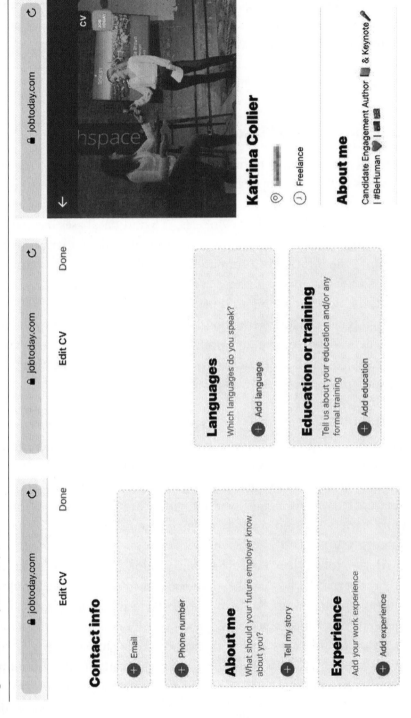

So though I've recommended removing compulsory boxes that force duplication, you may need to include optional boxes for instances where people don't have a traditional résumé and even use the information to create a document for your hiring managers.

Video job applications

With the rise of video in most aspects of recruitment, it was surprisingly hard to find examples of companies using video instead of a CV in the application, and I came across only one applicant tracking system specifically catering to video job applications, StartMonday, which caters to the hospitality and retail industry.

You may have concerns that watching video job applications would be more time-consuming than scanning résumés, but surely the need for an applicant to submit a video takes more thought and therefore reduces the volume of people who apply that are unsuitable or serial applicants?

This was something I put to Kristen Graham, Co-Founder of VideoMyJob, as they recently introduced VideoMyTalent to their product range, a tool for submitting video job applications. She shared, 'Coty Inc. posted a video job ad and then used our video response apply link. Instead of receiving their usual 8,000 plus applications to wade through, in two weeks they received 26 high-quality qualified and engaged application videos, which saved them an enormous amount of time sifting the wheat from the chaff.'

Children's Mercy, a non-profit paediatric medical centre in Kansas City, has a section on their career site called Introduce Yourself, which you can use if you are too busy to fill out an application (which is incredible candidate experience) or if you don't see a position that is right for you.[2] Because they believe in building careers not just filling jobs, they let candidates record and submit a video application, using their integrated video software provided by HireVue.

Strategic insight consultancy Flamingo wants to recruit people who are curious about the world, so they did away with CVs and instead ask candidates to submit a piece of work around what motivates them from a work or personal perspective, and to answer a question about what company they think is having an interesting impact on culture.[3] The answer can be given in 400 written words, as a video, an audio file or a link to a blog. The result is that they have seen someone's work and their thinking, which is not visible on an actual CV, and have accessed individuals they may not have seen with the old CV-based application process.

If you think your company could accept videos instead of a traditional résumé be sure to get your hiring manager's buy-in during the intake strategy session.

Application autoresponders

In Chapter 6, you learned about chatbots that can ease communication and even pre-screen candidates, and I shared Noa Ferber's experience of ditching the résumé, hoping to inspire your company to do the same. Hopefully, you have also had the opportunity to audit your application process and remove the barriers that stop diverse candidates applying.

Many recruiters though, for the foreseeable future, will be receiving applications via their database or applicant tracking system (ATS) and sending automatic responses to applicants. These application autoresponders have impact; take a moment to think about the wording of the tweet Demi shared and the emotion behind it.

After applying for a position, Demi shared an image of the email auto-response she received, which said 'Dear Demi, Thank you for applying for the role of [role], we will be reviewing your application and will be in touch should your background meet the requirements for the position. Thank you for your interest! Regards, Talent Acquisition Team' and to the image she added 'Pray for me, I want this job so badly!'

Demi is so excited about this job opportunity that she has gone to Twitter and shared an image of the email but do you think she will hear back?

You may not be surprised by the wording of the autoresponder and on the plus side, it does use her name and say thank you. On the downside though, it is dismissive, anonymous and missing the opportunity to keep Demi engaged and learning more.

Imagine how different it would feel if she had received an email or even a video thanking her sincerely for the time and effort she had put into her application, explaining the likely next steps and directing her to more information.

For zero investment, this could be improved by signing off with the name of the recruiter. With today's technology, you can add the name of each recruiter working on each role, and though some may be concerned about being chased, dealing with a few interruptions from super-keen applicants is better than the negative impact a cold response can have on engagement.

You could also use this opportunity to direct candidates to more information. Share job search or interview advice from your employees or even share a post on your own employees' funniest interview fails to show the candidate how approachable you are. Remember to direct them to your social media pages too.

By doing this you are adding value and with the sharp rise in candidate ghosting, whether ethical or not, you are already on your way to developing a good relationship with the applicant.

Mobile autoresponders

When the average open rate for SMS is 98 per cent it makes sense to integrate tools like Twilio or Zapier to your ATS or database so you can send a personalized text response, even including a gif or video to add that personal touch.[4] An alternative is ConveyIQ, which will send a rich media text to acknowledge the application. You can also design campaigns to keep in touch with candidates, which give visibility into the next steps and allow for the scheduling of interviews, all by text, and it includes the ability to ask candidates for feedback so you can improve the overall recruitment experience.

Telephone interviews

Most recruiters start the interview process at the phone screen or interview, though as I have already touched on with Yodel's chatbot and Noa Ferber's quiz examples in Chapter 6, there are ways to use technology to ensure the right people reach the initial phone screen.

My aim is to show you how you can use technology to help people decide whether they wish to continue or opt out of the recruitment process, so you conduct fewer but higher-quality candidate phone screens. This section also includes technology that aids you with your phone screening and ensures you are using technology to place the human first and improve the candidate experience.

Amp-up deselection

Recruiters spend a lot of time rejecting people at the phone screen when people could have deselected themselves at the job post/description or using a screening bot, like the Yodel example in Chapter 6. This time could be better invested in delivering an exceptional candidate experience for the people who are genuinely invested in continuing with their application.

Durham Police in the UK, in need of dozens of constables, created an excellent video from real bodycam footage and asked 'Do you really want to be a cop?'[5] It is emotive, credible due to the date stamps in the footage, and it will cause many to deselect through being confronted with the harsh realities of the role; perfect, recruiters will spend less time wasted sieving unsuitable applications. But also remembering the importance of the application process for those who do proceed, it is a good thing that the video mentions the paperwork police are faced with because the entire application process is outdated, requiring the printing and manual submission of forms, which could be stopping applicants who are genuinely interested in working for Durham Police from applying.

To increase the chance that the video will be seen add your videos directly to the job advertisement pages of your website and where possible, to increase conversion, use videos from your hiring managers. But if you cannot do that, you could use your application autoresponder to send them the video and ask them if they would like to proceed with their application.

Pre-screening tools for assessing 'fit'

There is a plethora of tools you can use to carry out pre-screening to assess if someone will fit your organization or team and this could potentially be a great way to reduce the number of phone interviews you need to conduct. But, unlike assessing hard skills, assessing an applicant's soft skills fit really comes down to being able to accurately identify the personality characteristics and cognitive abilities needed from each person carrying out the duties of the role.

Working out who is a great fit is definitely not something I've ever been great at; I have hired many people based on my gut, which is far from scientific! So I asked Dale Clareburt, CEO & Co-Founder of Weirdly, recruitment software that uses a customizable quiz to rank candidates against your ideal 'fit', what is essential for making this technology work for you and deliver a better candidate experience?

Firstly, Dale suggests that you measure what your candidates and employees are saying about the recruitment process and their employment experience. Without knowing what is and isn't working, you may be adding a step that isn't necessary, it is important that 'You only add a step into the recruitment process if it is simplifying it or providing more relevance and clarity to the candidate experience.'

Secondly, it is vital to understand the problem you are trying to solve and what you should measure. For example, if you aren't attracting and recruiting the right people, you need to define what that means; is it that they don't stay or perform, or a lack of diversity, and so on? It is critical to accurately diagnose the challenge that you are trying to solve, improve or evolve when using a pre-application tool or a new approach to a specific interview structure or process.

Dale described how

> Weirdly uses a methodology that uncovers what 'good' and what 'not right' look like, in relation to the values, attributes and traits, at both an organization level and across job families or departments. By rigorously running a discovery and diagnostic methodology we find the good oil that is really needed and then we drill down. All teams should run through a process like this before researching for or investing in pre-application tools and interview processes.

Delving further, Bas van der Haterd has written an excellent free white paper on assessment tools, based on his own experiences and available for download here: ta-live.com/whitepaper. Whatever tool you decide to use though, make sure that you start with an assessment of your needs or ask the technology provider to help you to do that if you are unsure, or you may end up investing money in a product that delivers the wrong outcome.

Audio, video and artificial intelligence pre-screening

This book has been written to improve how recruiters engage with people who possess skills that are in high demand, and those people are less likely to search for a job and more likely to be sourced by a recruiter, but if you are in high-volume recruiting, combining video and artificial intelligence (AI) could be beneficial.

Companies like Unilever are using video and AI to match graduates to roles; applicants are asked to film their answers to questions that pop up on their computer screen. Unilever uses HireVue Assessments to analyse candidates' recorded interviews and filter the applicant pool leaving only those most likely to be successful, based on video interview attributes, like facial expressions, body language, and word choice, which has been proven to be predictive of job success.[6]

Both successful and unsuccessful candidates receive and give feedback throughout the process, which crucially improves the candidate experience. In fact, now deployed in 53 countries, over 80 per cent of the candidate feedback is positive. In just one year, Unilever saved over £1 million, reduced recruiting time by 75 per cent, and hired their most ethnically and gender diverse graduate class to date.

As an alternative to video interviewing, JabaTalks provides an audio interviewing platform; you pre-record your interview questions, send them to the applicant and they can record their voice answer in their own time. Using audio can be less confronting to an applicant because they can focus more on their answers and less on their presentation. It also reduces potential bias and is more inclusive for those less comfortable with video technology.

Technical pre-screening tools

Recruiters often have concerns when it comes to online technical tests, for example, whether the applicant is actually the one taking the fully automated test, but offering real-time online tests with hiring managers can be extremely time-consuming and can usually only be conducted in office hours, and this inflexibility makes recruiting for highly sought-after technical positions, such as developers, even more challenging.

Wanting to provide human-first technical tests at times that suit his candidates, sourcer Mark Lundgren started using Karat; interviewer engineers, who methodically practise their craft to improve the candidate experience and maximize the predictiveness of each interview. He said that he is 'not a fan of online testing platforms because they can be very impersonal. With Karat a real person is asking the questions and guiding the coding test and we don't have any company bias as the interviewers are not working for us, we just receive their assessment and a video copy of the interview.'

Relevance is key or the consequences can be dire, as evidenced by developer Renata Jegereva's comment on LinkedIn bemoaning the fact that she was asked to complete an irrelevant technical test to proceed with her application.[7] 'Just happened to me: a contract I was keen to take based on the job description, spoke to HR, and before even speaking to the developers I was given a test that would take more than a working day to complete.' She went on to explain that the test was irrelevant because it was not in the technology framework required for the contract. Two days later she accepted a job with their biggest competitor because their hiring manager took the time to look at her GitHub profile. She added that she knows competent developers who refuse to take tests.

When it comes to technical screening tools there are plenty to choose from and as most recruiters are far from technical, this is best left to your hiring manager and technical team to decide upon, but recruiters can make sure the testing process is human-centric and beneficial to the overall hiring experience.

Some technical tests to try:

Codesignal Recruiter
CodeAssess
Codility
CodinGame
Devskiller
HackerEarth
HackerRank
Hundred 5
Interview Mocha

Lytmus
Mettl
Qualified
QuodeIt
Talview
TestDome
Tests4Geeks

Pre-interview rejection tools

To deliver a positive candidate experience, it is just as important to give closure to those who won't be proceeding to a phone or face-to-face interview, including those who demonstrate that they didn't read the job description! It is important to remember that a rejected applicant could reapply later when they have gained more skills or experience, that they will talk about your company with their network and possibly online, and, depending on what your company does, that you could potentially lose the candidate and their network as customers if they have a negative experience.

People won't forget how your company made them feel and though rejection by email is acceptable at this point, consider adding value by pointing them towards job search resources and offer to connect on LinkedIn. To go further, consider using a tool like Rejobify, that helps job seekers by putting them through a seven-day email job search course, or implementing CareerArc's Candidate Care portal, a comprehensive job search platform that enables video interview practice, skills assessment, résumé writing advice and more.

Scheduling, recording and transcribing tools

For those who proceed on to a phone screen, there are many tools available that automate call and interview scheduling. On my own website, I use Acuity, and many recruiters use Calendly, TimeTrade, x.ai and others to let people book their interviews directly into their calendar. But if you are looking for tools to do more than just schedule time here are a few to take for a test drive.

GoodTime can cope with complex interview booking schedules and even book your rooms. It can pick interviewers based on the requirements of the role and choose an alternate interviewer if one becomes unavailable. It syncs with your applicant tracking system and proactively scans for calendar conflicts, noticing when hiring managers become unavailable.

GoHire provides a central platform for recruiters to manage conversations across web chat, text/SMS, Messenger and WhatsApp, and also layers in automated interview scheduling and other chatbot features.

AllyO utilizes deep workflow conversational AI to fully automate the end-to-end recruiting workflow by intelligently engaging through texting over mobile and web. It takes the recruiting process to the applicant rather than bringing applicants to the recruiting process by enabling conversational job matching, intelligent qualifying of the candidate for the best-fit role, by automating interview scheduling and post-interview interactions, by driving retention through post-hire check-ins and by gathering actionable insights to improve overall recruiting performance.

Honeit, built by a recruiter for recruiters, makes it easy to schedule interviews, capture structured data during the live call and share interview answers directly to hiring managers in audio clips. Rather than frantically writing notes during the phone interview, you can record each answer, which reduces the chance of missing something important, which can happen on runs of back-to-back interviews. Sending the recorded answers to the hiring manager also gives them the opportunity to listen to the answer first hand. You can easily search for interviews and also track email opens, clicks and interview analytics.

Having received several WhatsApp messages from recruiters late on a Sunday night I was surprised to see a thread from recruiters asking how to hide their personal mobile numbers from candidates. But if you are concerned about your privacy, you could try an enterprise solution like Fuze that lets you use your laptop to make calls, or you could add a phone number to Skype or use Google Voice (in the US), or try searching in your mobile device's store and try one of the many for second-number applications. Whichever one you use, please consider the impression you make, especially about work–life balance if you work in-house, by sending texts late in the evening or on the weekend.

More advice

- Chris Russell assessed four automated interview scheduling tools: bit.ly/ChrisRTech
- Zapier looks at nine calendar scheduling apps: bit.ly/ZapierCST
- TechRadar shares its favourite dictation apps: bit.ly/TRDictApps
- Ikream assessed free iOS dictation apps: bit.ly/IKSpeechApps

---

The phone call

The phone call is your opportunity to use your tone of voice and knowledge to make a brilliant impression, succinctly share your understanding of the opportunity as gained during the intake strategy session, to reassure the candidate on the genuineness of the role and, most importantly, listen to the candidate to discover the information that isn't on their CV.

Senior Technical Recruiter, Amy Miller, recently wrote an article to help candidates understand the difference between a genuine recruiter call and a fishing exercise, and it is great advice.[8]

> A great recruiter will do more listening than talking in this first conversation, and want to know if the candidate is open to making a job change, if their skills and abilities are a fit for the hiring need, and find out the candidate's expectations. A recruiter should be able to share whether the role is the average compensation for the industry and expertise level, the chance of the candidate progressing to the next step in the hiring process, the timing of the recruitment process and more. All of this can and should be readily answered by the recruiter.

She goes on to add 'don't pretend to be technical if you're not.'

Similarly, Mark Lundgren shared, 'I want to understand the applicant's motivations and what hot buttons we need to push to be interesting to them. I ask a few questions I know the hiring manager will want to know the answers to or even ask, and I go through the recruitment process so they know the next steps.'

Remembering Talent Board's points on improving candidate experience from the beginning of the chapter, this method ensures you actively listen, set clear expectations and, possibly, give closure.

Face-to-face interviews

Bedelia shared on Twitter, 'So I went on an interview and the interviewer asked me why I was there. I said I was here for the interview, then realized it was *the* interviewer, and it gradually got more awkward from there!' To most, interviews are already uncomfortable situations, without the added confusion that comes if the hiring manager fails to make it clear who they are.

But considering the plethora of advice and technology available for job seekers to practise their interviewing, there is little available for hiring managers to use to hone their skills. This chapter is focused on technology but because many recruiters have experienced the frustration of an interview destroyed by an ill-prepared interviewer, here are some useful resources that could help if you don't have the budget to invest in training:

- Amy Miller shares insight for conducting interviews as a non-technical tech recruiter: bit.ly/AmyMillerTR

- Interview resources from Workable: bit.ly/InterviewsWB

- Five musts for your hiring manager, advice from HR consultant, Sharlyn Lauby: bit.ly/HMAdice

- Talentlyft has many resources for conducting interviews: talentlyft. com

- Lever's recruiting hacks: bit.ly/LeverRH

Of course, approaching your hiring manager and telling them that they need to improve is far from easy, even when presenting the facts and stats, so I asked difficult conversation expert and author,

Sue Ingram of difficult conversation consultancy Converse Well, for her top tip for starting this conversation.

> Approach the conversation calmly and respectfully. They will be effective at a lot of things, just not recruiting even though they will want to be. Introduce what you notice, make the conversation around the benefits to them of improving their interview techniques. Say something like, 'I notice that something is going wrong with the interview process because talented people are not accepting positions. I feel that must frustrate you a great deal. I believe some small tweaks in your approach will make a big difference in helping you spot talent other people overlook, saving you a lot of time whilst ensuring the right hiring decision is made and gaining acceptance from a strong candidate.'

Interview feedback

Ever been on a date that you thought went really well and then heard nothing? You send a text suggesting a second meeting and nothing. You keep looking at your phone, wondering if SMS is broken and then you start wondering 'what did I do wrong?' You start scrutinizing every minute of your date, trying to understand how you went from what felt like a great connection to radio silence. The lack of closure is disheartening.

Imagine a different scenario where you received closure for your date via email, in a similar fashion to the email template the largest professional network recommends recruiters use to reject interviewed candidates, how would this feel?

Dear [NAME],

Thank you for coming in to learn more about me as your potential [BOYFRIEND/GIRLFRIEND].

After conducting several dates, I have decided to offer the position to someone else with experience that's better aligned to the role. As you progress in your dating, please stay in touch and feel free to apply for future openings.

Sincerely, [YOUR DATE]

Obviously, I have changed a few of the words in the 'best-practice' email template to suit the situation but as our careers can be as important as our personal lives, it helps make the point. Interviewing is personal to the interviewee. The rejection is personal.

Have you ever been interviewed for a job, thought you did really well, and not got the job? Imagine the feeling of despondency when this happens time and time again. Imagine how depressing it is to be left wondering what you are doing wrong and wondering why the recruiter or company won't help you. It could be one minor tweak that is the difference between securing a role and not. As recruiters, isn't it our responsibility to help people into a job even if it's not ours?

Then why don't recruiters do this? It definitely baffles recruiter Evan Herman, 'I just got a great referral from a rejected candidate who I told in a timely matter after interview why we weren't moving forward with his application. I told him what experience he lacked and he then referred someone he knew who does have that experience! I don't know why more recruiters don't do this.'

Debating the point of calling a candidate with interview feedback, Talent Acquisition Lead at Servian, Mark Mansour shared how his team tackle it. 'Within 24 hours of an interview, we send an email to the candidate telling them that we have feedback and asking them to use a link provided by our ATS Lever, to book a time of their choosing into our diaries to discuss it.' Powerful because it puts the candidate in control of how they would like to receive feedback, they can reply and ask for it by email if they would prefer. He added 'And no feedback is feedback. Even telling them I am still chasing the hiring manager is appreciated.'

Delivering feedback needn't be complicated and it is a crucial part of our job to give closure and provide the best experience for the candidate that we can. In five steps:

1 Call the candidate or ask the candidate to book a time with you using Mark's method.

2 On the call, let them know the decision of your hiring team quickly.

3 Ask them if they would like to hear the feedback, most will say yes.

4 Pass on the reasons as constructively as possible.

5 Ask them how the feedback sounds, this gives candidates that chance to share their take on the interview and their experience as a candidate.

People never forget how you make them feel. Founder of Amplify, Lars Schmidt was recently in a conversation with someone he had interviewed and declined seven years ago; at the time he explained in detail why, and though the interviewee was disappointed he understood and ultimately agreed. 'He appreciated the respect and candour. Since then, he has loosely tracked what I've been up to and is now in a position to revisit us working together. This was a great reminder why feedback is so important and ultimately how openness and candour in delicate conversations can make someone feel.'

Gathering feedback

Hiring managers can prove elusive, which is why you must agree to timely feedback during your intake strategy session. Come to an agreement on the best way they will give their feedback, which could be a meeting, a call or using shared technology, but whatever the method, keep them accountable.

HR & Tech Recruitment Lead, Ellie Brown, regularly delivers sessions to her management team on giving and receiving feedback. These sessions include models they can use to lay out the feedback before delivering it ensuring that it includes relevant examples, how to have the courage to be honest, ensuring there is good intent and listening to the person's thoughts on the feedback. Delivering interview feedback isn't dissimilar.

Internally, Ellie's company has set service level agreements, with the manager agreeing to deliver feedback in a set time frame, and Ellie uses private Trello boards to gather feedback. Ellie recommends that you prompt your hiring manager's feedback with three questions: what they liked, what they didn't like and what questions they still have about the candidate. She added, 'To keep hiring managers accountable use stories of when they lost good candidates due to not being responsive enough!'

Talent Acquisition & Employer Branding Evangelist, Heidi Wassini, added 'Any candidate that you speak with should always be invited by phone and rejected by phone. I put emphasis on two or three things from the interview that will help the candidate to see that the match wasn't good and hopefully this gives them something to improve from for future interviews. I teach hiring managers to do the same; if your interview is a structured, competency and performance-based one, it is easy to deliver proper feedback.'

In the next chapter, you will find advice for using technology to take the candidate from accepted offer through to successful on-boarding and beyond, but as recruiters reject many more candidates than they hire it makes sense to discuss tools for measuring candidate experience here, but be sure to ask your hired candidates for their input too.

Candidate experience surveys

When Mark Mansour, the Talent Acquisition Lead at Servian, was recruiting his team, he asked them how they found the recruitment process. Fast, communicative and personal were words included in all the answers. He then set the benchmark, 'that's what I expect you to deliver to all of Servian's candidates.' His team's aim is to approach all candidates with the same tenacity, speed and zeal as they do the perfect candidate. They ask candidates for their feedback on the experience so that they can improve because 'candidate engagement is the lifeblood of recruitment.'

You are looking to gather feedback from the candidate about many aspects including:

- The length, fluidity and communication throughout the recruitment process.
- The candidate's understanding of the steps involved.
- If the realities of the job match the job description and information given during interviews.
- The behaviour of the hiring managers; were they prepared, punctual, communicative, etc?
- Was time given to ask questions and did the hiring process seem fair?

- How the recruitment process could be improved and if they would refer others.

- The opportunity to add anything else, essential to ensuring the candidate feels heard.

Most of this book has been written to give recruiters and sourcers tools or advice that they can use to impact their candidate engagement and to improve how they make people feel through the entire hiring process. But candidate experience is more than how a recruiter engages a person and it is not the sole responsibility of recruiters. It can be any touchpoint a potential employee has with your company; they could be a client, have seen your employer branding, experienced your hiring managers, how the receptionist treated them and more. Therefore it is not enough to keep feedback from candidates in your inbox or within the talent acquisition function, it's crucial to use it as data to improve the entire hiring process by all involved.

To go beyond using a survey to collect feedback, have a demo of one of these tools:

- Mystery Applicant: automates the capture of both candidate and hiring manager's feedback, helps you understand the expectations of both sides, gain insights to improve your recruitment strategy and benchmark yourself against other companies.

- Rant & Rave: can help you capture feedback from every candidate in real time along their journey, this gives you an authentic picture of how the experience is and an opportunity to improve immediately.

- Starred: has a candidate experience measurement option for both companies and recruitment agencies to help you improve the recruiting process and a candidate Net Promoter Score (NPS) to help you know who will refer you to more potential applicants.

- Survale: has a website button to capture pre-applicant feedback in real time; on the application it initiates automatic feedback campaigns to candidates, hiring managers and recruiters through the entire life cycle, and it gathers feedback from hired and declined applicants.

Talent Board is the leader when it comes to candidate experience and you will find a wealth of information to guide you on their website including research, articles, podcasts and webinars. Your company could also participate in the Candidate Experience Awards, which take place in North America, Europe, the Middle East, Africa and AsiaPac. They are more than awards, they allow your company to benchmark and improve the candidate experience.

Of course, the candidate experience doesn't end here with rejected applicants, the need for brilliant candidate engagement continues for those who have received and accepted an offer and on to their on-boarding. In the next chapter, you will hear about more ways you can use technology to put the human front and centre to reduce first day no-shows and disillusioned new starters.

Summary

- Candidate ghosting is happening because there are more jobs than available people and because recruiters haven't been working hard enough to create loyalty.

- Helping candidates deselect from the process will reduce the time you spend screening unsuitable applicants and give you more time to engage properly with the candidates who are the right fit.

- Your application autoresponders deserve more attention, as without it they could be leaving a great applicant feeling cold.

- All applicants deserve closure and without it, they can damage your company's reputation; use technology to help you humanize applicant rejections, and call all interviewed candidates to personally deliver feedback.

- Help applicants feel the process is fair by explaining it to them, and ask for and listen to their feedback.

- Be accountable for improving the hiring process by measuring candidate feedback but remember you are not alone so be sure to share the data with all who are involved in the experience a candidate has with your company.

How are you improving candidate experience? Tweet me @KatrinaMCollier using #RobotProofRecruiter

Notes

1 Spool, JM (2009) [accessed 12 April 2019] The $300 million button, UIE, 14 January [Online] https://articles.uie.com/three_hund_million_button/ (archived at https://perma.cc/4VWR-FZUQ)

2 Children's Mercy [accessed 12 April 2019] Careers [Online] https://www.childrensmercy.org/careers/ (archived at https://perma.cc/BS7Y-G2X9)

3 Rogers, C (2018) [accessed 12 April 2019] Brands are ditching CVs to find new ways of discovering diverse talent, Marketing Week, 11 May, [Online] https://www.marketingweek.com/2018/05/11/brands-ditching-cvs-diverse-talent/ (archived at https://perma.cc/CHJ7-WV34)

4 Mobile Marketing Watch (2014) [accessed 12 April 2019] SMS marketing wallops email with 98% open rate and only 1% spam, Mobile Marketing Watch, 6 August [Online] https://mobilemarketingwatch.com/sms-marketing-wallops-email-with-98-open-rate-and-only-1-spam-43866/ (archived at https://perma.cc/H67J-6WUY)

5 Durham Constabulary [accessed 12 April 2019] Do you really want to be a cop? Facebook [Online] https://www.facebook.com/durhamconstabulary/videos/362827594535299/ (archived at https://perma.cc/U7PA-2ZF9)

6 HireVue [accessed 12 April 2019] Unilever finds top talent faster with HireVue Assessments, HireVue [Online] https://www.hirevue.com/customers/global-talent-acquisition-unilever-case-study (archived at https://perma.cc/7Y4G-T6F4)

7 LinkedIn post from Craig Turner [accessed 12 April 2019] LinkedIn [Online] https://www.linkedin.com/feed/update/urn:li:activity:6491957594679242752 (archived at https://perma.cc/TH73-HEDL)

8 Miller, A (2019) [accessed 12 April 2019] Recruiting in Yoga Pants blog, 9 January [Online] https://www.recruitinginyogapants.com/ (archived at https://perma.cc/Y3YP-QNAB)

No more non-boarding

09

According to Jobvite's Recruiter Nation Survey, 75 per cent of respondents have seen a candidate change their mind after signing the offer.[1] Fifty-three per cent went on to say that it was because the candidate received a more enticing offer, yet nearly half said they would do nothing to convince them to start. It is concerning that so few recruiters would go on to attempt to uncover and address the concerns of the offered candidate, when not only is that a recruiter's job, it could uncover a problem in the hiring process that would prevent this from happening again.

In this chapter, you will learn how to use technology to improve the relationship you have with your candidate and the process of taking them from accepted offer through to successful pre- and onboarding. In this candidate-driven market, neglecting a candidate between offer and starting is likely to result in a non-starter. It is time to ditch the 'non' boarding.

The offer

If throughout the hiring process you have kept it candidate-centric, you have shown enthusiasm for your company and the job, you have proactively stayed in touch, listened and shown understanding of their fears and concerns, and you have paid attention to finer details like their commute time, values, career aspirations and personal interests, then giving an offer and receiving an acceptance should be a smooth process.

If you have worked hard to source, woo and interview this ideal candidate, start with your best offer. The cost of starting the recruitment process anew, and to the bottom line while the position remains vacant, is more expensive than starting with your best offer now. If you know salary could be a stumbling block, see if you can offer a golden handshake, relocation costs, more annual leave or flexibility, anything that shows you are serious and doing all you can to meet their needs.

If they don't immediately say yes to your offer, ask them how they feel about it and, once you have given them time to answer, when it would be best to reconnect. Like dating, you don't want to pressure them nor do you want to seem arrogant or aloof. Of course, you want an answer immediately but realistically changing jobs is a big deal so be sure to give them the breathing space they need to make their decision and contact them again at the agreed time.

Offers that delight

An offer of employment is best given on a phone call or even in person so that the candidate hears your excitement, something that a cold toneless email won't give them. If you must send an email, please include a video or better yet, a video from the team inviting them to join, with the aim of getting the candidate on a call. This is the time to lay on the human; it is a crucial time for the candidate, they will be thinking about the repercussions of making a poor job or company change, so be ready to offer patience, kindness and empathy, and gauge their enthusiasm.

Working for a leading technical consulting firm, recruitment manager Jeff Lovejoy is familiar with the battle to secure people with in-demand technical skills. Competing in a marketplace where candidates receive multiple job offers, he set out to find a solution that would stand out, be more human, and far more interesting than your standard welcome note from HR or even the CEO.

The solution: an augmented-reality job offer, which was surprisingly budget friendly, even on a global scale. Jeff shared, 'Have you ever received those wedding invitations that come to life? That's how we delivered it. We selected a company that provided a unique experience but also included reporting on things like open rates. All we needed to do was create a flyer with a welcome from the company on one side, including their unique QR code and instructions to download the app on the other side. The app revealed the job offer, which was a video of our CEO in a Pokémon environment welcoming the new candidate to our family.'

But did it work? Jeff told me it was a great success, 'We had candidates excited to show other people their job offer, which helped with conversion and expanding the visibility of our brand. Though it isn't the saving grace of hiring technical people as it is so competitive, it helped and a lot of the time it's the little things that help bring your organization over the top.'

Declined offer

Recruitment is a tough job; our 'product' is a human being. A human that decides whether they will or will not accept our job offer. They can say no. I remember my nos well and how I would take it personally, wondering what I had done wrong, and then have to work really hard not to apply pressure but instead delve deeper to find the real reason. It was usually one of these:

- A lengthy hiring process with little feedback or communication.
- The compensation and benefits were below what they expected.
- They didn't think the opportunity was right for them.
- Lack of work–life balance or flexibility.
- Realizing the poor location would lead to a nasty commute.
- An undefined career path or little opportunity for progress.
- They couldn't get a feel for the company culture and the reviews were unflattering.
- Negative press that went against their values.
- The dreaded counter-offer from their current employer.

Recruiters can fix or address many of these during the hiring process, even a nasty commute can be overcome with flexible hours or by offering work from home. The more you invest in improving your processes and creating better candidate engagement, the less often you will receive a declined offer.

On Hired's podcast, 'Talk talent to me', technical recruiter Viet Nguyen shared how they created an additional interview he calls the reverse interview.[2] The candidate can request another interview with any of the people they have met, in their own format, and giving them plenty of time to really see the environment and culture and ask their questions. Though the interview is optional, the majority of applicants opt for it.

Sometimes the touches that create candidate loyalty are small but their impact is huge. Imagine the surprise on job seeker Ellie Brown's face, when the CEO sent her a handwritten note with a copy of the book they had discussed during her interview. This gesture spoke volumes about the company and the potential and helped allay her fears when changing jobs after three years.

Viet gives candidates the opportunity to be heard on their terms, while Ellie's CEO showed he had listened. The same goes for counteroffers, you have to listen to what they say and gently remind the candidate of their reasons for looking to leave in the first place. Ask them to create pros and cons for staying or taking your offer, and ask if a salary raise will negate the reasons that caused them to start looking in the first place. If you approach this calmly and empathetically, hopefully it will be enough to convince them to join you, but if not they will remember how you made them feel and think positively about you and your company.

Be sure to survey all the people who declined your offer so you can improve your recruitment processes, and ask for their permission to stay in touch, they may regret their decision or refer others to you. If they are happy, you could even ask them to leave your company an interview review on Glassdoor or similar, to help others looking to join your company.

Accepted offer!

On LinkedIn, Talent Acquisition Partner at Swiss multinational pharmaceutical company Novartis, Anna Hodges, shared a video of her doing four cartwheels with the caption 'When most of the office is having an awesome time at Cycle, and your candidate accepts your job offer, what is there left to do? Yes! (Clearly I missed my calling as a gymnast!)'. This is certainly how I felt when an offer was accepted.

It is the best feeling, you've closed the candidate. Through the entire process you were actively listening, addressed all their concerns and at the offer, fantastic, they said yes!

'That's enough, right? They will turn up on day one.'

Not any more. Your candidates are being wooed by other recruiters with potentially bigger and better opportunities so it is not a time to rest on your laurels.

Speed is essential here; get the written offer out to your candidate as soon as possible. Ideally, within three days maximum, I used to deliver mine the same day to secure loyalty. You are looking to reinforce that your company is serious and that you are excited to have them on board. Until the candidate sees a written offer, it won't seem real, but as I said at the beginning of the chapter this is not the time to sit back and relax.

Pre- and onboarding

In the not too distant past, a recruiter could receive a signed contract back from a candidate, ignore them until just before day one, and they would still turn up and even tolerate spending the first few days doing paperwork, finding computer equipment and maybe even a desk. And people would stay. Back then the internet wasn't a great disrupter, it didn't offer the transparency and access to opportunities that it offers today's job seekers, people who are less tolerant of this kind of neglect.

Technology has shifted the power from the employer to employees and candidates and a poor pre- or onboarding experience encourages people to keep looking until they find a company that does treat them well and is concerned about their experience and initial impression.

Those who do invest in onboarding discover that:[3]

- 69 per cent of employees are more likely to stay for three years;
- 58 per cent who go through a structured induction are more likely to stay past three years; and
- having a standard onboarding process leads to 50 per cent greater new-hire productivity.

Pre-boarding

Between the signed offer and day one is the period called pre-boarding; it is one of the most neglected parts of the recruitment life cycle. The length is dependent on the person's notice period, which can be as little as two weeks or as long as three months, but it is plenty of time for the new joiner to replace your offer with another one.

Strengthening and keeping new starter loyalty starts now.

Technically it may not be your job but if you don't want to undo all of your hard work, take accountability for the process and get your hiring manager, HR, learning and development, legal and anyone else who should be involved, on the same page.

Get the paperwork done

Paperwork may seem tedious and something that could wait but getting it done now will reinforce commitment from your new starter and mean you can focus on more enjoyable and interesting things on day one. You will both also know that they are ready contractually and will be paid on time. This is usually HR or the finance department's responsibility but as they are not as invested in the new starter as you are, I recommend keeping tabs on them until you know the paperwork is on its way.

Strengthen the connection

Ted Hewett is an expert in employee engagement and was very happy at the company he loved, Reward Gateway, until he got the opportunity to combine his two passions, gaming and engagement. Knowing how hard the decision had been for Ted to leave, Play Consulting didn't take any chances during the short pre-boarding period. 'They set me up on the internal comms platform immediately so I could see what was going on and get a feel for the culture. Plus they invited me to their regular Friday evening Mario Kart tournament with beers, it was great.'

Oodle wasn't risking losing Ellie Brown either, not only had the CEO already wowed her with the book, she shared, 'They immediately added me to a WhatsApp group and even asked for ideas for a team night out – and they chose my idea! They also sent me cake pops with a note that said, "We can't wait for you to join Oodle! See you on the 28th!"'

Just by immediately including people in your internal communications, you are giving them a sense of belonging and reducing the anxiety that always comes before starting any new adventure. The best part, it is free to implement and could save your company a fortune in failed recruitment costs.

Can you imagine how daunting it could feel changing jobs after 13 years and the trepidation that you would feel during the transition from your current organization to a new one? From the moment Emma Crowe's new organization offered her the role, they ensured that Emma immediately felt part of the team by assigning her a buddy who was tasked with keeping her engaged and educated on culture and strategy.

> My buddy sent me some great information that enabled me to get up to speed more quickly than I would have without her support. She also arranged to meet me several times to aid my onboarding. Five of the team reached out independently to welcome me, including senior leadership, which really put my mind at rest. I felt that they were really excited for me to start which made me excited. My onboarding buddy was just fabulous and has made day one feel like day thirty one.

How your peers pre-board

Building an organization that is welcoming, inclusive and engaged is far from easy so I asked two people I know who are working hard to do that what they do to stop people pulling out of the process at this late stage.

Sophie Theen, Global Head of HR & Talent at 11:FS, shared the weekly touchpoint emails they send, from signed contract up until the day the person joins, to keep them engaged.

1 Rather than sending a bland email requesting background check documents, they share a story to make it more personable and to explain why it is needed.

2 The new joiner receives their email logins, which allows the team to include them on calendar invites for socials, meetings and introductions. They also receive access to the HR portal, which gives them the opportunity to learn more about the company, people and team.

3 Next is some reading: 'company Wiki access is granted giving them all sorts of information including company structure, achievements, and town hall presentations. It's very detailed.' [To create your own Wiki page see wikihow.com/Start-a-Wiki]

4 Day one expectations. 'They receive their first day instructions, time to start, who to ask for, what to expect, etc. We give them access to Slack and ask them to send us a photo, a bio and something we don't know about them so we can announce them in our Friday newsletter. We also announce them on Slack so everyone can welcome them'.

Patrick Caldwell, Head of People at FundApps, shared four things they do to keep a new starter engaged during pre-boarding.

- Including a handwritten note, they send a copy of the book *ReWork* by Jason Fried and David Heinemeier Hansson, because their CEO used this as inspiration when setting up FundApps.

- They invite them to company social events, team days and training workshops, 'This has had great feedback from our new starters because their first day isn't about meeting people from scratch.'

- They give them an insight into their onboarding, 'We have a task board called First 100 Days which is a guide of things to read and do; easing nerves by giving them a snippet beforehand.'

- About a week before, they tell the new starter what happens on their first day. 'It starts with coffee with their manager, and it is a very chilled day to get their IT set up and get their swag, and go out for team lunch, etc.'

The common thread is communication, availability and letting people meet the team before the start date. Other than time, none of these is costly to implement but they are costly if ignored.

More pre-board ideas

Right after the signed offer, use a phone app like GIF Camera or GIF Maker to capture the excitement of the team the new starter will be joining, and send it to them in an email. The recruitment team at

Lever[4] do this and they even copy in the entire company, which gives employees the opportunity to reply and welcome them further.

Have you ever spotted the photos of first-day desks on LinkedIn? As posts, they are usually exceptionally popular with likes in the tens of thousands and with hundreds of comments. The desks show that the computer equipment is ready, cell phone and stationery are supplied, and some company swag is ready to be enjoyed; people love being welcomed so warmly.

You could privately text or message a photo or video to your new starter of their new desk so that they know that you are ready and excited to have them join. Include their neighbour or an office shot so they know exactly where they will sit. You could even supply a floor plan showing names and where important things are like the kitchen and toilet. As well as being welcoming, it will allay potential first-day jitters.

It could be a great time to send them an organizational chart too. If you don't have one, try using MS Visio, or an online chart software like Lucidchart or MyDraw. OrgChart not only allows you to create rich charts, which are helpful for your new hires, it can also be used for workforce planning to help you see where you have vacancies now or in the future.

Hopefully, using the Chrome extensions from Chapter 7 and from actual conversations with the new starter you now know their interests and hobbies. It could be a great time for other employees with similar interests to say hello or, if you have company sports, ask them to join the team. If you know they have a pet, you could send them a pet bundle as CA Technologies does. Searching #LifeAtCA shows countless photos of happy pets in branded swag; not only is this great for a new starter and employee engagement, it is great for employer branding.

Help your new joiners relocate; your employees will have a wealth of tips and advice that you could gather and share in your intranet, Slack channel or Trello board. If you are regularly moving people though, consider using a relocation software like UrbanBound or Orion Mobility, which will create ease and security for new starters and relocating employees by connecting them with local suppliers, trades, schools and more, and take the hassle out of reimbursing expenses for your finance team.

Importantly, be sure to tell them what to expect on their first day. Include transport and parking options, arrival and finish time, what to wear and/or bring, and who to ask for. Outline the day so they feel relaxed, and ensure you tell them that you are ready and excited to welcome them.

Pre-boarding technology

Thankfully there is technology available to help you structure and automate the process of keeping in touch during this critical period.

Gemma Matthews, Head of Talent Acquisition at Reward Gateway, recommends Enboarder because

> It allows us to create global consistent on-brand and engaging messaging for our new hires, from the moment they sign the contract all the way through to month one in their new job. We share culture pieces, our benefits, what to expect on their first day, videos from the team and a welcome message from the CEO. Then when they join, Enboarder shares learning and development pieces and allows us to ask for feedback along the way.

Here are three others to try as recommended by your industry peers:

- Appical: an app that lets companies easily use videos, checklists, quizzes, interactive assignments or virtual reality to create an interactive pre-boarding process.
- Personably: can help you engage effectively, save time scheduling and ease the set-up of new starters' technology. They are growing and have interesting prototypes in the pipeline.
- SmarterMedium PerStart: focuses on onboarding new hires; bridging knowledge gaps, providing confidence for a successful start. It delivers a story-driven online learning experience prior to the start.

Onboarding

It's your first day. You've hardly slept. You wake overly early to ensure you will make it in on time. The new route to work worries you.

You don't know how the day will go. You are concerned you won't be liked or that you have made a huge mistake, the last thing you need to be is late.

As you're getting dressed your hands are trembling and you tell yourself it's OK, you've got this but still your heart races. The self-doubt is creeping in. The fear of the consequences if you find you don't succeed and end up out on your ear. The stress is palpable; change is hard.

You take a deep breath, pull your shoulders down and back. Head held high, you grab your phone, your keys, your bag and you head out the door into the unknown. You hope they are as ready for you as you are for this new chapter in your life.

But no

'I turned up and was asked to wait in reception. After 30 minutes, someone came to meet me – I was told my boss wasn't expecting me! I was taken to meet the team an hour later and told my boss had no time to meet me until the next day.' Kelly Swingler, Rule Breaker

'I walked into a job once where every single person that had been involved in my hiring process had left by the time I arrived. Nobody knew who I was, nor where I fitted into the scheme of things. I immediately wondered if I'd made a horrendous career mistake!' Russ Morgan, Programme Manager

'I remember starting my first day at a job where I was joining the senior management team and they hadn't given me the code to get in the door – I had to wait for a staff member to arrive to let me in. Needless to say, I didn't have an induction plan.' Sara Duxbury, Business Psychologist

'Starting a new job where the manager was too busy to induct you or show you around. Ended up sitting at my desk for two weeks without being given a single task to do! Then asked after two weeks what I thought the company needed. My first answer was an induction process!' Sarah Williams, Reward & Engagement Officer

This collection of quotes was gathered within minutes of posting one question on Facebook and LinkedIn, 'Ever had a first day disaster?' All replies are appalling, especially if you add the fact that

33 per cent of new starters know if they are going to stay or leave in their first week.[5]

But HR, the hiring manager, IT or legal, surely they are now responsible for the new employee experience? No, not any more. As long as people can take their mistreatment online and write reviews, which will impact your future hiring, it will be up to the recruiter to take accountability for onboarding and to help the organization shift its mindset.

Recruitment is no longer in isolation, it is now heavily impacted by the employee experience, so read on and encourage relevant colleagues to improve the experience for all new starters with these ideas.

Buddy/mentor systems

Earlier I mentioned how beneficial Emma Crowe found having a contact in HR who had been there to guide her through her notice period and into her first weeks. Such an easy system to implement too, especially if your employees are engaged and want the company to succeed.

Delighted to see the excitement in Employer Brand Strategist Shannon Smedstad's social media post, about being appointed as the 'onboarding buddy' for exaqueo's new employee, I had to ask her more about the programme.

As part of the exaqueo Buddy Program, for the first six months of employment, all new hires are matched by the CEO with a buddy. The overarching goals of the programme are to offer a warm welcome, to be a sounding board, offer guidance, and help the new starter get set up and working through their personalized onboarding workbooks. She describes how,

> Before getting the start date, we send a welcome email, a welcome note via snail mail, and conduct a welcome call that we use to write a blog post welcoming the new employee. We then have weekly calls for the first three months, then monthly calls in months four, five and six. As the buddy, I ensure my new hire job shadows people to learn our business and I check in regularly to ensure she's settling into our environment.

Jobvite's 2018 Job Seeker Nation Study, found that 30 per cent of job seekers left a job within the first 90 days with 34 per cent citing a bad experience and 32 per cent blaming company culture.[6] If those bad experiences include a cold welcome and a lack of support, then implementing a buddy or mentor system will go a long way to fixing this.

A mentor or buddy system gives new hires insider knowledge rather than throwing them in at the deep end and hoping they will swim. A long-serving employee knows who to ask and how to get things done, will have routines gained from experience and can lessen the new starter's steep learning curve. The mentor or buddy can explain all of those informal interactions and unwritten rules that make up the behaviours of people and culture of a company.

Importantly, the new starter will feel like they belong and are supported, reducing the likelihood that they will leave, and for the buddy or mentor, they get to feel like they are an important part of the recruitment process and positively impacting the employee experience.

Employee manuals

During pre- or onboarding, new starters are presented with the employee manual and the tone, language and vibe of the manual create an immediate impression. Unless you are in a highly regulated industry, there is probably little reason for it to be just a cold list of rules and regulations written by Legal. As much as recruitment has been changed by the internet and technology, so has the world of work and the tolerance levels of employees who want to work with purpose, have flexibility, and see a greater emphasis on physical, psychological and financial wellness.[7]

You want to give your employees a valuable manual that creates positive outcomes for employees and the company when clear, unequivocal policies are followed, and creates expectations for employee conduct that safeguards the company if employees do not meet those expectations. Your handbook should directly reflect how your company actually operates, its culture and its expectations.

Valve Software created an employee manual that is available on their website under Publications for all to see and published on their intranet for employees to edit.[8] They are welcome to add comments and suggestions that are taken forward into future editions.

I recommend you have a look at this quirky manual to see how they use words to offer guidance and understanding and explain their culture. For example, 'Why does your desk have wheels? Think of those wheels as a symbolic reminder that you should always be considering where you could move yourself to be more valuable. But also think of those wheels as literal wheels, because that's what they are.'

They go on to add that moving your desk around is encouraged and that there are no restrictions placed on an employee wanting to work nearer to the people that can help them best. They have even taken into consideration the fact that the regular movement of people and teams could be disorientating and explain that there is an online directory available, complete with a map, that tracks people's locations based on where they have plugged in their workstation.

Take a moment to think about your own employee manual or one of the worst you've had in the past and compare it to the feeling created by these words, 'What if I screw up? Nobody has ever been fired at Valve for making a mistake.' The manual then explains their history and that employees being given the freedom to fail is how they operate, it's an essential part of their culture.

Their manual won't be right for your company, yours has its own culture, but humanizing the legal jargon and offering a resource that helps new starters over their first six months to feel confident and supported, is something all companies could implement.

Deliver an extraordinary experience

In the 2019 HCM Trends report, HR Technology Analyst, Trish McFarlane wrote 'The idea of the candidate participating in a fully immersive experience is one that blends current onboarding practices and virtual, illusory experiences. Currently, organizations are beginning to embrace technologies that provide a customized experience for candidates and new hires.'[9] Trish predicts that in the future more organizations will incorporate how the candidate will look, feel and sound while working at the company.

Jennifer Candee from Mondelēz International shared that they built a hub that delivers a fully personalized onboarding virtual reality experience using an integrated series of photos, videos and 360-degree tours, which they use to engage people during pre-boarding.[10] The new starter receives a Google Cardboard virtual reality headset and instructions to download Mondelēz's app; combined they give the new hire the opportunity to choose what they'd like to see, which could include a tour of Cadbury's chocolate factory or the RDQI research centres and offices, for example.

Siemens use virtual reality for training to prepare technicians for future challenges and collaboration, and Accenture has a 360-degree virtual reality tour on their career website, offering a look into their lab just by moving your mouse around on the video.[11, 12]

It makes sense to use technologies that demystify life inside your company, especially when 43 per cent of the people leaving in the first 90 days say that the day-to-day role wasn't what they expected.[13] With the cost of virtual reality no longer prohibitive, could your company include it in your recruitment, onboarding, training and communication to deliver exceptional experiences? The uses seem limitless.

Onboarding resources

- Onboarding software provider Personably shares many tips under: bit.ly/EmpOnb
- Onboarding statistics for your business case: http://bit.ly/OnboardStats
- Remarkable onboarding strategies that inspire: bit.ly/OnbInspire and bit.ly/OnbInspire2
- An ongoing strategy for onboarding from Click Boarding: bit.ly/ClickOB
- Using VR in onboarding: bit.ly/VROnboard

Onboarding technology

The New Hire Momentum: Driving the Onboarding Experience research report found that 76 per cent of HR leaders feel that onboarding is under-utilized, yet 53 per cent of HR say employee engagement is improved when onboarding is improved, so finding a technology that supports your goals and encourages usage is crucial.[14]

Yet with hundreds of onboarding software providers, choosing one can be overwhelming. To put the human at the centre of your onboarding, demand more from your software by choosing one that can:

- Delight candidates with insights into the culture as well as ease the completion of documents, background checks and training.
- Provide you with the ability to automate the pre-boarding process so you don't lose your new hire before day one.
- Encourage managers to engage through gamification and send automated reminders to hiring managers to keep them on track.
- Share employee stories, journeys and career paths, and the directory and organizational and team structures.
- Gather feedback so new starters and employees feel heard.
- Nurture the employee and mentor/buddy relationship.

In research, I have seen both Enboarder and Click Boarding praised by talent acquisition professionals. Your new starters can tell you what they wished they had experienced during onboarding; I recommend you get clear on what you would like the software to achieve and relieve you of, and then ask your peers for their recommendations and experiences before test-driving software.

New starter stories

As part of onboarding, it is critical, in this new transparent world, to ensure that your employees are aware that social media, mobiles and the incessant need to share means a company's reputation is only as strong as the person who represents it at any given moment.

As critical as it is for your company to know that how it treats its people ends up online, during induction ensure that your new starters know:

- What your company stands for and how they represent it while performing their duties.
- That the company's values come before their personal values or intolerances.

- That they are paid for their duties and for the ability to represent the company with dignity.

- How the situation looks is often what becomes the social media story, even if it is false.

Your aim is to raise awareness and understanding, while avoiding implementing strict policies that curb creativity and productivity. Especially when the sharing of new starters' stories can deliver insight into the company and how it treats its people, attract more applicants, and at the same time increase the new employees' sense of belonging.

Travel company TUI does this very well with their UK & Ireland Graduates blog, which delivers stories of their career journeys so far, covering the training they have received, the charity events they've been involved in and the conferences they've attended.[15] They also give insight into the recruitment process, which they are now involved in for the next wave of graduates, and offer advice for future applicants.

Wanting to highlight their BGL Academy Apprenticeship programme, the financial services company BGL Group interviewed Ali Ayoub on their main blog, when he had been with the company for eight months.[16] He shares his experience and offers tips for anyone wanting to join the team, which encourages candidates to consider and even apply for the apprenticeship programme.

Could you implement a weekly Instagram takeover like Philips does on their @life.at.Philips account? They let employees share their photos and experiences during the week that include personal and work insights. Not only would you be showing your trust in your employees and letting their creativity loose, you would be easily creating and sharing genuine content on the most engaged social network.

Employee journeys, like all employee stories, give great insight into your company for those doing their research to see if you are a company worthy of their time, and they can also be beneficial in increasing employee referrals when employees share the posts with family and friends. In the next chapter, you will discover more about the different types of referrals and how technology can be used to improve the referral process and increase the number you receive.

Summary

- If someone says no to an offer, a recruiter's job is to be consultative and to find out why, because it could improve your hiring process or secure the hire.

- An offer is not a guarantee that someone will actually start so it is essential to keep in touch through the pre-boarding period.

- With 33 per cent of new starters deciding if they will stay or go in their first week, it is essential to deliver an excellent first day and onboarding process.

- Give new hires confidence and clarity through a buddy or mentor programme and access to insightful tools and resources early.

- Though onboarding isn't really a recruiter's responsibility by taking accountability for the experience, you will improve future hiring.

What surprised you in this chapter? Tweet me @KatrinaMCollier using #RobotProofRecruiter

Notes

1 Jobvite [accessed 12 April 2019] 11th Annual Recruiter Nation survey, The tipping point: A new chapter in recruiting, Jobvite [Online] http://web.jobvite.com/FY18_Website_2018RecruiterNation_LP.html (archived at https://perma.cc/K49N-23NV)

2 Stevenson, R (2018) [accessed 12 April 2019] Improve your close rates by offering your candidates a 'reverse interview', Hired, 2 November [Online] https://hired.com/blog/employers/conducting-reverse-interviews/ (archived at https://perma.cc/M3FM-A5RK)

3 Baumann, A (2018) [accessed 12 April 2019] The onboarding new hire statistics you need to know (with 2019 updates), UrbanBound, 20 April [Online] https://www.urbanbound.com/blog/onboarding-infographic-statistics (archived at https://perma.cc/CQW9-KMSB)

4 LinkedIn (2018) [accessed 12 April 2019] 23 Recruiting hacks for interviewing and closing candidates, LinkedIn learning, 24 January [Online] https://www.slideshare.net/LeverHiringSoftware/

23-recruiting-hacks-for-interviewing-and-closing-candidates-86654199 (archived at https://perma.cc/CQW9-KMSB)

5 LinkedIn [accessed 12 April 2019] Leverage learning to onboard top talent, LinkedIn [Online] https://learning.linkedin.com/content/dam/me/learning/EMW/lil-guide-leverage-learning-onboard-top-talent.pdf (archived at https://perma.cc/93GR-D2ET)

6 Jobvite [accessed 12 April 2019] 2018 Job seeker nation study: Researching the candidate–recruiter relationship, Jobvite [Online] https://www.jobvite.com/wp-content/uploads/2018/04/2018_Job_Seeker_Nation_Study.pdf (archived at https://perma.cc/8YJN-MZGZ)

7 Mercer [accessed 12 April 2019] Global talent trends 2019, Mercer [Online] https://www.mercer.com/our-thinking/career/global-talent-hr-trends.html

8 Valve Software [accessed 12 April 2019] Publications [Online] https://www.valvesoftware.com/hu/publications (archived at https://perma.cc/YTZ6-TQMY)

9 UpstartHR [accessed 12 April 2019] 2019 HCM trends report, UpstartHR [Online] https://upstarthr.com/what-are-the-2019-trends-in-hr/ (archived at https://perma.cc/C7AU-HBXA)

10 Candee, J (2018) [accessed 12 April 2019] MDLZ VirtuallyHere teaser long, YouTube [Online] https://www.youtube.com/watch?v=ZE_jGkI2iKs&feature=share (archived at https://perma.cc/3DLX-QY5E)

11 Siemens [accessed 12 April 2019] [Online] https://new.siemens.com/global/en/products/automation/industry-software/plant-engineering-software-comos/virtual-reality-training.html (archived at https://perma.cc/2PJM-U52W)

12 Accenture [accessed 12 April 2019] Accenture Careers 360 virtual reality tour, Accenture [Online] https://www.accenture.com/us-en/careers/360vrtour (archived at https://perma.cc/BAM7-2K46)

13 Jobvite [accessed 12 April 2019] 2018 Job seeker nation study: Researching the candidate–recruiter relationship, Jobvite [Online] https://www.jobvite.com/wp-content/uploads/2018/04/2018_Job_Seeker_Nation_Study.pdf (archived at https://perma.cc/77FK-PJCX)

14 Filipkowski, J (2018) [accessed 12 April 2019] New hire momentum: Driving the onboarding experience, Human Capital Institute, 15 January [Online] http://www.hci.org/hr-research/new-hire-momentum-driving-onboarding-experience (archived at https://perma.cc/9DCG-MSK5)

15 TUI Graduates blog [accessed 12 April 2019] TUI UK & Ireland Graduates: Our experiences working in the exciting world of travel! [Online] tuiukgrads.wordpress.com (archived at https://perma.cc/PXY5-R83S)

16 Ayoub, A (2018) [accessed 12 April 2019] Taking control of your career, BGL Group, 19 July [Online] https://www.bglgroup.co.uk/media/bgl-blog/july-2018/ali-ayoub-taking-control-of-your-career (archived at https://perma.cc/4HNM-ZHZF)

Referrals depend on you

10

Eighty-eight per cent of employers agree that employee referrals are the best way to hire and 85 per cent of job seekers use their networks when looking for jobs.[1] Yet this is the most challenging and often neglected part of most companies' hiring processes because recruiters still lack the procedures and technology that stop the referring employee and/or the referred applicant from becoming disillusioned, if not angry, about their treatment during the recruitment life cycle.

But there are more types of referrals that recruiters could be tapping into as sources of hire and in this chapter, you will discover more ways you can increase and manage your referrals with the right technology and a human-centric approach.

Employee referrals

You work at a good company, you are happy. Your work is the right kind of challenging and you are part of a vibrant team. The location is convenient, the environment healthy, I mean they even gave you a stand up-sit down desk.

You hear about a vacancy at your company and you think 'My mate would be perfect for this. Right skills and personality. Wow, it would be amazing to work with them. Can't wait to tell them.' So after work, you catch up at your favourite bar and you share the details. They are so excited! So are you, and your friend has said it is OK to refer them.

Just as you are about to send their information over to your recruiter, you have a minor wobble. This is your reputation on the line, you worry your friend may screw up. How will that impact on you? No, they are good. You have been friends for years and discussed your career and experience many times, all will be well. You submit their application.

Nothing.

You try to reach your recruiter. Nothing.

You are embarrassed. This is your friendship on the line. You were so excited. How could this company treat you and your friend like this? To think you were worried your friend would screw up.

Months go by and your friend, who is thankfully still speaking to you, adds this to Glassdoor, 'I applied through a referral, never heard back from the company. After checking regularly for three whole months my status changed to complete. If you take time to review the application, at least have the decency to inform an applicant of the decision regardless of what it may be.'

You hang your head in shame, you won't refer again.

You start looking for another job.

How did that make you feel? I wish it was a fake situation but it is far too often real. And similar reviews are easy to find on Glassdoor. Let's stop this and put the human back at the heart of employee referrals.

Why few employees refer

Currently, Natalie Glick, as Global Head of Sourcing at ThoughtWorks, a creative technology consultancy, is looking at their referral programme and kindly shared the feedback she received from surveying their UK and Indian employees; though the latter referred more their responses were similar.

- From those who had not referred in the last six months, this was due to a lack of awareness of the referral scheme, an absence of people to refer and, unfortunately, a previous bad experience (not necessarily at ThoughtWorks).

- Awareness of current hiring priorities is low and there is also a lack of awareness as to how to share jobs with their social networks.

- Those respondents who were unaware of the amount of the referral bonus also didn't know how to refer people via the applicant tracking system.

- Respondents in near equal number said they would give referrals if there was more information on current roles and confidence that the referral would not end up in a black hole.

- The majority of respondents would like to help and asked for bite-sized training on how to search LinkedIn or pitch a role, and also offered to spend time with recruiters.

- Asked what would be meaningful if referring wasn't just a monetary incentive, responses included: days off, holidays, more training and technology, evenings out, the joy of working with family and friends in the company, and recruiters responding to referred applicants.

These responses make sense. Your employees' day-to-day lives are focused on their duties, not recruitment. It a recruiter's responsibility to bring the referral scheme to life by gaining trust, sharing more information and training, and with transparent recruitment flows, so employees know how to refer and can see where in the process their referred candidate is at any time.

Employee engagement

In this section, I am making the assumption that your employees like what they do, where they work and will be willing to refer. If you are unsure whether your employees are engaged:

- Use an employee sentiment tool like HappyOrNot, the familiar smile rating system, TINYpulse, which can also measure candidate experience, or Officevibe, which sends a weekly email to employees to assess their moods and how employees feel about the company culture.

- For a deeper dive into employee engagement try Culture Amp's on-demand platform that is designed by psychologists and data scientists to help you build an employee feedback programme that will work for your specific company, or try people analytics tool Peakon, which has a continuous approach to employee feedback delivering the insights you need to improve your business in real time.

• Introduce stay interviews: sit down with employees and find out what it is they like about working for the company, what they don't like and what they would change if they could. Importantly, don't just listen to their concerns; real engagement comes when you address them.

Before you ask your employees for referrals, it is essential that you improve your employee engagement. A great starting point is Glen Elliott and Debra Corey's book, *Build It: The rebel playbook for world class employee engagement*, where they discuss the Engagement Bridge™, which is a proven model for building an engaged company culture.[2]

Increasing employee referrals

Findings by Drafted found that increasing the referral bonus doesn't significantly increase the number of employee referrals you will receive from your employees, though having a monetary award is better than not having one.[3] But simply having an employee referral programme is no guarantee that you will receive any so here are some ideas to increase their volume.

Talk about your programme more

As you saw in Natalie's data, many employees didn't know about the programme, or potentially they did and they had forgotten. Yet, only 29 per cent of companies regularly remind their employees of the programme, 11 per cent annually and 14 per cent biannually.[4]

Mark Mansour shared that at Servian they use a 65 inch screen in their employee area to welcome and share information and photos about their new starters, and to remind employees to refer. At their weekly stand-ups, where employees share what they will be working on, he mentions the open roles and referral opportunities. It works well for this SME; one employee has successfully referred 10 people.

I will never forget seeing the newsletter at Fletchers Solicitors; they print it and strategically place it for maximum visibility on the back of each toilet cubicle door and sensibly, they remind their captive audience of their employee referral programme. For the cost of printing a flyer, you could be reminding your employees to refer while making them feel more included by sharing your company news, birthdays and other events.

Don't forget to ask your employees who they would most like to work with again and encourage them to think of diverse former teammates too.

Immediate thanks and appreciation

Produced by our brains, the chemical dopamine plays a key role in motivating behaviour. It is released when we take a bite of something delicious, after we exercise and, related to referrals, when we have successful social interactions. It rewards beneficial behaviours, it motivates us to repeat them.

Creators of social networking sites use this to keep us engaged by using rewarding social stimuli like smileys, likes, and recognition from friends and contacts. Smartphones have provided us with a virtually unlimited supply of social stimuli; every notification has the potential to be a positive social stimulus and release dopamine.

As dopamine causes people to want, desire, seek out and search, and increases people's general levels of arousal and goal-directed behaviour, it is beneficial to provide instant appreciation to those who submit a referral.

Consider rewarding the people who are happy to sit down with you to help you source by going through their networks. Perhaps create a sourcing event over pizza and drinks; by gathering teams to source candidates together, employees will feel involved in choosing who is being hired and discover what you look for in candidates.

Provide instant recognition for referrals through the attainment of points toward a perk or lunch. Put their name in a draw for a raffle, though the prize will need to be strong to get them motivated. Perhaps offer one of a kind swag as a prize, or a training perk, or a donation to a charity. But definitely ask your employees what they would like as recognition of an application from their referral.

You will definitely want to introduce some form of gamification, to encourage a little bit of healthy competition and increase the number of referrals. There is software to help you, or it could be as simple as a chart on a whiteboard but ensure that your leaderboard is visible to employees and make sure that you personally thank your referrers at team meetings.

Choose user-friendly software

Time is our most precious resource and the more time it takes to open, search and submit a referral, the fewer you will receive. When choosing employee referral software you want it to:

- be easy for employees and recruiters to use and mobile-friendly;
- allow recruiters to proactively search employees' networks for an introduction;
- include gamification, a leaderboard and notifications to encourage the release of dopamine so employees refer;
- be easy to control so employees can publish to their wider social networks, which increase reach and diversity;
- have the ability to give immediate recognition and reward for the referral;
- provide transparency through the entire recruitment life cycle for both the employee and the candidate;
- potentially, sync with your applicant tracking system or database and be GDPR compliant;
- allow employees to refer people to the company even if there isn't an available job that matches their skills right now;
- offer easy-to-understand analytics so you can see what is and isn't working and therefore improve the referral process.

There are many employee referral software suppliers to choose from so be sure to test them against your list of requirements and keep the employee and candidate experience front of mind. Also, ask your peers for their thoughts and recommendations, you will find very helpful members in The Employer Brand Forum[5] or HR Open Source – HROS[6] groups on Facebook.

Technology that stood out during research:

- Talentry: not only gives your employees the ability to refer people easily but also makes it very easy to share roles to their social networks and break up the job posts with interesting peer-to-peer news and posts. Also, one of the few to push notifications via WeChat in China.

- Drafted: proactively allows recruiters to search through their employees' networks and easily send an email or message via Slack asking for the referral. It also learns from the feedback as to why people aren't suitable and avoids making similar matches in the future.

- Hollaroo: is interesting because it helps you build communities from initial engagement, through pre- and onboarding, with current employees while increasing referrals, assisting with internal mobility and keeping contractors, freelancers and your alumni engaged.

Prioritize referred candidates

Referrers don't want to annoy their family and friends by asking or sharing too many jobs and they put their reputation on the line when they do refer. They won't refer someone they don't like or who will make them look bad by not fitting the company so it is worth giving referred candidates the VIP treatment. Spend extra time reviewing their CV and profile, and if it isn't clear to you that they have the required skills ask the referrer, it could be that they do and they simply haven't updated their résumé. Be swift, communicate well, and if it is a no or not now, ensure the reasoning is communicated so you don't end up with a disillusioned employee or candidate.

Celebrate the referral hire

Everybody loves extra money in their pay cheque but being thanked and truly appreciated for a successful referral goes further and will encourage others to refer; remember the dopamine. Ask their manager or a senior leader to take them to lunch or give them some other extra recognition.

With their permission, share a photo of the referrer and referred hire in your newsletter, internal communication channels and, potentially, on social media. Consider asking the referrer to conduct an interview with their referred hire that could be made into a blog or vlog (video blog) welcoming the new starter to the company and giving current employees the opportunity to learn more about them, welcome them and hopefully feel inspired to refer more people themselves.

Internal referrals = engagement and retention

The people inside your organization have already mastered the skills required and understand what it is like to work at and fit into your company. And according to research from Professor Matthew Bidwell, those you recruit externally will need to be paid substantially more than your current employees and are more likely to leave.[7] Those employees you promote, despite a lower salary, perform much better in the first two years and have far lower departure rates, either voluntarily or involuntarily.

With a shortage of people with the right skills externally, it is worth looking within to see who could possibly be trained or seconded for a project, especially as it improves employee engagement by keeping people interested and productive and therefore improves retention.

On 'The #SocialRecruiting Show', Tracey Parsons compared recruiting to the cell phone industry, which is now at saturation point.[8] Cell providers have realized that the only way they can truly compete is to get people to upgrade, not switch. 'We have record low unemployment, we can't keep pouring more names in the top of the funnel and asking people to switch companies. We should be looking to "upgrade" our high performers instead of losing them to a switch or trying to switch someone in!'

It is often challenging to see and match the skills of your current workforce to a new role or projects, especially as people grow over time and gain new skills. This is where a tool like ProFinda, built for enterprise size companies, can be so powerful. Powered by machine learning it gives companies new perspective and insight into the skills, competencies, experience, client connections and motivations of all of the organization's internal talent, including current employees, contingent workers (gig workers, contractors or freelancers) and your former employees. This gives enterprises the ability to resource and project manage efficiently and swiftly, and employees the ability to share knowledge more openly, improving engagement.

If your company is open to job sharing, flexible working or job rotation, a technology like Tandemploy can connect colleagues within your organization for flexible collaborations and help with knowledge transfer and the opening up of silos, which improves employee engagement.

In the same way, you won't get employee referrals without reminding your employees about them, you won't gain internal referrals if your employees don't know what is going on in the company. Using Slack or an intranet, the communication within a platform like Reward Gateway, or if you have teams without desks, Yapster, will painlessly increase communication and engagement while letting your employees know of new opportunities. Some referral platforms offer internal mobility features but they tend to be reliant on the employee indicating that they are looking for a move and signing up for alerts, which will only work if you have a culture that indicates it is OK to be interested in internal moves.

Social referrals

By social referrals I don't mean those that come from your employees sharing your jobs to their social networks, I mean those that come from sharing relevant industry or peer-to-peer content as described in Chapter 4, the compelling human stories, the posts teasing someone with a hint at what life could be like if they worked for your company. This could be content your employees are sharing on your internal communications channel that, with permission, could be repurposed for sharing externally. For agency recruiters, these are valuable non-job posts, like industry news, recruitment tips, life inside your agency, and so on.

Social referrals could, of course, come from your employees' posts but they could also come from your own posts, your posts being shared by your clients or vendors, or even a stranger. In the following,

I have separated these categories out, and described technology that will help you share news and posts more easily.

As mentioned, referral tool Talentry can help your employees share your content on their social networks. The posts are automatically linked with suitable jobs, so people who see the posts and are interested can apply directly.

For small companies without enough of their own content or resources to produce it, I have always recommended finding and storing sources of relevant content on news aggregator site Feedly, and then using a scheduling tool like Buffer to regularly share content throughout the day on your social media channel. By using these in conjunction with a tool like Sniply or Rite.ly, you can add a call to action, in this case, your jobs. Unfortunately, this process is time-consuming and requires proactivity so even with the best intention it often gets forgotten.

Recently, I started using ContentApp, which is brilliant for saving time and reminding me to post via SMS. On the site, you search for content that is right for your target audience, the people you want to attract to your role, or use the Chrome extension to add new sources of content, and you decide where you would like to share your posts. You then have the choice to schedule content manually or share updates on the fly but the reason I am such a fan is that ContentApp texts me content that I can share, update or skip. Now I am consistently sharing quality news and updates and it is learning what content I like and sending better results all the time.

To gain the social referral you need a call to action so ContentApp adds a page from your own website, which could show your jobs or another kind of lead marketing magnet, and shows when someone clicks on the shared link. It is only a small interruption but a very effective one. For recruitment agencies, this is especially useful because they can share interesting articles to build their personal brand and attract more candidates while directing more traffic to their website.

There are also some interesting employee advocacy tools that you might want to consider, which allow approved content to be shared via employees' social networks. Before you select one for your company, I recommend looking at the information on Tribal Impact's guide to employee advocacy tools at bit.ly/TribalImpactEA. Also, ask how the tool can include a call to action because ultimately you want to draw people's attention to your roles.

For agency recruiters, have a look at a tool like Firefish Software, which can help you share great content to attract people and referrals that will direct them to landing pages with rich information and strong calls to action.

Community referrers

In the same way that the internet has been an extraordinary disrupter for recruitment, by giving companies direct access to people and agent recruiters greater reach than their own black book of contacts, the internet has also created an opportunity for people to become involved in recruitment without being a recruiter or even working for the hiring company.

Beyond the mainstream social networks and gig hiring sites like Fiverr, platforms have arisen that give communities of people the ability to refer people to opportunities, often for a referral fee:

- AnyGood? is a site where vetted professionals who have agreed to a set code of conduct, refer people they have worked with, with a written note of recommendation, to opportunities. AnyGood? actively manages the quality and diversity of the network and the members personally know the candidates they recommend. They also have a transparent flat fee pricing structure.

- Keycoopt: on top of being an employee referral and internal mobility platform, the French company has also created a platform for executive recruitment, giving you access to a network of co-operators willing to refer people to your roles from their LinkedIn and Viadeo networks. Consultants from the company also vet each candidate before passing the referral to the company.

- Drafted Communities: on top of their employee referral tool mentioned earlier, Drafted have created communities that people can join to make referrals. Some offer money or rewards, some do not. For the referrer, the process to join is very quick and upon syncing social networks it suggests possible matches.

Love your leavers

Ten years ago I left the most toxic company I have ever had the displeasure to work for. It wasn't like that in the beginning but over the course of five years, it went downhill. I was one of the biggest billers in the recruitment agency but by the time I resigned my team leader's boss and his boss had both stopped talking to me. My exit interview was farcical and only occurred because I ran into a member of HR in the lift. It consisted of six words, 'Oh, we hear you are leaving.'

Unwilling to accept this treatment, I asked to meet the CEO and spent an hour sharing what I should have been sharing in my exit interview. I will never forget his parting words, 'You will come back, won't you?' which reinforced to me that I had not been heard and why the agency's management was riddled with problems.

I was relieved to be out of there but a decade on I still remember exactly how I was made to feel. They are lucky this was before the days of company or agency review sites because I would have warned future applicants of the toxic atmosphere. I still feel resentment that my overall contribution to the company was ignored and in all these years since I have never referred clients to them.

It is obvious in customer experience; treat a customer badly and they vote with their feet. The last bad customer experience I received left me so inconvenienced that I now buy the same high-ticket items from their competitors and share a picture on Twitter to remind the company of the cost of their poor service. It may be less obvious in employee experience but treat your employees badly and they too will not refer paying clients or future employees, and akin to my tweet, they can write reviews online.

Departing employees

An employee's experience doesn't stop when they resign, it includes your exit interviews, how they are offboarded, and how they perceive your company and their treatment in years to come. Your alumni are an incredible pool for boomerang hires and referrals so let's look at how your company can put the human first.

For agency recruiters, think of your contractors as departing employees because the better you take care of them the more loyal they will be and the more likely to return or refer.

Exit interviews

For any employee who is leaving the company, it is wise to conduct an exit interview. As types of employment change though, you may want to extend this opportunity to long-term contractors and freelancers as well. If done correctly, exit interviews will help you assess the overall experience an employee or contractor has had and you will discover opportunities to improve your retention rates and company culture.

The exit interview is best conducted by a member of human resources but if you are a small company, anyone can carry out the exit interview except their direct supervisor, or you may want to outsource it to an HR consultant. In a private relaxed situation that encourages open communication, you are looking to:

- Find out why are they leaving: this is your opportunity to identify factors that could help future retention, which is a huge cost saving for any company.

- Find out what swayed them to accept the other offer: this could give you intel to use to improve engagement and attract new people.

- Provide closure: unlike in my example, be sure to ask if there is anything they would like to say, genuinely thank them for their input and leave them with a good impression.

- Potentially remind them of their legal obligations, if you have non-disclosure agreements, non-competes, patents and so on in place.

- Finish by asking what your company is doing right and what made them happy.

- Let them know that the door is still open and that you would like to stay in touch.

Ensure your employee or contractor leaves with the best possible impression of your company, and feeling that they have been heard and appreciated because they could potentially refer clients and candidates your way in the future.

Exit interview tools

Some will disagree with my preference for a face-to-face exit interview, saying that people will be unlikely to be as forthright as they would be in a confidential online survey. But I like that you have the opportunity to watch their body language and see if their words match their gestures or facial expressions.

To ensure that you create the lasting personal connection, that good feeling they will remember for years to come, consider using an online tool to gather the information you can then discuss in more depth in a face-to-face meeting or at a minimum, on a video call. Formstack[9], SurveyMonkey[10] and Typeform[11] have survey templates to get you started but be sure to customize it to suit the style of your company. For something more in-depth, which looks at all aspects of an employee's experience, look for a tool like Qualtrics, which can help you predict and mitigate against problems, and spot opportunities to improve.[12]

One of the drawbacks of online or in-person exit interviews is that people can come across as overly negative and resentful or unnaturally positive; to get a better idea of how the departing employee feels, it may be better to implement a more consultative interview that happens over a period of time during the offboarding or notice period.

Implement exit rituals

Tomislav Masle shared a video on LinkedIn of his departure from Apple; the employees lined up on either side of the stairs and clapped and hugged him as he descended and left.[13] It made me well up, due to the genuine emotion displayed and the supportive cheers of his peers.

Not for everyone, too cheesy for some, too intimate for others, but put in place some kind of routine that employees can expect to ease the discomfort of a departing colleague. Be it as simple as send-off drinks or lunch, a specially made cake or some embossed company swag, use it to show your appreciation for your departing employee.

Offboarding checklist

Of course, a departing employee has an impact on more than just the employee and their team, if they are offboarded badly, it can impact the morale of the whole company. With that in mind, it makes sense to create a checklist so that you:

- Efficiently communicate the change: not only to give your employees the heads up but to ensure impacted departments like HR, IT and legal are aware so they can take care of relevant procedures.

- Complete the paperwork: any legal or tax forms, for example.

- Start transferring knowledge as soon as possible: this may be to a new employee but more likely an existing employee who will need to cover their duties.

- Conduct the aforementioned exit interview.

- Recover anything that belongs to the company.

- Finalize any other matters: tie-up loose ends like email redirections, meeting invites and so on.

Further reading related to departing employees

- An article about stay interviews by Jock Purtle who prepares companies for sale and understands the impact of engagement on productivity: bit.ly/ExitInterviews2

- 'The ultimate guide to employee offboarding' includes a checklist: bit.ly/ExitIntCheck

- A great guide for using exit interviews to retain employees: bit.ly/ExitRetain

- Using exit interviews to reduce turnover: bit.ly/ExitInterviews3

- Interesting piece about reputation management during layoffs: bit.ly/OffboardingReputation

Alumni referrals and boomerang hires

My Uncle Rob worked for an Australian bank for well over 30 years, patiently waiting for his turn for promotion while working extremely hard and remaining loyal. It was a different time, a job for life was possible. He didn't receive the same loyalty from his employer though, in fact as he neared his retirement, Uncle Rob was treated abysmally by the company he had given his working life to. His loyalty was overlooked and underappreciated by his employer.

Yet today, in a very different employment world where employees can see the countless other job opportunities available online and move on if they don't feel that their work is fulfilling or if they feel under-appreciated, many managers feel betrayed when an employee resigns. They question their loyalty and many swear that they will never be welcomed back for such a 'betrayal'.

But rewarding longevity of tenure is no guarantee that someone is being productive and disregarding an employee who resigns could cost you future referrals, their re-employment and/or, depending on what your company does, customers.

From a recruitment point of view, the people who worked with you gained skills and unique experiences that they will take into their future career and deepen. It could be that in a few years time, your company has a role that would fulfil their career aspirations or keep them better engaged and that they could be attracted back and rehired as a boomerang (returning) employee. From a referral point of view, if you take care of your leavers and keep in touch with them, they may one day return and they will certainly help you by sharing your jobs or pointing people your way.

Boomerang hire realities

Your people can be found and tempted to other job opportunities as easily as you can find people to tempt to your jobs, so naturally employee turnover is increasing compared to five or ten years ago. But as turnover increases, the pool of your ex-employees and therefore your potential rehires also grows.

The benefits of rehiring an ex-employee include:

- They are not a stranger: your company will have performance records and know whether they fit into your company from their previous employment.

- They hit the ground running: unlike a brand-new employee, they don't need time to get settled in and learn all the quirky nuances of the company, the processes and management style.

- You can hire them quickly: being a known factor, the interviewing process can be reduced.

- Higher retention: they are not going to return if they hated the company, plus they have seen employment life on the other side and realized that your company is better than your competitors.

- Bring a fresh perspective: their return is likely to encourage other employees to stay when they realize how good they have it and they will also bring in new knowledge and experience.

The potential negatives:

- It is essential to find out if they have resolved the reasons that made them leave so they don't leave again.

- They may not be comfortable with or resistant to changes in processes and procedures that happened in their absence.

- Potentially, they could reignite old grudges with co-workers or past managers.

- HR bias: because the boomerang applicant is known they may be hired over a more suitable but unknown applicant who is overlooked during the interview process.

Avoid burning bridges

If you don't love your leavers you will miss the opportunity to rehire them, receive referrals from them, or worse they could write negative online reviews that impact your hiring process for years to come. Loving your leavers is more than giving them a nice send-off, it is keeping in touch and being genuinely interested in how their career is progressing.

Swedish Technical Recruiter, Sofia Broberger, knows how to love her company's leavers, she interviews them for Swedish television network TV4's blog.[14] Six months after they have left the company she asks if they are happy to be interviewed for the blog, 'I especially like their answers to the question "What's your favourite memory of your time with us?" because Sweden's biggest morning news show, *Nyhetsmorgon*, is produced right in the middle of the building so they always have some funny memories to share!'

The aim of these posts is to provide transparency, honesty, credibility and career development by showing that if you join TV4 you will grow. Sofia shared that the alumni blog posts generate the most traffic to their career site and that 'they give good insight into us as a company, what it's like working for us and what type of experience you'll gain. They are way better than traditional testimonials.'

On the blog, you will see other interviews from new hires and team managers, mixed in with technical and general blog posts, and the occasional job. If your company is open to boomerang hires, this could be such an easy way to reopen the door to their employment.

Create an alumni network

Your alumni need to have a reason to visit and engage in the network you create, so you are looking to create a platform or channel that allows people to:

- network and knowledge share;
- be kept informed of industry, company and alumni news;
- see employment opportunities;
- receive perks and benefits as they did as an employee;
- hear about alumni events;
- discover CSR and volunteering opportunities.

Regularly add engaging content   Remember the dopamine; make posts interactive. Consider adding surveys and polls asking for feedback, and share relevant news stories, pictures and videos, ensuring that posts can be liked, shared or commented upon. Like Sofia does on TV4's blog, interview your alumni, and consider making it a podcast for use by the alumni and externally.

Make it user-friendly   Look for a software provider that has:

- A mobile app so it is easy for users to access out of hours or during their commute.
- Instant messaging so alumni can keep conversations out of their overloaded email inboxes.
- The option to add groups, which will encourage sub-communities to form based around interests and hobbies, which will keep the network active.
- A content library: somewhere you can find, store and organize content ready for sharing.
- An easy way to share new jobs and manage alumni referrals.

G2 Crowd[15] and Capterra[16] detail the many different alumni management software available to take for a test drive and it is definitely worth the time to ask your peers for their recommendations too.

Be transparent   On Deloitte's Alumni page on their US career sites, there is a clear call to action for referrals.[17] The dedicated website page details the referral programme including who is eligible, how rewards are paid and exactly how to submit the referral. Grant Thornton is also clear about its employee referral payment, which is a set figure and donated to one of the 13 charities listed.[18]

Sodexo, a French food services and facilities management company, state on theirs that alumni have access to 10 per cent more job opportunities than external job seekers, which is quite an incentive to become involved if you liked the company and would consider returning.[19] As part of the alumni, people are kept updated on events, training and even opportunities to volunteer with staff.

By sharing information about their alumni programmes publicly, these companies are not only reminding their leavers to get involved, they are also showing future employees that the experience of their employees matters from start to finish and beyond.

Further reading

- SHRM details information on some of the sizes of alumni networks and the top three drivers for a successful programme: bit.ly/SHRMAlumni
- Vendor Enterprise Alumni shared the results of their 2018 survey and how important it is to make sure your alumni network is more than a place to hear about jobs: bit.ly/CASurveyResults

In a candidate-driven market, referrals are an easier way to gain and keep the attention of people with skills that are in demand but before you start doing the work to increase them, improve your processes and supporting technologies. It is essential to keep both the referrer and the applicant happy with a transparent smooth process and excellent communication so that you don't jeopardize losing future referrals.

Summary

- There are many different types of referrals and no matter which referrals you are trying to increase, they all rely on the effort of the recruiter to be a success.

- Clear communication and transparency are vital if any employee referral programme is to succeed.

- Harness the power of dopamine by using instant recognition and awards and gamification in all of your referral programmes.

- Social referrals will only happen if the recruiter becomes known, liked and trusted and this will only happen through the sharing of interesting content and proper engagement with people.

- In a tight labour market like this, it is important to consider hiring your ex-employees and losing any misconceptions held about boomerang employees.

- By creating an engaged alumni network, recruiters have the opportunity to re-hire ex-employees and receive referrals, but to be engaged it must be easy to access and contain engaging content, groups and events.

How are you changing your referrals? Tweet me @KatrinaMCollier using #RobotProofRecruiter

Notes

1 ReferralPrograms [accessed 12 April 2019] 2017 Referral programs benchmarks report [Online] https://www.referralprograms.org/report (archived at https://perma.cc/7Q3Z-W6HQ)

2 Elliot, G and Corey, D (2018) *Build It: The rebel playbook for world class employee engagement,* John Wiley & Sons, West Sussex, UK

3 Ranade, V (2017) [accessed 12 April 2019] The referral programs benchmarking report, Drafted, 23 October [Online] https://blog.drafted. us/benchmarking-report/ (archived at https://perma.cc/H4N3-S6MP)

4 CareerXroads [accessed 12 April 2019] [Online] https://cxr.works/ research_reports/research-directory/employee-referral-programs/ (archived at https://perma.cc/4V3L-HX92)

5 Facebook [accessed 12 April 2019] The Employer Brand Forum (closed group), Facebook [Online] https://www.facebook.com/groups/ employerbrandforum/ (archived at https://perma.cc/C5TQ-MULZ)

6 Facebook [accessed 12 April 2019] HR Open Source – #HROS (closed group), Facebook [Online] https://www.facebook.com/groups/ hropensource/ (archived at https://perma.cc/4VW9-SG8R)

7 Wharton University (2012) [accessed 12 April 2019] Why external hires get paid more, and perform worse, than internal staff, Knowledge@Wharton, 28 March [Online] http://knowledge.wharton. upenn.edu/article/why-external-hires-get-paid-more-and-perform-worse-than-internal-staff/ (archived at https://perma.cc/Y3V6-FY3P)

8 The Searchologist, The #SocialRecruiting Show [accessed 12 April 2019] Does candidate experience matter? The #SocialRecruiting Show [Online] https://www.thesearchologist.com/candidate-experience-2/ (archived at https://perma.cc/R2HN-ELEM)

9   Formstack [accessed 12 April 2019] Employee exit survey template, Formstack [Online] https://www.formstack.com/templates/employee-exit-survey (archived at https://perma.cc/7ZR5-E2RG)

10 SurveyMonkey [accessed 12 April 2019] Employee exit template, SurveyMonkey[Online] https://www.surveymonkey.com/r/Exit-Interview-Template (archived at https://perma.cc/3QW5-UZTL)

11 Typeform [accessed 12 April 2019] Exit survey template, Typeform [Online] https://www.typeform.com/templates/t/exit-survey/ (archived at https://perma.cc/JD9V-Q3E7)

12 Qualtrics [accessed 12 April 2019] Your guide to employee experience programs, Qualtrics [Online] https://www.qualtrics.com/uk/experience-management/employee/ (archived at https://perma.cc/J78H-UM7K)

13 LinkedIn post from Tomislav Masle [accessed 12 April 2019] LinkedIn [Online] https://www.linkedin.com/feed/update/urn:li:activity:6441562694708457472/ (archived at https://perma.cc/N3WE-XJC5)

14 Broberger, S (2018) [accessed 12 April 2019] Why you must love your leavers! Sofiabroberger, 6 August [Online] https://sofiabroberger.se/2018/08/06/alumni-interviews/ (archived at https://perma.cc/F453-PP5T)

15 G2 [accessed 12 April 2019] Best alumni management software, G2 [Online] https://www.g2crowd.com/categories/alumni-management (archived at https://perma.cc/S4RN-585N)

16 Capterra [accessed 12 April 2019] Membership management software, Capterra [Online] https://www.capterra.com/membership-management-software/ (archived at https://perma.cc/AHK8-8BQJ)

17 Life at Deloitte [accessed 12 April 2019] Alumni referral program: Refer a friend, get rewarded, Deloitte [Online] https://www2.deloitte.com/us/en/pages/careers/articles/alumni-referral-deloitte-us-join-deloitte.html (archived at https://perma.cc/UM8H-LV7Z)

18 Grant Thornton [accessed 12 April 2019] Referral rewards: Alumni referral bonus policy, Grant Thornton [Online] https://grantthornton.referrals.selectminds.com/info/rewards (archived at https://perma.cc/GY7Y-ZKJ9)

19 Sodexo [accessed 12 April 2019] Welcome to Reconnexions – Sodexo USA's alumni community, Sodexo [Online] https://www.sodexoalumni.com/ (archived at https://perma.cc/ZR3M-BJ9X)

Conclusion

As you have heard, the role of the recruiter has been irreversibly changed by technology and the internet. How many more hats you are required to wear to succeed; you are sourcers, recruiters, marketers, community builders, and accountable for more steps in the process than ever before. One false move, in this new search-engine-led world, and your recruitment becomes more challenging and you, as the face of the company, are left to deal with the mess.

You have learned throughout this book that you need to put the human first and keep technology in its supporting role, so you drastically improve your candidate engagement, response rates and your overall recruitment. The formula for this is:

1 *Be a candidate-centric recruiter* – the internet shifted power from the company to the employee or candidate, so recruiter behaviour and reputations are more critical than ever. Candidates now have greater choice; develop your robot-proof soft skills to keep candidates happy and assured.

2 *Look like a recruiter worth talking to* – candidates are looking at your online presence so complete your profiles, look friendly and approachable, inject some personality, share updates and rich media that help you become known, liked and trusted, and follow the social media etiquette.

3 *Don't forget your hiring managers* – encourage them to complete their social media profiles and to showcase their work on the sites where potential employees are active. Ensure hiring managers are respectful of every candidate so that candidates don't deselect themselves for the wrong reasons.

4 *Look like a company worth talking to* – Google for Jobs presents company reviews right where most people begin their job search, Google. Share compelling peer-to-peer human stories. Walk through

your recruitment process and remove obstacles to a smooth application, interview and hire.

5 *Your intake is the most crucial part* – in the intake strategy session, it is essential to learn all you can so you can gain the attention of people with skills that are in demand, and allay their fears with your understanding of the role, team and company. Also, be ready to push back if you think that unconscious bias is reducing your talent pool unnecessarily.

6 *Human-first job posts gain attention* – use the information from the intake strategy session to create job posts and advertisements that are all about the candidate. Get creative with your colours, images and/or video, to evoke emotion and action. Maximize visibility by being creative with their placement, sometimes online is not be the best place for your advert.

7 *Use robot-proof messages* – with one chance to make a first impression, ensure each email or message is personalized and relevant. Be conscious of how you address your potential candidate and sign off with full transparency. Try using video and SMS messages to stand out and definitely follow up.

8 *Keep applications and interviews pain-free* – helping candidates deselect from the process will reduce the time you spend screening unsuitable applicants. All applicants deserve closure and without it, can damage your reputation. All interviewed applicants deserve feedback.

9 *Reduce non-boarding* – a job offer is not a guarantee that someone will actually start and it is essential to deliver an excellent first day and onboarding process; consider implementing a buddy programme. By taking accountability for pre- and onboarding, you will improve future hiring.

10 *Referrals depend on you* – any type of referral relies on the effort of the recruiter to be a success and needs clear communication and transparency. In a tight labour market, it is important to consider hiring your ex-employees so look to create an engaged alumni.

Competing in the future

Technology is evolving rapidly and impacting how people want to work and how we will hire in the years ahead – who knows what surprises recruiters have in store? One thing that is certain though, it makes little sense to remain reactively fighting for the same people in an ever-dwindling pool of people with the skills you need. To remain competitive in the future will involve a change to proactive recruitment through greatly improved people analytics, workforce planning and talent intelligence.

People analytics

People analytics, sometimes called talent or HR analytics, is the method of analytics that can help managers and executives make decisions about their workforce. It applies statistics, technology and expertise to large sets of talent data, and technology is making it easier for HR to integrate data from its employees into their decision-making processes. Having better insights to guide succession planning, career mobility, retention strategies, talent acquisition strategies, and learning and development programmes increases the effectiveness of human resources.

Workforce planning

Workforce planning is a core business process that aligns changing organizational needs with people strategy. In the future, as technology takes over transactional tasks, leaders will be looking for human-led and technology-enabled workforces to gain a competitive edge. The workforce will be different, an extended talent ecosystem made up of talent pools spanning multiple generations and including direct employees, contractors, freelancers and more. Though transformation and new technology will mean fewer people doing some jobs, it also means that new roles will be created, giving companies an opportunity to place their existing people into new roles and increase their engagement through learning. To compete in a tough recruitment market, companies need to get more proactive with workforce planning.

Talent intelligence

In 2014, research from PwC found that mismatching talent is costing the global economy $150 billion per annum.[1] By placing the wrong jobs in the wrong places, the wrong skill sets in the wrong places, trying to hire people into difficult locations and so on, there is a lost opportunity to generate $130 billion of additional productivity globally and to avoid recruitment costs of $19.8 billion, caused by taking longer to fill roles and higher incidents of failed recruitment.

To address talent mismatch Philips formed a Talent Intelligence function. Since forming in 2016, the team has impacted billions of euros' worth of decision making and saved a substantial amount of external research fees. Toby Culshaw's team consider the feasibility and risk associated with business planning and strategy from a labour market perspective. 'Given the increase in complexity in today's world, Philips had a growing demand to provide effective talent intelligence to help determine the organization's buy versus build strategy, talent strategy and location strategy. We are very much a consultative and decision-influencing function rather than a business process.'

As for the future, Toby added 'If people are a company's competitive advantage and we are shifting from a talent war to a skills war then I would see effective talent intelligence being fundamental in winning that war.'

Keep up with change

I have talked a lot about the change to recruitment over the course of the book and I couldn't have done it without the input of the thriving recruitment communities that exist exchanging ideas and solving problems. To stay informed, I recommend that you get active in some of the following places, some mentioned previously, so you can find help from your peers and be inspired to be a better recruiter.

- Groups on Facebook: SourceCon, Secret Sourcing Group, Sourcers Who Code, Recruiters Online, Growth Hacking Recruiters, Storytelling Recruiter and The Employer Brand Forum
- Reading and community: ERE, SourceCon, RecruitingDaily and #ChatTalent
- In-house recruiters: DBR channel on Slack
- Agency recruiters: The RecruitingGym
- Podcasts: start at Hung Lee's 'Big List of Podcasts to Follow in 2019'
- Shows: RecruiterZone on Crowdcast

Listen to your peers, offer help, ask questions and be respectful of others, even if you don't agree with their thinking. To grow and thrive in your chosen network, you will want to pay it forward and help people keep the network safe for the exchange of ideas and opinions.

As for technology

The plethora of recruitment technology available is truly breathtaking and I have not seen it captured better than by Nathan Perrott, VP Digital Marketing Solutions at AIA Worldwide, in TalentBrew's RecTech Hype Cycle, which you will find at bit.ly/RTHypeCycle19. In an effort to explain what technology is useful, relevant and worth exploring, the RecTech Hype Cycle will help you cut through the noise. It is designed to help you understand what is hot, what is not, what is new and what is next. I urge you to download a copy and bookmark the page because they update it regularly.

If you only take away one thing about recruitment technology, please let it be that when you are looking at new technology, you ask for proof that it will save you time, money and hassle, and that it will make recruitment better for you, the candidate, your hiring manager and the company. That it will actually solve the problem you are hoping to ease. Look for vendors who actively engage with the recruitment community, either with recruiters and sourcers as advisors or who are former recruiters themselves. Nobody understands the pain points of recruitment like we do.

For HR and recruitment technology know-how, follow these people:

- Anna Ott: an HR tech expert helping practitioners and HR tech buyers connect with the right solutions.

- Alan Walker: CEO and Founder of Udder. Alan helps companies buying talent tech to make the right decisions, and vendors selling talent tech to build the right solutions.

- Bill Boorman: Founder of #Tru unconferences, speaker and an advisor to many recruitment technology companies, he needs little introduction.

- Chad Sowash and Joel Cheesman: known for 'The Chad & Cheese Podcast', there is little these two don't know about the world of technology and recruitment.

- Chris Russell: Founder of RecTech Media, advises on the recruiting technology ecosystem, through his consulting practice and his great RecTech Podcast and webinars.

- Clair Bush: Founder of the recruitment marketing consultancy, AM-Bush, can help you to strategically align your brand, resources and technology to get results.

- David Green and Iain Baillie: experts on people analytics, HR and future of work, both at Insight222.

- Hung Lee: my ex-colleague of old, Co-Founder of Workshape.io, the matching service for technical talent, and Curator of Recruiting Brainfood.

- Jackye Clayton: Director of Customer Success at HiringSolved, helps recruiters get to grips with the latest and greatest technology

- Jim Stroud: a long-time member of the sourcing community and an out of the box thinker, author, vlogger and podcaster at JimStroud.com

- Karen Azulai: Co-Founder of HRTechnation, she advises HR startups and writes about new technologies impacting the HR industry.

- Louise Triance: Founder of UK Recruiter and host of 'The Rec Tech Showdown' on RecuiterZone, where she interviews recruitment technology founders.

- Martin Burns: VP at HireClix, is a talent acquisition strategist consulting on talent acquisition strategies, technologies and branding.

- Matt Charney: a marketing and communications professional with incredible knowledge of talent and technology who refreshingly says it as it is.

- Steven Ehrlich and Nathan Perrott: both at AIA Worldwide, are visionary when it comes to talent acquisition technology and employer branding.
- Wendy McDougall: Founder and CEO of Firefish Software, helps recruiters reach, engage and recruit people through technology.
- William Tincup: at the intersection of HR and technology, he is a writer, speaker, advisor, consultant, investor, storyteller and teacher.
- The 300 women listed in RecruitingDaily's '300+ Women in HR Technology Worth Watching'.[2]
- Any of the advisors or mentors behind Udder, a mix of consultants and practitioners with extraordinary experience.[3]

Final thoughts

There is still an incredible amount of 'us and them' in recruitment between in-house and agency, with opinions of both sides that may or may not be true. To a candidate, none of that matters, they give recruiters the same reputation. To technology, none of that matters, vendors will try to replace parts of your job whether you work in-house or in an agency. It is time to lose the 'us and them'. It is time to embrace all of the recruitment community, to learn from each other and exchange ideas. It is up to the recruitment industry as a whole to improve. Will it ever be fixed? Unlikely, we are human! But it can be better and it can deliver a better experience for people than it does today.

When the automatic machines threatened to replace tellers, I was working in the bank, yet decades later there are still tellers in the bank because, for some people, it is important to deal with a human even for such a mundane transaction as withdrawing cash. At the supermarket, some of you will prefer a human cashier and some self-checkout. So, do I really think that people will ever want to deal with a machine for something as critical as their career? No, I don't.

But in the words of resourcing leader, Ben Gledhill, 'candidates are not scared of technology, recruiters are.' Though it is unlikely that all of a recruiter's job will be replaced by technology any time soon, it is time to stop technology hampering where it could be helping. To improve candidate engagement and ensure you truly are a robot-proof recruiter, place the human first, be curious and learn about recruitment technology, but keep it firmly in its supporting role, always.

Notes

1 PwC (2014) [accessed 12 April 2019] Talent mismatch costs global economy $150 billion, PwC Press room, 8 April [Online] https://press.pwc.com/News-releases/global-economy-misses-out-on-150bn-due-to-talent-mismatch/s/c433d953-6669-41c1-9225-fd63ac9298d6 (archived at https://perma.cc/SQD9-QEQ4)

2 Tincup, W (2017) [accessed 12 April 2019] RecruitingDaily Presents: 300+ women in HR technology worth watching, Recruiting Daily, 8 March [Online] https://recruitingdaily.com/300-women-in-hr-technology-that-you-should-follow-and-support/ (archived at https://perma.cc/2TJX-G82T)

3 Udder [accessed 12 April 2019] Team – the brains behind Udder, Udder [Online] https://udder.rocks/who-we-are/ (archived at https://perma.cc/Y7EA-ZSE6)

INDEX

Note: Numbers, acronyms and the @ symbol are filed as spelt out; 'Mc' is filed as written; the symbol # is ignored for filing purposes. Page locators in *italics* denote information contained within a figure or table.